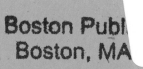

D0131235

The Will Eisner Companion

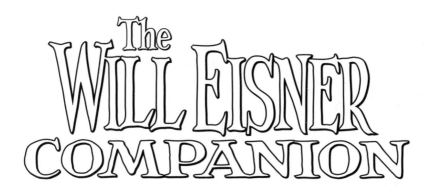

OTHER WILL EISNER TITLES AVAILABLE FROM DC COMICS

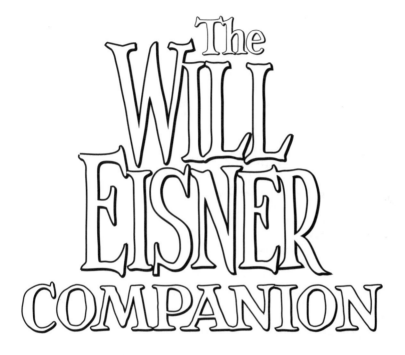

The WILL EISNER COMPANION

THE PIONEERING SPIRIT OF
THE FATHER OF THE GRAPHIC NOVEL

N. C. Christopher Couch
and Stephen Weiner

Introduction by Dennis O'Neil
Afterword by Denis Kitchen

DC COMICS   NEW YORK

Dan DiDio VP-Editorial
Charles Kochman Editor-Licensed Publishing
Amie Brockway-Metcalf Art Director
Paul Levitz President & Publisher
Georg Brewer VP-Design & Retail Product Development
Richard Bruning Sr. VP-Creative Director
Patrick Caldon Sr. VP-Finance & Operations
Chris Caramalis VP-Finance
Terri Cunningham VP-Managing Editor
Alison Gill VP-Manufacturing
Rich Johnson VP-Book Trade Sales
Hank Kanalz VP-General Manager, WildStorm
Lillian Laserson Sr. VP & General Counsel
Jim Lee Editorial Director, WildStorm
David McKillips VP-Advertising & Custom Publishing
John Nee VP-Business Development
Gregory Noveck Sr. VP-Creative Affairs
Cheryl Rubin Sr. VP-Brand Management
Bob Wayne VP-Sales & Marketing

Published by DC Comics, 1700 Broadway, New York, NY 10019. A Warner Bros. Entertainment Company.

Hardcover ISBN: 1-4012-0422-8
Softcover ISBN: 1-4012-0423-6
Printed in Canada

First edition
10 9 8 7 6 5 4 3 2 1

Visit DC Comics online at www.dccomics.com
Visit Will Eisner online at www.willeisner.com and www.deniskitchen.com

With those who hold that a comic strip cannot be a work of art, I shall not traffic.

—Gilbert Seldes, *The 7 Lively Arts*, 1924

To Dave Schreiner—brother-in-law, mentor, friend.
—N.C.C.C.

This book is for my mother.
—S.W.

TABLE OF CONTENTS

ACKNOWLEDGMENTS

I hope that somewhere Dave Schreiner knows how deeply in his debt I am. He brought so much of Will's work to everyone, editing the Kitchen Sink Spirit comics and writing about the stories in each issue. Dave had just begun working with Will on his latest graphic novel when he passed away in the fall of 2003. I wish Dave were here to see this book—he'd let me know what was good (and not so good) about it.

And thanks to Charlie "the K" Kochman, for friendship, for making this book happen, and for taking the time to make sure everything turns out "OK."

Amie Brockway-Metcalf is the perfect designer for any project with Will's art; thanks once again for creating a design that is simultaneously classic and fresh. Thanks to Lesley Stone, whose fabulous work as production artist really put it all together. And to Dale Crain, who shared so generously his expertise and resources from his painstaking work on DC's Spirit and other Eisner works.

Many, many thanks to Mark Chiarello, who must be a wizard since he conjured up time in his too-many-hats schedule to do the magical and loving all-new coloring for the Spirit's origin and Gerhard Shnobble stories in the color section.

Thanks also to Randy Scott, who keeps track of more comics than any human being should in the Michigan State University Libraries Comic Art Collection Reading Room Index (www.lib.msu.edu/comics/rri), for doing the excellent index to this book.

Thanks always to Will, whose work is "the best to think" in our field. Thanks to Denis Kitchen, for everything, and to Jackie, for even more than that.

N. C. CHRISTOPHER COUCH

I first thought of writing some kind of book about Will Eisner after reading Gary Groth's interview with Neil Gaiman in *The Comics Journal* no. 169. Groth and Gaiman talked about why there was so little comics' criticism. It almost immediately occurred to me that one reason there was so little analysis was that few cartoonists had created a large enough body of work to warrant careful study—but I knew that Will Eisner was one illustrator who had. Shortly thereafter, I called the only professional cartoonist I knew, Scott McCloud, who offered to help me in any way possible.

Eventually, the project landed with Kitchen Sink Press. After Kitchen Sink went out of business, DC Comics picked it up. It has been a long journey, and I'd like to thank my editor, Charlie Kochman; my co-writer, Chris Couch; Denny O'Neil for his most excellent introduction; my agent, Judy Hansen; especially Will Eisner, for creating a body of work worthy of serious study; Denis Kitchen, who carried this project with him as he moved from the role of publisher to author representative, making sure this companion became a reality. And lastly, I would like to thank Rachel who helped me every step of the way.

STEPHEN WEINER

INTRODUCTION

by Dennis O'Neil

Do not seek to follow in the footsteps of the wise.
Seek what they sought. —Basho

It's difficult to know exactly how and where to begin writing about Will Eisner because, after spending quite a few recent hours looking at his work, what I *feel* like doing is simply seeking him out and strewing rose petals in his path. Or maybe bowing to him. Or maybe just murmuring "Thank you."

But doing any of that would only embarrass Will and would *not* serve to introduce the book you hold, which is what I've promised to do.

So, here's a start, in the form of a recommendation: If you know anyone who absolutely despises comic books, who is convinced that their existence is eroding the moral and spiritual fiber of the nation because all they *do*, these paragons of trash, is present crude images glorifying adolescent power and revenge fantasies, show them anything Will Eisner's done in the past 25 years. Ask them to quiet their preconceptions and simply read the stuff as they would read Philip Roth, John Updike, John Dos Passos, J.D. Salinger, John Steinbeck, William Faulkner, Eugene O'Neill, Arthur Miller—any modern storyteller who deals honorably with the travails of being human.

You might not convert your skeptical friend. The form could be a problem. Will Eisner does sequential art, usually known as comics, and some people just can't seem to be able to like, or grasp, or understand comics, regardless of how much they try. There's something about the *language* that is comics, a unique amalgam of word and image, that irritates and defeats them. Some of us can't seem to enjoy poetry; for others, it's jazz, or ballet, or opera, or macramé. Name an art form and you can find someone who just doesn't *get* it. *Can't* get it. So it is with comics.

But if your skeptical friend doesn't have an inherent dislike of comics *per se*, looking at Eisner's work will pretty quickly eradicate any notions about comics' inherent trashiness. Of course, specialty shops are full of comics that *are*, in fact, full of the aforementioned adolescent power fantasies, though they are certainly no more pernicious than most popular culture fare, and maybe less so. Most of them, these days, feature costumed vigilantes with "powers and abilities far beyond those of mortal men," to quote the opening of an old television show. They're called "super heroes" and you'll get no patrician disdain of them from me. Certainly a lot of them are, shall we say, less than first-rate entertainers but, as Theodore Sturgeon said when someone told him that ninety percent of science fiction is crud, ninety percent of *everything* is crud.

It is entirely possible to work honestly and honorably in the super hero genre, to use it as a vehicle for saying whatever the artist and/or writer has to say, subject to the limits that apply to *all* arts, the vision and talent and skill of the creative people. Jazz, now heard in the same concert halls that feature symphony orchestras, was once considered to be whorehouse music, not fit for decent people's ears, and the stories of men like Dashiell Hammett, Raymond Chandler, and James M. Cain, in my father's day published as amusement for the lip-movers among the reading public, is now the subject of doctoral theses. Like the work just mentioned, super hero comics, too, are acquiring respectability, discussed and indeed taught in the world's great universities. Time doesn't improve our collective ability to look at art, but it does move us past the prejudices that prevent us from seeing what's there.

Which brings us back to Will Eisner. Between 1937 and 1940, at the beginning of his career, he worked on a number of different characters, including a couple of super heroes. Then, in 1940, he created his own variation on the form. This new creation was called the Spirit and his adventures appeared weekly—yes, *weekly!*—as a comic book supplement to Sunday newspapers. Look at examples of Eisner's *Spirit* work and you'll see that the title character (real name Denny Colt) was in fact a super hero, but just barely. The Spirit wore no cape, no tights, no high boots, no emblem blazoned across his chest, not even any flashy colors except for a red necktie. He *did* wear a mask, and that was Will's concession to his syndicate's desire for a costumed evil fighter like Superman and Batman, who were then making DC Comics prosperous, but the rest of his garb consisted of a man's suit, maybe bought off the rack somewhere, and shoes, gloves, and a hat.

In the beginning, for a mercifully short time, he got around in a flying car, perhaps a first cousin to Batman's Batmobile. But he was never the flying car type any more than he was really a super hero. His foes, like himself, tended to dress in recognizable, if not downright ordinary, clothing and they didn't wield death rays nor harbor ambitions to rule the world. They were driven by greed, fear, ambition, and various kinds of desire—the same impulses that drive you, me, our families, friends, and the guy down the street. Denny Colt? Well, he was their self-appointed nemesis using traditional detective's tools: wit, ingenuity, courage, toughness, intelligence, and, yes, the occasional application of fisticuffs. Everything in *The Spirit*, with the possible exception of that anachronous flying car, was human-scaled. Denny Colt wouldn't have had much to say to Superman, but he could have spent a pleasant evening in the company of Philip Marlowe.

Superman and Batman and their legion of imitators were and are the reincarnations of mythological deities: icons. Will Eisner was never very interested in icons. But frail, fallible, suffering human beings—these fascinate him.

In the early fifties, as the comic book business was imploding because of changing retail practices and being criticized by politicians, psychiatrists, and editorial writers, among others, for corrupting the nation's youth, Will retired *The Spirit*. He went on to ventures that made him a bona fide success outside the esoteric world of professional comics and then, when he was able to do so comfortably, he returned to his first love, which he was now sometimes calling "sequential art." But not to *The Spirit*. Denny Colt remained pasturing in crime fighter Valhalla while his creator began the work—the *vocation*—that he continues to this day. Beginning with *A Contract with God*, published in 1978, Will devoted himself to telling tales of his people, the immigrants who settled in New York City's outer boroughs and points north and west—brave and silly and stupid and venal and noble and tormented folk who struggled, often in vain, for a share in an American dream of happiness and fulfillment.

They would not be out of place in the streets Denny Colt walked, so many years earlier. There is a straight line between *The Spirit* and whatever's on Will's drawing board this afternoon. Now, let it be stated, with all possible pomp and fanfare, that I revere *The Spirit*—but the current work is why I want to strew rose petals in Will's path. The current work is better.

There are a number of reasons for this. The first, obvious one is that Will no longer has to make concessions to genre. *The Spirit* was heroic melodrama, and readers had a right to expect the elements of that sort of fiction: good guys, bad guys, murders, assorted other felonies, the occasional *femme fatale* and, above all, the socko finish—villainy emphatically vanquished, tranquility restored and justice served, all due to the efforts of an avenging paladin who is noble of heart, pure of motive and, oh yeah, a hell of a brawler. In his early years, Will did this kind of story and did it as well, probably, as anyone. But even then, his plots, his sense of ambience and the ordinary-guy quality of his hero indicated that although he was honoring the genre conventions, he was not a prisoner of them.

So that's one reason why Will's later work is superior: the caged bird sang but the uncaged bird really let 'er rip! But the second reason, I submit, is why Will Eisner is distinctive among the world's storytellers and deserves the sobriquet Artist—note the capital A and let it be writ in Day-Glo. Will has taken strip cartooning, that disreputable stepchild of the arts, and perfected it into a unique narrative tool. He uses cartoons' simplicity and plasticity and the exaggeration of form they allow for as devices for limning character, giving his paper-and-ink people plenty of body language and then carrying the process a bit further—exaggerating that body language in precise ways so it becomes a glimpse of their souls. There aren't many analogies, either inside or outside cartooning, for what Will does. We're not discussing caricature here—rather, something like caricature's smarter older brother, a graphic strategy that not only exaggerates the exterior but uses exaggeration to suggest the *interior*.

To get a rough understanding of what, exactly, Will achieves, remember that all art, with the possible exception of some experimentation, involves a process of conscious selection; the artist decides what to include in his painting, play, film, comic book, whatever, and equally important, what to exclude. With that in mind, imagine that Will Eisner is a kind of wizard observing reality and stopping time at the micro-instant when the people he's watching are at their most expressive and *then*, using his eldritch powers, manipulating the scene—the people and the other graphic elements—to heighten their expressiveness even further: twisting, turning, stretching, compressing, and erasing until some Platonic ideal of hyper-expressivity is achieved. Then he flattens that scene onto a piece of paper. If you're a wizard, like Will, you repeat this process as often as necessary until you have a collection of time-frozen images. Next, you assemble them chronologically, and—*presto!*—you have a visual narrative—a world lit by lightning flashes that, if put together with skill and vision, can focus our attention and tell us deep and profound truths. It can also be immensely entertaining.

Although they're exaggerated, the better to reveal their inner selves, the creatures who inhabit Will's lightning-lit world are familiar to us. We know them, or someone very much like them.

They do not meet their fates in empty space. Like nature, Will Eisner abhors a vacuum and so, more than any cartoonist ever, he gives his characters real locales to inhabit, cityscapes and interiors rendered with either meticulous attention to particulars or deftly suggested with a precise detail or two. Will stands at the altar of Kipling's God of Things as They Are. I imagine him saturating himself with whatever's around him, looking, all the time, at *everything*, and remembering it and deriving enormous satisfaction from recreating it on paper. As I mentioned above, Will has little interest in either gods or monsters, nor does he have any desire to visit Narnia, Oz, Mars, Krypton, or anywhere that isn't on a map you can find in a child's atlas. Oh sure, Denny Colt *said* he lived in "Central City," wherever that might be, but who does he think he's kidding? We know a New Yorker when we meet one! And ever since Will did *A Contract with God,* he doesn't even pretend to set his stories anywhere other than New York.

What I've discussed in the last few paragraphs is only a partial inventory of the technical aspects of Will's work. I haven't mentioned how he integrates word balloons into the design of the panel; nor how he uses the lettering itself to suggest the inflections of human speech; nor, speaking of speech, how as a writer he evokes the rhythms and vernacular of his characters' talk. All that, and more, is worthy of notice and, if you're interested in learning how to do comics, instead of merely *appreciating* them, those things can reward study. But if Will Eisner were merely as good technically as he in fact is, we'd enjoy his stuff, we'd even applaud him, but I'm afraid I'd save my rose petals for someone else. As you've gathered by now, I consider Will to be quite a lot more than a superb technician.

Let me repeat: Will Eisner is an Artist.

He has a vision of the human condition and the means to communicate that vision to us. It is essentially a tragic vision, though not a morose one, and that may be why he no longer does melodrama; in the world that Will has been presenting for the last quarter-century, problems are not solved by violent action and big, fluffy endings are impossible. This is *our* world, focused and purified and magnified, displayed for our amusement. We might be well advised not to analyze it further, but to do what Will Eisner wants us to do. Turn pages. Experience. Enjoy.

DENNIS O'NEIL

Dennis O'Neil is an award-winning comic book writer and editor.

WILL EISNER: A SELECTED CHRONOLOGY

March 6, 1917
William Erwin Eisner born in Brooklyn, New York.

December 8, 1933
Eisner's first published work of art appears in the De Witt Clinton High School newspaper, illustrating a story on the "Forgotten" Ghetto.

1934
Eisner becomes art director of *The Medallion*, a literary magazine at De Witt Clinton High modeled on *The Masses*.

April 1934
Eisner becomes art director of *Eve* magazine, "Dedicated to the modern American Jewess," and fired shortly after the first issue appears.

1934
Eisner works in the ad department of Hearst's *New York American* newspaper.

1935
Eisner contributes a weekly comic strip starring Spunky to his high school newspaper *The Clintonian,* his first published comic strip; Eisner begins to create sample comic strips for newspaper syndicates, notably the comic detective strip "Harry Carey" and the serious crime strip "The Flame."

1936
Eisner sells the comic detective strip "Harry Carey" (renamed "Harry Karry") and "The Flame," recast as a pirate adventure, to John Henle's anthology comic book *Wow, What a Magazine!*

1936
After the failure of *Wow, What a Magazine!,* Eisner and Samuel "Jerry" Iger form the Eisner and Iger Studio, a comic book "shop" created to produce features for a variety of other publishers. Staff and freelancers included Lou Fine, Jack Kurtzberg (Jack Kirby, later co-creator of Marvel's Fantastic Four), Bob Kane (creator of Batman), Mort Meskin, et al. The Eisner-Iger Studio created its own syndicate, Universal Phoenix Features, which marketed comics overseas to the comic weekly Wags (U.K. and Australia), including Eisner's own series "Hawks of the Seas." Eisner and Iger features appeared in U.S. comics, either as reformatted reprints of syndicate material or in the form of original features.

March 1937
"Muss 'Em Up," a seven-page one-shot story, appears in *Detective Picture Stories* no. 4, story and art by William Eisner, published by Centaur.

September 1938
Sheena, the Jungle Girl, appears for the first time in *Jumbo Comics* no. 1, published by Fiction House; the concept and character were created by Eisner, although the first story was written and drawn by Mort Meskin.

September 1938
"Hawks of the Seas" appears in the U.S. for the first time in *Feature Funnies* no. 12, published by Quality Comics.

1939
Eisner signs on with Everett "Busy" Arnold of the Quality Comics Group to form a new shop to create features for Quality Comics and a newspaper comic book supplement for the Des Moines Register and Tribune Syndicate.

December 1939

Feature Comics no. 27 published by Quality Comics, featuring the first Doll Man story, a character created and written by Eisner (credited as William Erwin Maxwell), with art by Lou Fine.

May 1940

Crack Comics no. 1 published by Quality Comics, featuring "The Man Who Can Fly Like a Bird," the first Black Condor story, a character created and written by Eisner, with art by Lou Fine.

June 2, 1940

The debut appearance of the Spirit appears in the first Weekly Comic Book, a newspaper supplement created in Eisner's studio and circulated to newspapers by the Des Moines Register and Tribune Syndicate. In the origin feature, detective Denny Colt is put in suspended animation by the evil mastermind Dr. Cobra. Colt is declared dead and sets up shop as a masked crime fighter in his tomb in Wildwood Cemetery, adopting the name the Spirit. Commissioner Dolan of the New York City police department appears in the first story; appearing for the first time in the second section (June 9, 1940) are Ellen Dolan, the commissioner's daughter and the woman who will win the Spirit's affections, and Ebony White, the controversial African-American sidekick. In addition to the lead feature, each supplement contained two backup strips, "Lady Luck" and "Mr. Mystic."

August 1941

Military Comics no. 1 published by Quality Comics, featuring the origin and first appearance of the military aviator Blackhawk and his team—characters created and written by Eisner, art by Charles "Chuck" Cuidera.

Autumn 1941

Uncle Sam Quarterly no. 1 published by Quality Comics, featuring "Forged Faces," the first Uncle Sam story, a character created for comics by Will Eisner, with art by Eisner and Dan Zolnerowich, inks by Lou Fine. In a conversation on September 29, 1998 with Steve Darnall, author of the 1997 Alex Ross graphic novel *Uncle Sam,* Will Eisner said this about his adaptation of the Uncle Sam symbol for use in comics: "We were living in a time when it was necessary to have heroes who were capable of superheroic capacity, because the enemy was superheroic. I was 22, 23 years old [in the days prior to World War II], and Hitler seemed invincible. We needed an invincible hero to fight an invincible enemy."

October 13, 1941

The Spirit daily comic strip is launched. Although featuring the same characters as The Spirit comic book, it shared no continuity with the Weekly Comic Book Section stories. The black-and-white strip ran for three years, ending on March 11, 1944.

May 1942

Eisner drafted into the U.S. Army, reports for duty at Fort Dix, New Jersey. Transferred shortly to Aberdeen Proving Ground, Maryland. There he begins military artistic career, producing editorial cartoons and a weekly strip for the base's newspaper. Eventually transferred to the Pentagon, where he produces comics and articles for educational Army periodicals related to ordnance and vehicle maintenance.

Fall 1945

Eisner discharged from U.S. Army, returns to New York City, working on the Weekly Comic Book Section and *The Spirit.* He retakes personal control of *The Spirit,* moving to put his personal stamp on the series once again by expanding the range of situations and characters. Publishes his first new story, "The Christmas Spirit," on December 23. Eisner also begins to add new assistants to the studio, including Marilyn Mercer and Jules Feiffer.

June 12, 1946

Origin and first appearance of the Octopus in *The Spirit*. The Octopus is the first great postwar villain in *The Spirit,* Denny Colt's own Dr. Moriarty, and an Eisnerian metaphor for the continuing influence of Fascist ideology after World War II. The Octopus goes on to poison urban water supplies and steal atomic secrets, and is opposed not only by the Spirit but also by organizations with an international scope including the U.N. and an insurance company modeled on Lloyd's of London.

October 6, 1946

First appearance of P'Gell, the French woman of mystery who would become the archetypal femme fatale in *The Spirit*. Like other Eisner heroines (or anti-heroines), P'Gell pursued a variety of careers, not only as a confidence woman, but as a business woman and a single mother.

1948

Eisner founds his own company, American Visuals, as a basis for continuing his educational cartooning and writing for the Defense Department, done during his World War II service, and to expand the concept of educational comics to other contexts. One of his first non-Army products is *Baseball Comics* no. 1, which failed to make a hit on the newsstands and was cancelled after the first issue. It was reprinted in 1991 by Kitchen Sink Press (a second issue followed featuring an unpublished 1948 story).

September 5, 1948

Publication of *The Spirit* story "Gerhard Shnobble," about a man who flies because he believes he can; this is the most commented-upon and frequently reprinted *Spirit* story, and the subject of a 1995 Danish mural and poster. [See color section for a reprint of the entire story.]

1950

Will and Ann Eisner get married.

1951

The Army begins publication of *P*S, The Preventive Maintenance Monthly,* which became artistically and financially the most important product of Eisner's American Visuals company. The digest-size magazine featured characters and approaches Eisner had developed during and after World War II in such venues as *Army Motors* magazine, including safety pinup Connie Rodd and incompetent every-GI Joe Dope, the exemplar of doing the wrong thing in maintaining military equipment. Eisner continued to produce the magazine until 1972.

October 5, 1952

The last *Spirit* section is published. Eisner had turned more and more work over to assistants in the last few years of *The Spirit,* as his own company, American Visuals, occupied more and more of his time, and proved more commercially viable. After the failure of E.C. Comics artist Wally Wood to meet deadlines on the feature, Eisner decided to end it and concentrate on his Defense Department assignments and other educational and commercial comic work.

1965

Award-winning writer/artist Jules Feiffer, a former assistant of Eisner's, publishes *The Great Comic Book Heroes,* a book that became one of the first huge successes of the 1960s comics nostalgia craze, and the archetype for all subsequent genre analyses to follow. Based on an article Feiffer wrote for *Playboy,* the book included lavish praise of *The Spirit,* and helped reawaken interest in Eisner's creation.

1965

Eisner serves as president of the Bell-McClure Syndicate, which circulated comic strips and features to newspapers around the country.

January 9, 1966

The first new *Spirit* story since 1952 appears in the *New York Herald Tribune,* a five-page story satirizing New York City mayor John Lindsay during his campaign for re-election.

October 1966

Harvey Comics publishes *The Spirit,* the first of two magazine-size comic books reprinting Spirit stories from the 1940s with new pages by Eisner.

1971

Eisner attends the Creation Con, a comic book convention in New York City, and meets Denis Kitchen, an underground comic book artist and publisher. Two issues of a Spirit underground comic are published by Kitchen's company, Kitchen Sink Press.

1972

Readers are treated to a rare glimpse of Kitchen Sink's "subterranean headquarters" when Eisner illustrates the cover for the underground comic *Snarf* no. 3 (Kitchen Sink Enterprises, 1972).

1973

Eisner teaches cartooning at Sheridan College, Ontario, Canada, and he and the students create a new Spirit story, "The Invader," published by Tabloid Press.

1974–1993

Eisner teaches illustration and comics at the School of Visual Arts in New York.

April 1974

After several Spirit stories are reprinted in the horror comics magazine *Eerie* to favorable reader response, the Warren Company begins publication of *The Spirit Magazine* (there were 16 issues in all, published through October 1976). *The Spirit* will be reprinted continuously henceforth by a variety of companies, making it the single most frequently reproduced series of comic book stories in the United States.

1975

The Spirit makes an appearance in a story in Warren Publishing's *Vampirella* magazine no. 50, featuring a scantily clad alien vampiress. Written by Bill Dubay with art by Ramon Torrents, the story features Denny Colt rising from the grave.

1975

At the International Salon of Comic Books, Eisner wins the "Grand Prize of the City of Angouleme" for Lifetime Achievement.

1976

When the Warren Company discontinues publishing magazine-format comics, Eisner rejects an offer from Marvel Comics to begin reprinting *The Spirit* and signs with Kitchen Sink Press to continue *The Spirit* reprint series, beginning a nearly thirty year affiliation with this independent comic/popular culture publishing company. Eisner also publishes *Will Eisner's Spirit Casebook of True Haunted Houses and Ghosts,* a 160-page paperback from Tempo Books, with the Spirit serving as a "host" for true, mostly English, ghost stories, acting much like the Crypt Keeper in E.C. Comics's *Tales from the Crypt.*

1978

Eisner publishes *A Contract with God,* a 183-page work that features four linked short stories. Eisner popularizes the term "graphic novel," which will become a major feature of the discourse that begins in the 1980s attending the artistic and economic repositioning of comic art in the United States. Eisner publishes the work with Baronet, a New York trade publisher, not with a comic book or humor publisher—again symbolically repositioning the medium in literary and economic spheres, and paving the way for Art Spiegelman's Pulitzer Prize-winning *Maus* and other works that would be published and marketed using the term Eisner coined. In addition, *Contract* marks Eisner's return to creating his own comic art, as opposed to contract assignment, and begins a dual exploration of short stories and longer works in the medium that will comprise what is usually referred to as Eisner's "mature" period.

1985
Eisner publishes *Comics & Sequential Art,* one of the first and still one of the best books on creating—and understanding—comics, based on the illustration and comics courses he conceived for the School of Visual Arts in New York.

1986
Will Eisner publishes the graphic novella *The Dreamer,* a roman à clef of the early days of the comic book industry, and the forerunner of Michael Chabon's Pulitzer Prize-winning novel *The Amazing Adventures of Kavalier & Clay.*

1987
Eisner publishes *The Building* and *New York, the Big City,* collections of short stories that first appeared in Kitchen Sink Press's *Will Eisner Quarterly* magazine, notable for their more universal exploration of urban dwellers, rather than a focus on Jewish life in New York, as in *A Contract with God;* Kitchen Sink Press releases the first Spirit record, featuring the song "Ev'ry Little Bug," based on the April 27, 1947 Spirit story.

Fall 1987
The Spirit made-for-TV movie premieres on ABC, starring Sam Jones (who had starred in the 1980 Flash Gordon film) and directed by Michael Schultz. Steven E. de Souza is credited with the final script; Harlan Ellison and William Friedkin had written earlier teleplays for the film that were not used.

1988
Eisner publishes the graphic novel *A Life Force,* an examination of the microcosmic effects of macrocosmic forces as the Depression and the rise of the Nazis affect the residents of a Bronx tenement neighborhood.

1988
Dave Olbrich, an editor for Eternity Comics, creates the Eisner Awards, designed to honor the best creators in comics and promote the medium by publicizing to non-comics fans the best the art form has to offer. In 1990 the awards began being presented at Comic-Con International's annual comic book convention in San Diego, California.

1989
Eisner publishes *City People Notebook,* a collection of urban short stories with a strong wordless component.

1991
Eisner publishes the graphic novel *To the Heart of the Storm,* an autobiographical work dealing with anti-Semitism in America in the 1930s and 1940s; Eisner also publishes *The Will Eisner Reader,* a collection of short stories from Kitchen Sink Press's *Will Eisner Quarterly* magazine.

1992
Eisner publishes *Invisible People,* an urban series of linked short stories dealing with working-class hope and despair.

1995
Eisner is awarded the Milton Caniff Lifetime Achievement award by the National Cartoonists Society.

1996
Eisner designs a mural based on the Spirit story "Gerhard Shnobble," which is painted on a building in Copenhagen, Denmark; a print of the mural is issued as well.

1997
The Spirit: The New Adventures begins, a comic book series devoted to new Spirit sto-

ries by contemporary creators, including Alan Moore and Dave Gibbons (*Watchmen*), Neil Gaiman (*Sandman*), and Eddie Campbell *(From Hell)*, edited by Catherine Garnier from Kitchen Sink Press. The series ends at issue no. 8, with the demise of Kitchen Sink Press.

1998

Eisner is honored by the International Graphic Novel Conference on the twentieth anniversary of the publication of *A Contract with God*, organized by N. C. Christopher Couch, and covered in a feature article in *The New York Times*.

2000

DC Comics publishes Eisner's *Minor Miracles*, a return to the thematically linked short story format he began with *A Contract with God* and continued through key works like *The Building*; *The Spirit Archives*, the first complete reprinting of Eisner's masterwork in full color, begins with the first of 20-something volumes, published by DC Comics.

2001

Eisner publishes *The Name of the Game*, a dark and deeply personal graphic novel that he had worked on for a half-dozen years. It depicts the social and economic divisions in New York between Jewish communities of different European origins and the tensions and prejudices that can affect marriage and friendship across these divisions. *The Name of the Game* is a fictional work located in the same social networks potrayed in Stephen Birmingham's nonfiction bestseller *Our Crowd*.

2002

Eisner receives the Lifetime Achievement Award from the National Foundation for Jewish Culture in New York. This is only the second Lifetime Achievement Award that the NFJC has given in its 40-year history.

2003

Eisner is honored as the "Father of the Graphic Novel" with an invitation to give an address entitled "The 25th Anniversary of the Graphic Novel" at the University of Massachusetts in Amherst, celebrating his pioneering publication of *A Contract with God* in 1978. Eisner's address is covered in an article in *The New York Times* by Steven Lee Beeber, and the anniversary is also observed with programming at the San Diego Comic-Con and numerous articles in the comics press.

2003

Eisner publishes *Fagin the Jew*, a retelling of the story of Oliver Twist from Fagin's point of view, setting a new direction in his work that will be continued in his next graphic novel, *The Plot*. Published by Doubleday, *Fagin the Jew* is Eisner's first book to be published by a New York trade house since *A Contract with God*.

2005

Eisner is invited to give the annual Robert and Pamela Jacobs Distinguished Lecture in Jewish Life and Culture at the Center for Judaic Studies at the University of Massachusetts in Amherst.

2005

W. W. Norton to publish Eisner's *The Plot*, his first nonfiction graphic novel, depicting the story of the anti-Semitic forgery The Protocols of the Elders of Zion. The Protocols was created by the Russian secret police for Czar Nicholas II and extensively used by the Nazis in propaganda leading to the Holocaust. Eisner's work demonstrates the means by which the forgery was created, traces its history, and serves as a warning about its renewed circulation in anti-Semitic propaganda and politics in today's world.

THE HUMAN SPIRIT

by N. C. Christopher Couch

In 1940, comic books had existed for all of seven years. During this short period, the new artistic medium had grown at blinding speed. By 1940, most of the conventions that still characterize comic books had been developed by the talented pioneers of the first generation of creators. In 1940, one of the most innovative of these creators began to extend the creative reach of the medium by challenging these conventions in a new comic. This creator was Will Eisner, and his comic was *The Spirit*.

The first comic books reprinted strips from newspapers, but within a few years of M. C. Gaines's *More Fun* (usually identified as the first comic book to be sold on newsstands), comic books had come to include all-new and original material. The real success of comics, however, had been guaranteed, in a sense, by a development that no one could have predicted. There was nothing like it in newspaper comic strips. The financial future and public acceptance of this new type of publication was guaranteed by the creation of the first and most important costumed super hero, Jerry Siegel and Joe Shuster's Superman.

When the Man of Steel burst on the scene in 1938, this new archetype demonstrated that this new kind of newsstand magazine could sell thousands upon millions of copies to a diverse market by featuring original material and new characters created only for the comic book medium. In 1939, Batman followed Superman into this new four-color world, and the future of the genre seemed assured.

Of course, there were already other heroes in comic strips. For example, Terry Ryan of "Terry and the Pirates" (by the master, Milton Caniff), was a tough and resourceful hero who was up to any challenge, and whose adventures were artistically striking and innovative. Science fiction provided readers with heroes, like Buck Rogers in the glorious Sunday pages drawn by Russell Keaton. And literary heroes moved into the pages of comics as well, like Edgar Rice Burroughs's Tarzan, whose earliest depictions were the atmospheric and illustrative strips by Hal Foster, who would later create Prince Valiant.

But comic book heroes were something new. It wasn't just the costumes, or the derring-do of the crime fighters who punished evildoers and protected the innocent. These were heroes who were powerful, intelligent, and incredibly resourceful at fighting crime and injustice. But they were also heroes who, in a very real sense, lived in the same world that the readers inhabited. Superman's adventures didn't take place in exotic Asian locales like Terry Ryan's, or in the jungles of Africa, like Tarzan's. The Man of Steel may have come from outer space, but he fought crime and injustice right here on Earth, in a big gritty metropolitan city. It was called Metropolis—but it was also Any City, U.S.A. Batman, who made his debut in 1939, found himself in Gotham, and while it was New York for all intents and

purposes, it was also a city with the problems and hopes of any American town: Gangland crime. Political corruption. Poverty. And hopelessness in the wake of the Great Depression. Even the Amazon Princess Wonder Woman came to the good old U.S.A. a year later in 1940 to bring ideals of equality to the everyday life of men, women, and girls and boys.

Comic books had romance and action, but the heroes had a quality of involvement in everyday life that wasn't lost on the fans. This "reality" was something readers couldn't get in the adventure comic strips that ran in the newspapers, and it appealed to kids and grownups in every walk of life. Comic books offered real heroes who lived in real cities and towns, and readers embraced this new form of entertainment.

Newspaper editors took notice. How could they not? Everybody loves the funny papers, but when comic books started selling millions of copies a month, the editors couldn't help but wonder if maybe, just maybe, it might not be a good idea to include some kind of comic book in their papers as well. The placement of magazines in newspapers had a long and successful history. In the 1890s, Joseph Pulitzer, the great pioneer of populist newspapers, had included tons of pictures in his *New York World*, and then added a general-interest magazine that was a huge success and led to all the newspaper magazines we have now, from the *New York Times Sunday Magazine* to *Parade*. Pulitzer followed this up with the addition of a free humor magazine, and included in it the first comic strip, R. F. Outcault's "The Yellow Kid," in 1895. Thus the Sunday funnies were born.

The Spirit Weekly Comic Book Section emerged from same spirit of innovation. When comic books roared out of the starting gate in the 1930s, this hot new medium burned up content so fast that it was impossible for individual artists to keep up with the demand.

Some of the most resourceful creators founded studios, where teams of artists and writers worked together to create a steady flow of new stories, new characters, and new adventures to keep the readers coming back for more. These studios, usually called shops, were run by an artist of talent and attracted the up-and-coming creators, many of whom would later come to dominate the field.

Considered to be one of the best shops at the time was the one founded by Will Eisner and his friend Samuel "Jerry" Iger. Between 1936 and 1939, some of the artists who would become the best in the business worked in the Eisner-Iger Studios: Bob Kane, who would later create Batman; Jack Kirby (then named Jack Kurtzberg), who created superb World War II–era comics featuring Captain America, and later some of the best comics ever: The Fantastic Four, Kamandi, and the New Gods; and the elegant Lou Fine, famed for his comics featuring the Ray and the Condor. Ever an innovator, Eisner led the shop into the creation of an international comics syndicate that sold original comics to British and Australian publishers, as well as creating page after page, feature after feature, for American comic book publishers. Eisner created characters and launched features that have stood the test of time, from the aviation team Blackhawk to the blonde and magnificent Sheena, beautiful jungle queen who, years later, continues to appear on syndicated television.

The comic book experienced commercial success soon after its birth in the 1930s. It is also an artistic medium that has attracted artists and writers who were, and are, devoted to the genre as a unique—and often misunderstood—medium of expression. Few creators have been more devoted to the cultural importance of "sequential art" than Will Eisner. From his earliest days in comics, breaking into the field with his first sales in 1936, Eisner has believed in its potential. Eisner's family background may have provided a unique advantage that helped him come to this early understanding of what comics could be: His father painted scenery for another popular medium that has recently received recognition for its pivotal role in American and world culture—

the Yiddish theater. Eisner himself studied with some of the greatest American illustrators, such as George Bridgman, at the Art Students' League in New York City. But his devotion to comics has never wavered. This led to his founding of the American Visuals Company in the early 1950s, the most successful creator of educational comics ever. It also led to his creation of the graphic novel medium in 1978, with the publication of *A Contract with God*, the first-ever graphic novel. And when the chance came to create a comic book to be included in the Sunday newspapers, Eisner not only jumped at it, he created what is probably the single most influential comic book ever published in the United States, perhaps in the world—*The Spirit*.

In 1939, comics entrepreneur Everett "Busy" Arnold asked Eisner to join him in the Quality Comics Group, another shop. Arnold wanted Eisner to be the creative force behind a comic book supplement that would be circulated to the nation's newspapers by the Des Moines Register and Tribune Syndicate. A syndicate is a company that provides comic strips and other features to newspapers, and in this intensely competitive business these companies are always looking for the best and most innovative features to sell. Newspaper editors had observed the success of comic books and, not wanting to be left behind, were open to buying a comic book as a free supplement for their Sunday editions. Eisner was the ideal choice to create such a weekly comic book. He had developed a reputation in comics for being superb at meeting deadlines (there is perhaps no deadline more unforgiving than that of a daily newspaper). Also, Eisner was famous for closely supervising the comics that his studio produced. He went over every script and every page of art, and if there was something that wasn't up to his standards, he'd have it redrawn or he'd redraw it himself.

The new Sunday Comic Book Section (later renamed The Spirit Section) was a good package for readers. Each week the section's logo proclaimed that it offered "Action, Mystery, and Adventure," and like this tripartite banner of attractions, the section included three different features. All were created by Will Eisner, but only the Spirit was his own, written and drawn by Eisner himself, albeit with a little help from the assistants in his new studio. The two backup features that appeared when The Spirit Section began were Lady Luck, an Irish-American adventuress and crime fighter who dressed all in green, and Mr. Mystic, an American who had the wisdom of the yogis at his disposal for his encounters with criminals.

Each Spirit section was sixteen pages long, all in color, and printed on newsprint just like the Sunday funnies or the interiors of comic books. It was nearly the size of a newsstand comic book, but it didn't have a separate cover on slick paper. Instead, it was what's called in the business "self-covering," so the first page acts as the cover, but it's also the place where the story begins. This could have been a limitation but Eisner, ever the innovator, turned this feature into a plus, making the first page a showpiece almost every week. These *Spirit* "splash" pages have become some of the most famous comic book art ever done. Sometimes they were dark and moody, sometimes very humorous, sometimes uproariously funny. And instead of having a monotonous, repetitive logo each and every week, Eisner prided himself on innovative ways to incorporate the title into the story. Sometimes the logo would be a billboard with the Spirit's name on it; sometimes all the letters would be turned into buildings in a cityscape; sometimes the logo would appear on a newspaper, its letters washing down into a gutter in the rain.

This approach to the logo treatment didn't always sit well with Busy Arnold, and sometimes he and Eisner even heard complaints from the copyright and trademark office. "How can we trademark this when it never looks the same?" they were asked. But Eisner kept on his own path. And he did the same thing with his hero, the Spirit. Because this was a comic book, the editors who were buying it expected certain things, features that they thought would help their new Sunday supplement compete with the comics on the newsstand. The hero had to have a costume, and he needed a secret identity. What good is a comic book hero without these conventions, they argued.

So *The Spirit* contained both "concessions" to the genre in his origin story, which appeared on June 2, 1940. Handsome, young private detective and criminologist Denny Colt tracks down the evil genius Dr. Cobra in his Chinatown lair where he's perfecting a new and poisonous chemical concoction. Denny is accidentally doused in this liquid and goes into a state of suspended animation, so the whole world thinks he's dead. But he revives in Wildwood Cemetery, and reveals his secret only to his friend, Police Commissioner Eustace P. Dolan. Denny decides to use his new "deceased" status as a tool to fight crime, creating a new identity as the masked crime fighter the Spirit!

Of course, a crime fighter can't operate entirely alone. The Spirit soon found himself in a world populated by friends and partners, loyal allies who helped him in his mission. He was opposed, sometimes outwitted, often beaten up but never ultimately defeated by adversaries who were some of the most dastardly villains ever created. And somehow he always ended up surrounded by gorgeous women who were bowled over by his charms, even though he had no idea just how smitten they were.

From his origin story to his last case on October 5, 1952, the Spirit's closest collaborator, the guardian of his secret identity, and the man who was a real father figure to Denny Colt, was the pipe-smoking police professional Commissioner Dolan. With his striking combination of bald head and widow's peak, his everburning pipe and three-piece suits, Dolan was usually the calm center of the Spirit's crime-ridden world. In his most action-packed adventures, the Spirit could always count on Dolan to come in at the end and haul away the criminals in cuffs. Dolan was an Irish cop at heart who began his career by pounding a beat, and

worked his way up to commissioner. But one of Eisner's themes throughout the dozen-year run of *The Spirit* was corruption in the cities, and the evils of machine politics. Dolan's finest hours may have been when he stood up to bribe-taking politicos like Ward Healey, no matter the consequences to his career. Before World War II, Dolan even found himself running for mayor to support his convictions, but fortunately after his victory, he found a reformer to serve in his stead. After the war, his ideals inspired his daughter, the beautiful and strong-willed Ellen Dolan, to run for mayor—and she won!

Blonde-haired, blue-eyed, tall and commanding, Ellen Dolan was the Spirit's first and only best girl. When the Spirit began, Ellen was a college student. She was also one of the few comic book characters who grew up and changed over time. Surrounded by men and women who fought crime, policemen and detectives, insurance investigators like Silk Satin and Detective McDool, Ellen Dolan learned the ways of criminals and those who hunted them. When she ran for mayor of Central City, she not only had to beat her political opponents, she also had to overcome the opposition of the Spirit, who couldn't understand why a woman would want to be mayor. But she proved to be the new broom that swept Central City clean, and her mayoralty provided a bully pulpit for Eisner's subtle but clear calls for cleaning up urban politics.

Is *The Spirit* a feminist comic book? Feminism wasn't a word that was in anybody's vocabulary between 1940 and 1952, the years that the Spirit appeared in the nation's newspapers. But it would be difficult, if not impossible, to find any other sustained body of work in American popular culture (or perhaps even in literary, artistic, or theatrical works) that featured so many strong, independent, intelligent, and fascinating female characters. Of course having Ellen Dolan run for mayor is remarkable enough in the context of America after World War II, when the entire culture seemed to be focused on getting American women out of the factories and workplace, ending the era of Rosie the Riveter and turning them into consumer housewives in a time of *Leave It to Beaver* and *Father Knows Best*. Ellen's mayoralty took on even more social and emotional power because of Eisner's long concern with municipal corruption and its pernicious effect on the lives of city dwellers. That a woman took on this eternal problem made this series of stories all the more powerful.

The Spirit was a detective, and even though he had a secret identity, he's certainly in the great tradition of American detective fiction that features hard-boiled dicks like Dashiell Hammett's Continental Op and Sam Spade, Raymond Chandler's Philip Marlowe, and John D. McDonald's Travis McGee. And a detective always needs to meet

up with femmes fatales, but usually all they can do is be femme, or fatale, and the detective either sends them to jail, like Sam Spade, or unites them with their maker, like Mickey Spillane. Where but in *The Spirit* are the femmes fatales professional women? The most femme and most fatale of them all is the lovely P'Gell, named for the Place Pigalle, the red light district of Paris that entranced so many American GIs in the aftermath of World War II. She was an international adventuress, often married and frequently—and mysteriously—widowed. But she didn't remain an adventuress, or not solely an adventuress. Within just a few installments, she became the headmistress of Miss Vitriola's School for Girls, which soon became known as P'Gell's School. And while her lovely teenaged daughter, Saree, learned things other than the three Rs from school, her mom, P'Gell, proved herself to be a professional administrator who rose to a series of financial and legal challenges to keep her school open. As Eisner described her, "P'Gell deals with life as it develops. I never could really deal with a hero or villain, male or female, who was totally one-sided. As far as I'm concerned, they were all multifaceted."

Despite her incredibly feminine and sexy name, Silk Satin was one of the most accomplished of the women who fell in with—and fell for—the Spirit. After World War II, Satin first went to work as an agent for the United Nations, and after the wounds of the world were beginning to heal, moved on to a more lucrative post as an insurance investigator with the top-dollar company Croyd's of Glasgow, the company that would insure anything. Satin also had a daughter, Hildie, whom she had rescued from the Nazis.

Not only were the femmes fatales in *The Spirit* professionally accomplished—they were mothers. Single mothers. Mothers who worked. Thirty years before the publication of Betty Friedan's groundbreaking *The Feminine Mystique*, forty years before the '80s, the decade of the woman devoted to having it all, fifty years before the political fund called Emily's List devoted itself to electing women to public office, the heroines of *The Spirit* were living the concerns that would dominate the discourse that we call feminism. But hey, it was just comics.

In 1942, Will Eisner was drafted into the army. It was inevitable, and while Eisner and his partner Busy Arnold had planned for this eventuality, there was no way that Eisner could be directly involved in the weekly creation of *The Spirit* while he was in the service. As a result, he left the feature in the hands of two veteran creators: Manly Wade Wellman, a writer who is well known as one of the first great generation of science fiction writers, a contributor to the golden age of the SF pulp magazines like *Amazing Stories* and *Thrilling Wonder Stories*; and Lou Fine, one of the most talented comic artists of his generation. Fine was a perfectionist whose art was as complex and exciting as some of the best comic strip artists, like Alex Raymond of Flash Gordon fame. Eisner himself continued to create comic art, but for the Pentagon. His skills were recognized by the army, and he created posters, comic strips, and drawings about machines, maintenance, and ordnance throughout World War II, educating many GIs through one of the best educational media ever created—the comics—helping to train soldiers, probably even saving lives.

After the war in 1946, Eisner more and more felt he had to deal with an issue that was raised in *The Spirit* by Denny Colt's kid sidekick, the African-American character Ebony White. Ebony joined the Spirit almost at the beginning, meeting the detective as a cab driver who helped get him to the scene of the crime in some of his earliest cases. Following

the template set in the comics, he gradually became a kid sidekick. Ebony's appearance and speech patterns were based on the depiction and dialect used by black entertainers in films and by white performers in blackface on the vaudeville stage, but his personality and accomplishments were never those of the demeaning characters who were so often used for comic relief. Ebony was a full and intelligent partner in assisting the Spirit in solving crimes. After the war, Eisner felt even more strongly that African-American characters should not be stereotyped, and Ebony soon gained an even fuller range of professions. He went back to school, and his accent was moderated. He organized art shows, directed films, and in general became an ever-more accomplished assistant to the Spirit. Eisner also introduced other African-American characters to the feature, characters who had no accents and were professionals, like Lt. Oren Grey, who collaborated with the Spirit on several cases. Eventually, a new kid was introduced, a baseball-playing towhead named Sammy, who pitched in to help the Spirit catch bad guys for several years after the war. Ebony also continued to appear from time to time.

No hero would be complete without some dastardly villains. What would Superman be without Lex Luthor? Sherlock Holmes without Professor Moriarty? Batman without the Joker? The first villain Denny Colt met was the aforementioned Dr. Cobra. In fact, there would have been no Spirit without the evil scientist. His plot against the city, creating a toxic substance to poison the water supply, led to the creation of the Spirit. But probably the feature's most memorable villain was the Octopus, a European criminal, a collaborator with the evil Axis powers of Fascist Germany and Italy, who devoted himself to recreating his international criminal network after the Allied victory. No one knows what he looks like, because he always wears masks that cover his entire head, sometimes multiple masks that he pulls off like nested Russian dolls. His signature feature is his mysterious pair of gloves. "My master criminal is a multiple character," Eisner has said. "His triple-striped gloves gave me the chance to let the reader in on the secret. There's also something very threatening about gloves, especially if they're associated with a villain." The Octopus is never captured by the Spirit, and in some ways he is the mirror image of our hero. Like Holmes's Moriarty, he's a villain who is as smart and strong and analytical as the detective. Like the Spirit, he wears a mask. In fact, both he and the Spirit wear gloves. The Octopus is a worthy opponent for Denny Colt as he creates a new life for himself.

The villains, the femmes fatales, the police, and the criminals are only some of the stars in *The Spirit*. It's the rare hero who's sure enough of himself to step aside and let the ordinary people take center stage, but the Spirit is just that exceptional. The working people of Central City, the messengers, the construction workers, the kids, are just as likely to be the central characters in a Spirit story as an international villain. The best-known of these is the most ordinary of all, Gerhard Shnobble. Gerhard Shnobble had one unusual talent: he could fly. And his flight was achieved not through any magic or mysterious technology, but through his own belief that he could do this, even though he was completely ordinary in every other way. This parable about the uniqueness of each individual and the ability of anyone, no matter how ordinary, to have a dream and realize it, is one of the true classics in the Spirit series.

Quite frankly, *The Spirit* is one of the greatest comic books ever created. And it contains all the elements that make comics great. Denny Colt becomes the Spirit, and lives in a secret hideout in Wildwood Cemetery. But his real life takes place in the streets of Central City. He tangles with international criminals, but he's also on the lookout for municipal corruption. He's the object of affection of femmes fatales, but he's also a friend to kids like Ebony, Sammy, and the marvelously spoiled Darling O'Shea. He's like the super heroes who came to four-color life every month in the comic books, a hero you could look up to but also somebody who walked down the same streets you do. And in *The Spirit* series, the hero would often step out of the way and let the ordinary people, like Gerhard Shnobble, take center stage to live out their dreams.

The Spirit wears a mask, and he has a secret identity, but he's a man of the people. He takes his lumps from villains, and loves real women who live in the real world. But the greatest thing about the Spirit is that he's both a hero and a human being at the same time. And that's the greatest thing about the world we all live in: the human Spirit.

Acyd Test: The Spirit gets called by Riverbend cop Dick Whittler to help out in a case involving international femme fatale P'Gell, who has taken a post teaching French at the local university. She wants to steal Professor Acyd's Metal Alloy Test, but when the Spirit outwits her and her "strongarm boys," she simply marries the professor—or, at least, she tries. The bogus preacher is none other than Chief Whittler, and P'Gell ends up in jail, albeit briefly. (9/10/50)

Atomic Bomb: When the atomic age began at the end of World War II, popular culture responded with atomic advertising slogans. Eisner mocked these kitschy coinages in a story featuring Goldberg's Atomic Frankfurters and Joe's Food, "served with atomic speed." Despite the humor, this was a cautionary tale, based on the fears of some atomic  scientists that an atom bomb could set off a chain reaction that would destroy the entire world  (2/3/46). In another satire of the postwar world, a broadcast by Gabriel Horn (a parody of New York radio personality Gabriel Heatter) chases Revolutionary War veteran Abe Pewter back to the past when he announces "Atomic scientists predict we are on the brink of doom!" (4/28/46). Atomic bombs explode in Eisner's satire of filmmaker Billy Wilder's Academy Award-winning depiction of alcoholism, *The Lost Weekend*. In "The Lost Fortnight" (6/30/46), sidekick Ebony is addicted to soda pop, and pawns a top-secret device the Spirit has given him to guard in order to feed his habit. Fortunately, in this auteur outing where Ebony is both director and star, only the hideouts of femme fatale Gurka Fyfe and her escaped war criminal henchmen are bombed, and thus only bad guys are harmed. Media frenzy over atomic bomb stories was parodied when Murmansk Manny showed up in Central City for a U.N. Security Council meeting with the "cosmic answer," a scientific formula more important than the atomic bomb, and reporters swarmed over him and everyone else in sight (2/2/47). Hiroshima on August 6, 1945, site of the second atomic blast in Japan that ended World War II, is one stop on the voyages of the haunted *S.S. Raven,* a killer ship even the Spirit cannot bring to shore. (9/21/47)

Autoplane: The Spirit couldn't fly like Superman, and he wasn't a high-flying athlete like Batman, who could swing from building to building at great heights. To get to crime  scenes, or to get the jump on crooks, in the Spirit's earliest adventures he drove and flew an autoplane, a classic red roadster that could sprout wings and take to the air.

Ball, Rolla: Television first appears in the Spirit's world in "Roller Derby" (2/12/50), starring the lovely Rolla Ball, when Central City gets captivated by televised female athletes on roller skates. When gangster Waxie Tallow wants Rolla to throw the race, the cameraman who's in love with her catches the evil deed on film. But Bascome Birch is disappointed when Rolla still won't marry him because she's moving on to a new televised sport: she's been signed as a lady wrestler.

Bandito, Signor: An Italian private detective comes to Central City to retrieve a locket that had belonged to Benito Mussolini, also known as *Il Duce* (the leader), Fascist dictator of Italy during World War II. Mussolini's corpse was hung upside down by his betrayed countrymen at the end of the war and, in Eisner's story, the locket contained a map showing the location of his treasure vault and fell into the hands of femme fatale P'Gell. Fortunately, the Spirit manages to get his gloves on it. (5/25/47)

Batt, Captain "Blind": A criminal version of Captain Ahab (from Herman Melville's *Moby Dick*), Captain Batt had led a crew of illegal whalers during World War II, and set out on a pirate voyage after the war to collect the whale oil, meat, and bones he and his gang had hunted. His nefarious plot is spoiled by the Spirit, but the real hero of the story is Denny Colt's new Inuit sidekick, Blubber, who guides the city-dweller detective through the dangers of the arctic. Batt is finally done in not by the Spirit, but by an angry, wounded whale, like Ahab. In 2001 Eisner retold the story of Ahab and Moby Dick in a children's book (see page 157). (2/17/46)

Bells, Awsome: In 1938, Orson Welles and his Mercury Theatre created what is probably the single most famous radio broadcast in history, a 1939 production of H.G. Wells's *The War of the Worlds*. Updated and set in contemporary New York and New Jersey, the show caused widespread panic when listeners thought the alien invasion was real. Welles later directed the film *Citizen Kane* (1941), a fictionalized biography of media mogul William Randolph Hearst, widely considered the best American film ever made. Welles became a larger-than-life celebrity, a media presence whose personal recognizability continued even when his acting and directing output faded. Eisner satirized Welles's famous radio broadcast (and subsequent corpulent presence) in "UFO" (9/28/47), but with admiration for the man and the artist. "Orson Welles was a tremendous influence on me," Eisner explained. "He was a genius and I was an ardent fan. What Welles was trying for in his work was the same thing I was trying for: believability."

Bendbagel, Guthrie, Jr.: Fate, chance, and the lives of ordinary people are themes Eisner explores at length in his graphic novels, and also with poetic clarity in *Spirit* stories like those of Gerhard Shnobble (9/5/48) and Guthrie Bendbagel, Jr. In the midst of this *Spirit* story about a scam cooked up by a crooked jeweler, Mr. Gem, and the sleazy European Prince Gunnar Metternix, Bendbagel is a messenger who tries repeatedly to deliver a jeweled tiara, the focus of the plot, until he accidentally dies in a hail of bullets fired by some of the conspirators. Bendbagel, and by implication all human beings, compared in this darkly humorous tale to the common housefly, living a short life at the mercy of events. In his 1988 graphic novel *A Life Force*, Eisner uses cockroaches as a similar symbol. (3/10/46)

Bierce, Ambrose: Several years before the famous E.C. Comics adaptations of stories by science fiction writer Ray Bradbury, Eisner adapted in *The Spirit* powerful supernatural short stories by two earlier American masters. "The Damned Thing" (1894), renamed "The

By the light of a tallow candle which had been placed on one end of a rough table, a man was reading something written in an old, greasy, worn account book.

AMBROSE BIERCE

Thing" when it appeared in newspapers (7/25/48), is by reporter, writer, and dark humorist Ambrose Bierce (author of *The Devil's Dictionary*). It's the story of the horrible mauling death of Hugh Morgan at the hands of a mysterious being, witnessed by a young reporter. "The Fall of the House of Usher" (8/22/48), written by Edgar Allan Poe in 1839, is the story of Roderick Usher and the destruction of the cursed and haunted family manse. Each story is read by the Spirit to Ebony.

Black Queen: The first of the strong and beautiful femmes fatales the Spirit would tangle with, the Black Queen is a high-powered lawyer who sets the standards of intelligence and professional accomplishment that her successors will uphold. She beats Slot Gorgan's murder rap to recruit him to boss the rackets with her, though the Spirit sees that Gorgan ends up in the slammer and the dough goes to school lunches. Then the Black Queen ups the ante, getting all of the city's gangs to work together to steal fifty million dollars from New York City's U.S. Subtreasury. In her final story, the Black Queen becomes a cold-blooded murderess, killing chemist Herman Keil and jeweler Abner Ames with her deadly kisses, then doing herself in while in jail in order to avoid the electric chair. (6/16/40; 7/7/40; 10/13/40; 11/10/40)

Bonehead, Cadaver B.: Central City's inspector of cemeteries, Cadaver B. Bonehead is reluctantly forced by boss pol Ward Healey in "Mr. Bowser's Selection" to run for mayor so his featherbedding relatives can keep their patronage jobs in the city's bureaucracy. (11/9/47)

Bones, Skinny: A *Spirit* femme fatale inspired by the beautiful actress Lauren Bacall, who offered to come if whistled for by Humphrey Bogart in Howard Hawks's *To Have and Have Not* (1944). Skinny was appealing enough that Eisner did a gorgeous original cover drawing of her for *The Spirit* comic book no. 22 (August 1950), which served as the basis for a 1986 serigraph released by Kitchen

SKINNY BONES

BORSCHTBELT'S BUTTERMILK

Sink Press. Skinny first appeared as the moll of mobster Glut Mutton. After the Spirit puts Glut away, Skinny hooks up with the equally gorgeous brunette Dulcet Tone to take over the hoods controlling the black market. But when Skinny realizes Dulcet is double-crossing her, she rats out her partner to the cops and tries to knife her in a fight in the harbor. Locked up for murder, Skinny goes free when Dulcet reappears. (6/9/46; 7/7/46; 7/14/46)

Borschtbelt's Buttermilk: The borscht belt or borscht circuit refers to the hotels of the Catskill Mountain area to the north of New York City. These hotels attracted primarily Jewish vacationers from the city, the nightclubs launching and nurturing the careers of many comedians and entertainers from Henny Youngman to Barbra Streisand. Borscht is a type of eastern European soup, most characteristically made from beets, but also from cabbage, potatoes, or other vegetables, and the name is a joking reference to the amounts of such soup supposedly consumed at these hotels. A Spirit-ed satire of liquor advertising, "Distinguished Men prefer Borschtbelt's Buttermilk" (8/18/46), is a multilayered joke in which a nonalcoholic beverage is advertised like a high-priced drink, but it's named after a district featuring primarily middle- and working-class hotel nightclubs.

Boxing: From the 1920s through the 1940s, sports writers like Ring Lardner were media stars, and their work appeared in newspaper sections along with almost equally famous sports cartoonists, including Willard Mullin, Leo O'Melia (who later worked for DC Comics), and a young V. T. Hamlin, the creator of the "Alley Oop" comic strip. Early on Eisner tried his hand at sports cartoons, but the vogue for them had ended. Eisner felt his style had something in common with sports cartoonists: "Probably one of the reasons I was accepted by the military as a cartoonist [after being drafted in 1942] was because of the rugged style. I was more in the tradition of Willard Mullin, the sports cartoonist. Bill Mauldin and Jack Davis are in that mold, too." The Spirit met several boxers in his career: Dipsy is a sad case, a patsy who has his nerves deadened by a character who, neither trainer nor gambler, is a ghoul who just likes to see the boxer kill other guys in the ring (3/23/41). Professor Bones brings twenty-five years of scientific training to bear on Nasdrov the Invincible, but it turns out the Spirit is the invincible one (11/16/47). When the Central City Police Department caps off a drive to aid the poor with a charity bazaar at the fairgrounds, one of the carnies, fight promoter Merry Andrew, figures to make off with the proceeds by slipping a Mickey Finn (slang for a knockout drug) into the free punch. He becomes "The Man Who Laid the Spirit Low," but when Musclehead McSneer forces him into his gang, it turns out the Spirit still packs a

punch. The narrative of this story is not derived from boxing movies or stories, but from popular poetry like Hugh Antoine D'Arcy's "The Face on the Barroom Floor (1887)," and the whole story is told in panel-less settings below Eisner's verse (2/15/48). The darkest portrait of boxing is the story of Porker, the fight promoter who manipulates the brothers Herbie and Marty Gritt into meeting in a fatal bout in the ring. (12/3/50)

Brown, Brains: The smartest kid in P.S. 23, Brains Brown needs Ebony's help with a report on crime. When they examine the criminals in the rogues gallery at police headquarters, they see a picture of Truant Officer Frend, placed there by a wag. The two boys capture Frend at school. In their pursuit, they aid the Spirit in capturing a crooked contractor, political boss Mr. Bubble, who has cornered all the contracts to build postwar schools. The kids inadvertently lead the Spirit to Bubble's henchmen in the boiler room, where they are digging under the school to make it collapse. (9/15/46)

BRAINS BROWN

Brown, Sawbuck: A poor orphan whose first name is slang for a one hundred dollar bill, Sawbuck Brown is one of many orphans in Eisner's fiction. "I think it must come out of my readings of Horatio Alger books when I was a kid," Eisner has said. "I supposed I identified a little bit with those books." In Alger's mid-nineteenth century tearjerkers, poor-but-honest orphans are always lifted from their misery by a good deed that brings them a wealthy patron. Sawbuck's fate is changed the first time he uses a gun. He wings Officer Klink, a young patrolman. Then the cop and the Spirit combine to show the boy the horrors of criminal life, saving him from joining Benny Zilch's gang. (11/2/47)

Bubble, Mr.: A corrupt political boss and contractor, Mr. Bubble, like Ward Healey, is a big-city type that Eisner knew well from growing up in the Bronx. "We always considered them the enemy. They were the guys you needed to know to get things done. The political machine was very powerful. You couldn't fight City Hall, but if you could get a contract at City Hall, that was the thing to do." Mr. Bubble burns down P.S. 43 to get a contract to rebuild it, then he heads the Citizen's Committee, a group devoted to putting the Spirit out of action. Mr. Bubble gets the citizens so worked up about stopping this vigilante (who also makes life harder for the bosses) that one of them shoots Commissioner Dolan in an attempt to frame the Spirit. Finally, Mr. Bubble nearly ends the Spirit's career, getting evidence

MR. BUBBLE

that he is Denny Colt, but then he's murdered. It looks like the rap is going to be pinned on the Spirit, but Ebony steps in and proves that the thug Case Phingle bumped Mr. Bubble off. Phingle killed Bubble to take over his rackets, a suitably ironic end for a corrupt political boss. (9/15/46; 10/6/46; 2/8/48)

Bustle, Olga: Actress Jane Russell's career was launched by aviation pioneer and industrialist Howard Hughes during his brief Hollywood career, when she starred in *The Outlaw* (1943). Famed for being "well-endowed" (and for wearing the Hughes invention, the "uplift bra"), Russell's notoriety launched a thousand satires, including Ms. Olga Bustle, "The Girl with Those Big, Big Eyes!" whose first starring role is in *Outcast*. Olga's agent,

OLGA BUSTLE

Format Finn, sets her up with a big contest, "The Girl American Men Would Like to Be Cast Away with on a Desert Island." As in any good screwball comedy, the Spirit ends up with Olga on Birdrock Isle, and she falls for him big time, ignoring the real contest winner, the criminal Mr. Dusk. Olga ends up behind bars for her blackmailing ways, and Dusk ends up adrift on the waves. (9/1/46)

Caliban, John: Alias Mr. Midnight, Caliban is based on the actor John Barrymore, patriarch of the theatrical family whose lineage extends to actress Drew Barrymore. John Barrymore was famed as "the profile" on account of his classic good looks, and renowned for his Shakespearean roles, especially Hamlet (thus this character is named after the sprite from *A Midsummer Night's Dream* and addresses his prop skull as Yorick). Caliban's *Spirit* turn is a classic mystery story à la John Dickson Carr, where Caliban demonstrates the perfect crime, murdering Ellison Wright without weapons or personal contact. (7/14/40)

JOHN CALIBAN

Capp, Al: One of the most famous comic strips of its day, "Li'l Abner" featured the hillbilly inhabitants of the town of Dogpatch, somewhere in the Appalachians. It starred the tall, dark, and innocent Abner Yokum, his folks Mammy and Pappy, and his gorgeous blonde sweetheart Daisy Mae. Abner's favorite comic strip is the strip-within-a-strip "Fearless Fosdick," a satire of Chester Gould's square-jawed detective Dick Tracy. Al Capp (the nom de plume of Alfred Gerald Caplin) was lauded by critics, including author John Steinbeck, for his strip, and a successful Broadway show and film were made from it in the late 1950s. In 1947, Capp asked Eisner to engage in a fake feud in their strips, and thus *The Spirit* featured the parody "Li'l Adam, the Stupid Mountain Boy" (7/20/47). Just as Eisner was creating this story, *Newsweek* contacted the artist about plans to feature him in an article. The "Li'l Abner" satire ended up getting national publicity in this weekly news magazine in the issue of 7/21/47. Eisner later concluded that the well-connected Capp knew in advance that *Newsweek* was going to write about the Spirit. "When the article came out, I suddenly realized that Al had somehow heard about it and correctly figured it as a way to get a free ride," Eisner recalled. "He

AL CAPP

never did anything in his strip about *The Spirit*." The story, which features Li'l Adam and Fearful Fooznick and includes the attempted murder of cartoonist Al Slapp, also takes pointed aim at the syndicates that circulate comic strips to newspapers and the money they make from the cartoonists who create the strips. Like Capp, Eisner had included a detective comic as a strip within a strip, "Gumshoe Gus" (7/27/41), credited to cartoonist Pink Perkins. Early in his career, Eisner himself had done a funny detective strip called Harry Carey, renamed Harry Karry when it was published in the comic book, *Wow, What a Magazine!* in 1936.

Caramba: Deep in the jungles of South America, there's a place where every criminal has a second home, the resort "Caramba" (11/10/46). Vacations for the Octopus, rest and

CARAMBA

relaxation for Mr. Carrion, they're to be found in Caramba, where the travel brochures offer "Gunplay, Murder, Gambling, and Interesting Characters." You can book your trip on Croox Tours (a pun on the famous Cook's Tour Company), and see the statue of Jack the Ripper in the town square (11/17/46). "The Eisner Travel Agency" (8/1/48) guarantees that any story set here will be a lighthearted romp.

Carrion, Mr.: In 1945, when Eisner returned to *The Spirit* after his stint in the army, he gave his new stories a real flavor of postwar America, where meat was still rationed, many young men were still in or just out of uniforms, and consumer goods were in short supply as factories were just beginning to shift from war production. Mr. Carrion, a scoundrel always accompanied by his beloved pet vulture Julia, got his name in his first appearance (4/21/46), where he scammed the families of missing-in-action heroes of World War II, exploiting the memory of those who were all but certainly dead, and killing their widows with grief and shock when he disappears with their money without giving them any information on their missing loved ones. ("Carrion," of course, means dead, decaying flesh, the food of scavengers like vultures.) In later stories, Carrion becomes a villain who preys on other criminals, often on the docks or in seafaring settings. His first true master criminal's hideout is located on a Pacific island that he steals from the infamous Dr. Scalppel with the Spirit's unwitting help (it's not just a great hideout, it's also loaded with gold). Later Mr. Carrion returns to Central City to kidnap the Spirit and Dr. Silken Floss to help exploit a powerful new drug discovered on the island. Floss, however, outwits him and uses the drug to cure the Spirit of temporary blindness. Long before transgressive fiction was fashionable, Eisner found a certain subversive pleasure in the Carrion character: "I was never absolutely sure of Carrion's gender, his sex. In 1947, in newspapers or anywhere else, you very carefully did not call much attention to abnormality, but here I had him being all involved with a buzzard." Carrion's lighter side is revealed in a Valentine's Day story, "To the Spirit with Love" (2/18/51), where Carrion tries to help Ellen Dolan get the Spirit to finally marry her by pretending they're engaged, only in the end to return to the "gay comradery" of his beloved Julia. (4/21/46; 5/19/46; 9/14/47; 1/25/48; 8/1/48; 11/20/49; 3/12/50; 3/19/50; 3/26/50; 1/14/51; 2/18/51; 5/6/51)

Castanet: A beautiful South American villainess who is recruited by the Octopus to assist him with looting Montabaldo, the mysterious Inca treasure island that rises from, and falls back into, the sea. Castanet becomes the Octopus's assistant in diving to retrieve the Inca treasure, but the Spirit intervenes, carried to the site of the sunken city by Capitan el Muerto—a real ghost of a Spanish conquistador, who provides his ghostly galleon as transportation to end the looting, perhaps making up for his misdeeds of the past. Long before the looting of Pre-Columbian sites became an international issue in the 1960s, leading to the UNESCO Convention on antiquities in 1972, the Spirit was doing the right thing. Castanet wanted to do some "right things" with the Spirit, too, after saving his life when the Octopus wanted to kill him. Eisner created a strong, beautiful Spanish woman in this character. (1/25/48; 2/1/48)

Central City: Batman fights crime in Gotham City. Superman keeps Metropolis safe. Private eyes usually work in real cities. Philip Marlowe would be out of place anywhere but L.A. Sam Spade fits Frisco like a glove. Spencer is as Boston as baked beans. Nero Wolfe barely leaves his townhouse, much less New York. The Spirit started out in a city plainly identified as New York, but shortly it got a nom de plume that made the Spirit more like his costumed fellows in the

comic books: Central City. But for all intents and purposes, Central City is New York, with its docks and harbor, international business, culture and politics, and even local machine politicos who are straight out of New York's Tammany Hall.

Chapparell, Sam: The Spirit seems to have a penchant for running across characters lost in time, like Simon Smudge and Abraham Pewter. These Methuselahs gave Eisner a chance to explore different periods of history and varied locales, as he does in the story of Chapparell and his gang of outlaws who've retired to the Western mountain town of Boot Camp, where the healthful air lets them live 100 years. When Sam is dry-gulched by his gang (sent out to die with only one canteen of water and his gun), he stumbles into the town of Lope, where sheriff Omar Trent is the only man in the West old enough to recognize him. When Ellen Dolan tries to turn the town into a hospital for sick children, the villainous Quirte opposes her and the Spirit at every turn because he wants the loot Chapparell left behind. (10/10/48; 11/14/48)

Christmas Spirit: In 1940, Eisner began what was intended to be a yearly series of Christmas stories, in which the Spirit devotes himself to celebrating the holiday, preferring to "leave crime and criminals to a more potent Spirit—the Christmas Spirit!" Eisner's holiday stories were done in part for newspaper editors, because they always liked seasonal features, but the Christmas stories were always particularly close to Eisner's heart. In the first Christmas Spirit story, Black Henry and Simple Simon plan to rob the Pauper's National Bank on Christmas Eve, but when they find out that the big deposit they stole was destined to buy toys for needy children, they sneak back into the bank and return the stolen money. During Eisner's wartime service (1942-45), no Christmas or other holiday-themed stories appeared, but Eisner returned to the theme in 1945, just after

his discharge, with the story of Horton J. Winklenod, a sheltered department store magnate who discovers late in life that there is no Santa Claus. Santa Claus himself makes several appearances, most notably when he's kidnapped by two hoods and they end up helping distribute Christmas presents around the world. (12/22/40; 12/28/41; 12/23/45; 12/22/46; 12/21/47; 12/19/48; 12/25/49; 12/24/50; 12/23/51)

Clach, Steven: Steven and his brother, the brilliant but mad scientist Sam Clach, lived a quiet life in their mansion until Nifty Nick, the hoodlum, managed to take over the place for a hideout. But it seems that the house has its own ideas about who gets to live there, in a story with one of the most distinctive of the early *Spirit* splash pages. (12/8/40)

Cobra, Dr.: The first criminal mastermind the Spirit faced, Dr. Cobra unintentionally creates the Spirit when criminologist Denny Colt tries to apprehend him but gets splashed with the doctor's latest experiment and appears to be dead. In "The Return of Dr. Cobra" (6/9/40), Cobra tricks Ellen Dolan and her boyfriend Homer Creap into assisting his escape from the Spirit. When the Spirit corners the devious criminal, he takes a leaf from the Spirit's book and fakes his own death with a grenade. The names Eisner chose for his villains are always appropriate, and his two premier evil supercriminals are no exceptions. The Octopus extends his "tentacles" through criminal organizations that spread across Europe and America. The venomous Dr. Cobra poisons Denny Colt, although the detective uses his own apparent death to become the crime-fighting Spirit. The evil doctor is adept at slithering out of the Spirit's grasp, disappearing into the urban jungle only to return with his menace undiminished. (6/2/40; 6/9/40; 10/13/40)

Colt, Denny: The detective Denny Colt really appears only once in the Spirit, in the "origin" issue (6/2/40). When this young private eye wakes up from a state of suspended animation induced by Dr. Cobra, Colt takes the opportunity to let the world think he's dead. Like Superman with his Clark Kent secret identity, Denny figures it will be easier to fight crime if no one knows who he really is. Eisner didn't want a costume, and it hardly seems that the small mask Denny wears would hide his identity. Except that people see what they expect to see, and most of us don't expect to see dead men walking around. Denny Colt truly becomes the Spirit. He doesn't have an apartment, or a mansion like Bruce Wayne, who becomes Batman in the Batcave. He lives only in his hideout in Wildwood Cemetery. Only Dolan knows his true identity, and really after Dr. Cobra does his dirty

DENNY COLT

work, Denny is the Spirit for all intents and purposes. There is rarely tension in the series about revealing his secret identity. Even his love life is that of the Spirit, as femme fatale after femme fatale falls for the handsome masked crime fighter that they know only as the Spirit.

Compote, Tooty: Tooty might seem to get his name from his red, bulbous, alcoholic's nose, and that's part of it, but he's also a caricature of author Truman Capote, whose novel *Other Voices, Other Rooms* launched his career in 1948. The jacket photograph of the twenty-three-year-old writer captured much media attention and became the basis for Eisner's character. Tooty is a little man who discovers that he can kill people just by telling them to "Drop Dead," and Mangles the Mobster wants to use him to replace all his thugs. But Tooty falls for Mangles's beautiful mouthpiece, Slip Claws, who almost goes along with him until her legal scruples get the better of her. Tooty's power is a gentle satire of super hero conventions, and he's ironically undone when another unlikely character proves to have the same abilities. (10/3/48)

TOOTY COMPOTE

Conscription, i.e. the Draft: Eisner was drafted into the army in 1942 and left *The Spirit* in the hands of his studio employees, Manly Wade Wellman and Lou Fine. When the United States passed a conscription (draft) law in 1940, the Spirit also joined up, but instead of becoming a cartoonist for the military, as Eisner did, he became a secret agent, joining a mysterious U.S. government organization called "the Espionage." In "Conscription Bill Signed" (10/27/40), the Spirit and Ebony round up a batch of spies. "Well, Ebony," the Spirit says as the sun sinks behind the gnarled outline of Wildwood Cemetery, "I'm working with Uncle Sam now...working to preserve on Earth the one place were men may live in freedom and in peace...America!" Eisner achieved the rank of Chief Warrant Officer during his wartime service, and he returned to civilian life, and *The Spirit*, in 1945.

Craft's Casino Pirate Ship: Like the ship in the Cary Grant film *Mr. Lucky* (1943), the Casino is an illegal gambling ship anchored in Central City's harbor. Ebony is kidnapped by the pirate-costumed gang who man the ship when, inspired by a pirate adventure show on the radio, Ebony sails out into the harbor and is rescued by the Spirit, who brings the thugs to justice. (8/25/46)

HOMER CREAP

Creap, Homer (also spelled **Creep**): Before Ellen Dolan discovers that only the Spirit can hold her affections, she has a nerdy, bespectacled boyfriend who constantly finds himself in trouble only the Spirit can spring him from. Homer fails to appreciate how lucky he is to be going out with the lovely Ellen, but what can one expect from a creep? When the Spirit "renovates" Ellen at her engagement dinner, removing her glasses and fixing her hair, she falls in love with the masked detective. "Now that she is beautiful, it's gone to her head," Homer explains to the Spirit, letting him know she had decided to become a chorus girl under the name Daisy Kay. The Spirit decides to help Homer out by kidnapping Ellen and letting her fiancé rescue her. When aircraft designer Arthur Sleet is killed, bad girl Poppy and her hypnotic henchman pin the crime on Homer, till the Spirit saves him—egged on by Ellen, who can't stand to see him with another woman! Homer soothes his broken heart by going to Cuba, where he marries a lovely Latina, Peppi Tamale. Unfortunately, Peppi's brother Pancho, the Beeg Bool, is unhappy about this. The newlyweds flee to Central City, where the sombreroed Pancho manages to start a riot that helps the Spirit and Dolan wipe up a bunch of mobsters. Homer comes out such a hero that Pancho approves his sister's union. (6/9/40; 8/11/40; 9/29/40; 1/19/41)

Daily strip: From October 13, 1941 until March 11, 1944, the Eisner studio produced a black-and-white daily *Spirit* comic strip that was syndicated by the Register and Tribune Syndicate, the same outfit that circulated the *Spirit* section. Eisner wrote and drew the first few weeks of the strip, then turned it over to Jack Cole, whose famous elastic detective, Plastic Man, would shortly be sharing *Police Comics* with *Spirit* reprints. After Cole left, Eisner's studio carried the daily through the next few years, with Bill Woolfolk doing most of the writing and Lou Fine the art. Expanding a Sunday strip franchise by adding a daily strip is the natural order of business, and it made sense to follow standard procedure with the Spirit. But the tiny canvas of a daily strip (even in those days of larger strips) was just too small for the kind of art that characterized the Sunday *Spirit*, and the venture was abandoned.

Daufan, M.: Monsieur Daufan (a pun on *dauphin*, the French word for prince, best known in American humor from the novel *Huckleberry Finn*) appears in Central City chasing P'Gell, who met, married, and was mysteriously left widowed by Waldo Portier. Unfortunately the real Daufan had been murdered himself, and the impostor is none other than the Octopus, who murders both Homer and Milissy Portier, tries to frame P'Gell for it, and escapes with the loot. (12/1/46)

Dolan, Ellen: She was the girl next door, the only child of Police Commissioner Dolan of Central City, a blonde, blue-eyed, all-American beauty who won Denny Colt's heart with her beauty and innocence, but her evolution from Deanna Durbin to Hildy Johnson to Hillary Clinton makes her one of the greatest female characters in *The Spirit*. In the early years, Ellen is the perfect only child, a willful girl who wants everyone around to pay attention only to her. Her first boyfriend is the useless Homer Creep, a bespectacled, noodlespined milquetoast who constantly has to be helped out of jams by the Spirit. Ellen is just too strong for him. She begins to fall for the Spirit, and one of the first things she does to establish her own identity is to start her own business—big surprise, it's a detective agency! Her first case involves Professor Ravel, the expert bomb maker, whose latest device has failed an army test. He's been kidnapped, and an impostor tries to get Ellen to cover the kidnapper's tracks. The Spirit solves the case, but he and Dolan agree "a girl as

ELLEN DOLAN WITH JULIA (LEFT) AND MR. CARRION

smart as her should have a career" (4/27/41). Then Ellen becomes a leader in the Ladies League Against Crime and captures criminal Guerilla Gage, leading to headlines about the "Lady Vigilante" (1/4/42).

When the Spirit and femme fatale Silk Satin secretly carry a baby out of wartime Japan in 1942, Ellen is obsessed with the idea that she's lost her man to another woman. Her relief is palpable when she realizes that the baby is a genuine orphan of war and not a love child.

Ellen's not above creating false emergencies or pretending to be a damsel in distress to get the Spirit's attention, or to spurn the Spirit for a handsome swell from an escort service to make sure her man gets good and jealous. Later in the strip, she becomes a fast-talking, quick-witted heroine, reminiscent of those in the best cinematic screwball comedies. For example, her quick application of a baseball bat to the Spirit's noggin and some strategically sprayed ketchup provided the setup that solved the Thorne Strand mystery (1/23/49). In "Ellen Dolan for Mayor" (11/12/50), Ellen became one of the most modern women in comics when she ran for mayor of Central City. The Spirit tried to stop her, but she ignored him and won the election, serving as the city's leader for the rest of the run of *The Spirit*.

Ellen and the Spirit never married but in one fantastic series of panels, inspired by the surreal dream and hallucination sequences in films of the 1940s, the Spirit dreams about what it would be like to be married to the commissioner's lovely daughter. Disturbed by questions about matrimony from Commissioner Dolan's aunt, Mathilda Dolan, the sleeping Spirit sees a future where he and Ellen have a horde of kids. Ellen insists that as a responsible husband and father, he should only chase criminals one night a week!

The crime fighter did pop the question to Ellen after he and a detective from the force were stranded together on an ice floe. Detective Bob Carson reveals that he's planning to ask Ellen to marry him. After their rescue, the Spirit tells Ellen, "He's just not your type." Then the Spirit continues, almost unintentionally proposing by explaining that if Ellen's going to marry someone, it might as well be him. Dolan's Aunt Mathilda tried to get the two hitched, and there are various other close calls and apparent proposals over the years. But these two lovebirds have yet to tie the knot.

Dolan, Eustace: Commissioner Dolan's father is the first of the family to drop the Hibernian O' (son of) from their name. His forebears, Patrick and Michael O'Dolan, came to America in 1810, and Dolan's grandfather Pat Jr. was the first to join the police. Eustace was born in 1880, and followed his father into the force in Central City in 1908. Unlike Pat Jr., Michael O'Dolan's son was a wild seed, an adventurer who made and lost fortunes and built a grand waterfront house in Central City that's left at last to the commissioner and his daughter Ellen. In old Irish fashion, this freebooter was called "The O'Dolan," and when Ellen tries to move into the manse, she finds his ghost and that of his boon companion and retainer Tim O'Leary. (4/11/48; 4/18/48)

Dolan, Eustace P.: The police commissioner of Central City, Dolan joins other prominent fictional police department heads like Batman's Commissioner James Gordon as the in-house ally who is relied upon not only for help in solving the toughest cases, but for friendship and advice. In the case of Dolan and Denny Colt—the Spirit—the relationship is one in which the older police veteran is really a father figure to the young crime fighter. Eisner was persuaded by his partner in the Quality Comics Group, Everett Arnold, to give the Spirit a secret identity. To help pull this off, Dolan becomes the key figure in helping

...WHEN HE DIED, HIS SON, YOUNG DENNY, FOLLOWED IN HIS FOOTSTEPS.... WELL, SINCE MY ONLY CHILD WAS A DAUGHTER, HE SORT OF BECAME A SON TO ME AND I HELPED HIM IN HIS CAREER OF CRIMINOLOGY!

Denny Colt maintain the impression that he has died, just as he will be the key source of cases for the Spirit over the years. Dolan can reach Denny Colt in his hideout in Wildwood Cemetery by means of a secret buzzer that summons the Spirit to police headquarters when he is needed to lend a hand with the latest case. From his very first appearance— in the initial panel of the opening story—Commissioner Dolan was an integral part of the entire *Spirit* series.

Dolan is a widower, raising Ellen by himself. Dolan is also a doting father who raises Ellen to be a strong and independent woman who eventually becomes mayor of Central City. In the early years of the strip she goes away to college, and when Ellen returns she starts her own detective agency. Although worried about her, Dolan tells the Spirit that a father shouldn't interfere because a girl needs a career. Dolan runs for mayor twice, winning both times. He never holds the office for very long—he can't resist returning to his beloved police department—but it's clear he cares about his city. When Ellen runs for mayor, the Spirit tries to stop her in every way possible. Her father, however, becomes her advisor and strongest supporter.

Balding and distinguished, always dressed in a suit and tie, Dolan projects the perfect image of a police commissioner. As a crime solver and supervisor of the force, he always comes off as a seasoned professional. This image provided a great source of jokes for Eisner when he began meeting more and more comic fans at conventions and public events in the 1970s and 1980s. At that time, before Eisner's graphic novels were recognized for their important contributions to world comic art, the most frequently asked question of Eisner was "When are you going to do more Spirit stories?" Eisner would explain that when he was doing the original series, it was easy and fun because he looked like the Spirit, but thirty or forty years later it would be hard to go back because now, "I look like Commissioner Dolan!"

BAH!

Dolan, Mathilda: It's no wonder Ellen Dolan's such a pistol when you see the rest of the Dolan family, from wild Texan Pappy Dolan to his five-times-married sister Mathilda. She tells her niece Ellen that she's got to trick the Spirit into marrying her: "Every man that was ever married was duped into it...they love it...the beasts." One of Mathilda's favorite tricks for getting a man hitched—kissing him with drugged lipstick on—backfires when the justice of the peace turns out to be a gangster. But Mathilda makes the best of it by marrying mobster Hinkey. When Hinkey flees to Mexico, Mathilda chases him down. Unfortunately, her arrival has a negative effect on him—he collapses and dies! The same fate had befallen her second husband, Harry, killed when he got wrapped up in a window shade. Next she sets her sights on Central City's Mayor Blast. A committed user of powerful beauty aids to keep her looks, including Pool's Toadstool Cream, Mathilda's still the marrying kind when, at age forty-five, she's engaged to gangster Glut Mutton and uses the occasion of their marriage to almost get the Spirit to pop the question to Ellen. Fortunately for her, and maybe for him, the Spirit sends Glut directly to jail from the altar. (3/1/42; 4/19/42; 11/1/42; 6/9/46)

AT THE DOLAN HOUSEHOLD, LATER THAT DAY...

OH, AUNT *MATHILDA*, IT'S ALL SO THRILLING! ...AND YOU LOOK SO BEAUTIFUL!

...AND WHAT ABOUT *YOU?* WHEN IS THIS BIG *BOY* WONDER GOING TO GET WISE AND PROPOSE?!

Dolan, Pappy: No one would ever suspect that the calm, pipe-smoking, urbane Commissioner Dolan is a native of "uncivilized" frontier Texas. When Pappy Dolan first appears, he's called Dead Duck Dolan, and serves as the sheriff of Borderville. Pappy lost track of his young son when Eustace ran away from home while his father was out with a posse. But now, in "Dead Duck Dolan" (3/2/41), he's come to the city to give a little paternal advice: shoot criminals, don't have meetings about stopping crime. And Pappy and the Spirit do just that when they take down the Fink Frazer Mob. It turns out that Commissioner Dolan sprang from a whole rowdy, cussin', shootin' clan of Dolans when Cousin Sam'l, Cousin Juke, Onkle Curd, Cousin Pewter, and Nephew Sump call on Dolan and the Spirit to rescue Dolan's Pappy, who's being held prisoner in the town of Tarnation ("Civilization's End") by the Calicos, with whom they've been feuding for generations. Turns out Pappy wasn't kidnapped, but eloped with the homely Purina Calico. In the end, the Spirit manages to revive the feud by discovering oil on a disputed patch of land. In "The Feud" (3/3/46), Pappy Dolan is unceremoniously replaced by Eustace Dolan in a revision of continuity. The commissioner's "new" father is a policeman, like his son, rather than a frontier sheriff.

Dusk, Mr.: A psychopathic villain, Mr. Dusk and his beautiful, savage wife Twilight represent the dark and murderous side of the human psyche. Dusk has an underground lab and a fascination with crime. He hopes to find a kindred "spirit" when he shows off his lab, his knife-throwing wife, and Gotha, the powerful servant he created in a bizarre experiment, to the masked crime fighter. But Dusk finds out the Spirit doesn't share his view of murder as a "fine art," and naturally tries to kill him, shortly ending up in custody. Dusk and Twilight escape for a one-night party, and collect some  party pals: Nothing, the Little Man Who Wasn't There, Hazel the Witch (who later adds the surname Macbeth), and a gnome—Ebony! With his big bowtie and insect-feeler hairdo, Dusk reappears after the war as a scheming mob boss who gets stranded on a desert island with Hollywood babe Olga Bustle, only by now the villain has become more comic foil than psychopath. (6/15/41; 10/26/41; 8/16/42; 9/1/46)

Eall, Slippery: Eall and two other hardened criminals, Bellows and Dapperish, make a break from Central City's prison in one of the darkest, most rain-splattered, noir *Spirit* stories of all (11/30/47). (The deep architecture and dizzying aerial shots led to its publication  in the three-dimensional comic book *Will Eisner's 3-D Classics featuring the Spirit* from Kitchen Sink Press in 1985.) Eisner's assistants were the models for Eall's co-conspirators, and escape artist Slippery was modeled on Eisner himself. The trio returns in a snowy fable about stolen ice and a fence (12/14/47). Trying to get their freedom by turning in Goldbrick and his smuggling partner Oliver J. Tarif, they blow the deal when their sticky fingers adhere to some of the diamonds, hoping to keep the jewels for themselves.

Ebony (see **White, Ebony**).

SLIPPERY EALL

Eisenshpritz: Eisner's use of rain and running water in urban landscapes and interiors has been nicknamed Eisenshpritz, a combination of Eisner's name and the word spritz, like spritzer. The term was coined by Harvey Kurtzman, the founding editor of *MAD* Magazine. The shift of vowels from Eisner's name recalls spas like the ones in Eisenbad, Germany, making the term more redolent of water. Eisner first explored its dark and atmospheric possibilities in *The Spirit*'s cityscapes, especially in the famous title pages—known in the industry, coincidentally, as "splash" pages—where rain and water running in the gutter would often provide atmospheric effects and structural elements that were as crucial to the story as the city itself.

In one of his most famous splash pages, the opening to the story of Slippery Eall, Eisner suggests one aspect of water's symbolic meaning: "Crime is a man-made stream...it is a dirty gutter stream that grows in the night and flows for a brief glittery distance, catching all it can in its muddy current...until it spills, at last, into the trap" (11/30/47). Eisner continued this use of rain and water in the graphic novels, particularly notable in his first graphic novel, *A Contract with God* (1978). There is also an aquatic element in the villains the Spirit faces, including the prewar nemesis who is crucial to the Spirit's origin, the Squid, and the postwar nemesis the Octopus, although Eisner says he did not do this intentionally. A third frequent villain, Mr. Carrion, is often associated with seaports or appears sailing on a raft. In the story of the blackmailing Actor Adam and his girlfriend Flossy, water spiraling down a sink's drain or through a water cooler becomes a metaphor for the vortex that consumes criminals and brings them to a bad end ("The Vortex," 9/8/46). "Comics don't have music or sounds or smells, so one of the most powerful tools available is using a universal experience. If you can reach a reader on the level of experience, then you have developed a valuable contact; you've made your case," Eisner has explained. "One of the reasons there is so much rain in *The Spirit* is that people understand the feeling of rain; the annoyance of being outside while it's raining. It's all part of setting a level of common communication."

Eisner in *The Spirit*: Will Eisner drew himself into *The Spirit* a number of times, beginning with the famous splash page showing Eisner drawing...a *Spirit* splash page! This story breaks through the fourth wall into Eisner's studio, but never reveals the artist's face

(5/3/42). It shows Eisner drawing the splash page at his drawing board in the studio surrounded by memos about deadlines. Another famous story involves Eisner and his assistant Jules Feiffer, who went on to become a playwright, a Pulitzer Prize-winning cartoonist, and Academy Award-winning screenwriter. In this story, Feiffer kills Eisner in a dream story, and takes over *The Spirit* strip (12/31/50). Although not appearing as himself, Eisner served as his own model for the criminal and escape artist Slippery Eall. (12/14/47)

Eisner's studio: Throughout the run of *The Spirit*, Eisner was assisted by several talented individuals, especially during the time he served in the U.S. Army, among them: John Belfi, Phillip (Tex) Blaisdell, Chris Christiansen, Jack Cole, Martin DeMuth, Jim Dixon, Jules Feiffer, Dick French, Lou Fine, Jerry Grandenetti, Abe Kaenegson, Jack Keller, Robin King, Alex Kotzky, Joe Kubert, Andre LeBlanc,

EISNER IN THE SPIRIT

Marilyn Mercer, Klaus Nordling, Ben Oda, Bob Palmer, Don Perlin, Bob Powell, Sam Rosen, Aldo Rubano, Sam Schwartz, John Spranger, Manny Stallman, Manly Wade Wellman, Al Wenzel, Wallace Wood, and Bill Woolfolk.

"Every Little Bug" (also **"Evvy Li'l Bug"** and **"Ev'ry Little Bug"**): If *The Spirit* has a theme song, this would be it. The distinctive ditty was first developed in a *Casablanca*-esque scene where the thug, Glut Mutton, asks for Gam to play it and play it again on the piano in his hideout. The song grows another verse or five when Gam is inspired by the lovely and deadly Dulcet Tone. Gam is a conflation of ivory ticklers from two Humphrey Bogart movies: Sam, played by Dooley Wilson in *Casablanca* (1942), and Cricket, played by Hoagy Carmichael in *To Have and Have Not* (1944). Eisner quotes Bogart in *Casablanca* correctly, "Play it, Sam," not "Play it again, Sam," as in the title of the 1969 play (and later, a movie in 1972) written by and starring Woody Allen. The tune finally came to full life when Ebony decides to pursue a career as a lyricist, encouraged by his crush on the pretty blonde Rosie Lee. Bill Harr, an old army buddy of Eisner's, was trying to crack the commercial song market in New York and dropped by Eisner's studio. "The song was there in the first place as an opportunity for Ebony, to get more use out of him. The more I used him, the more I liked him," Eisner recalled. "I just handed the lyrics over to Bill and asked him to set it to music." The sheet music was actually published by one of Harr's publishers, the Robbins Music Corporation, in 1947. The song was finally recorded and released in 1987 when Kitchen Sink Press produced a 12-inch picture disk containing this and several other related songs. (6/9/46; 7/7/46; 4/27/47)

Fairy Tales: Juvenile delinquency is the topic addressed in the updated fairy tales of "Cinderella" (10/5/47) and "Hanzel und Gretel" (7/13/47), "a public service feature...based upon the requests of public-minded citizens who feel that juvenile crime is largely a result of deficiency in the wholesome literature we used to enjoy." In a prescient and rare commentary on the media outcry that would lead to the creation of the Comics Code in 1954, Hanzel and Gretel are the kids of hijacker Fosgnov Slash. The children are rescued from their sad background by the Spirit, and an upper-crust couple is given custody of them. (In 1949, Eisner presented a satire of psychologist Fredric Wertham, a key figure in the persecution of comics, in the person of Dr. Worry.) In "Cinderella," Ma Harridan is a restaurateur with two daughters who are perfect ladies, Prudence and

nce upon a time there lived, in Central City, a poor hijacker named FOSGNOV SLASH... he had come upon hard times and so lived in abject poverty with his two children and their stepmother, a former première danseuse at the Gaiety, named MINNIE the MINK.

FAIRY TALES

Desire, and a youngest stepdaughter who is stuck in the kitchen in order to keep her pick-pocketing of the customers down to a low roar. Her fairy godmother sets her up to go to the policeman's ball as a cover for her man, sleazy Snaky, to rob the Eagle National Bank, but the Spirit gets the goods on her "when the slipper she left sticks the rap on her like porous plaster." The best-known *Spirit* fairy tale certainly is "The Story of Rat-Tat the Toy Machine-Gun" (9/4/49), about a nameless boy who falls in with the Carbunkle Mob, following them around carrying a toy machine gun. When the Spirit comes to the gang's hideout, the kid finds his real heart: he can't shoot the Spirit, even with a toy. And when the gang comes back, the kid and Rat-Tat save the wounded Spirit by almost miraculous means. The poetic narrative, vertical page design, and illuminated capitals as well as the driving storytelling make this a Spirit classic. The Pied Piper of Hamelin provided the key plot element for the story featuring the "Oldest Man in the World." (10/19/41)

Fallon, Sparrow: An appealing heroine, Sparrow motivates a passive, drifting soul named Bleaker Moore to become a man. Moore had been dragged into a life of crime by the beautiful Powder Pouf. Sparrow goes to jail to take the rap for her embezzling father, and ends up as Powder's cellmate. Bleak falls in love with the lovely Miss Fallon during a jailhouse visit to Powder, who's trying to corrupt Sparrow. "'Fate' never gave me a chance...I'm going to make my own breaks," says Bleak, who then rescues Sparrow from Powder and her gang. Eisner, who read all the great American short story writers, said, "O. Henry wrote a lot of stories about helpless but good girls, very fine, decent girls, but married to weak men. That's Sparrow Fallon." Her name of course is derived from the expression fallen sparrow, which comes from the Bible passage, "Not even a sparrow falls but my Father in Heaven takes note of its passing." (Matthew XI:39) When Sparrow is set to marry Bleak, Rosie, a dame from his criminal past, surfaces. Bleak had driven for bank robber Carbine Carson, and Rosie was the boss's moll. One day, Rosie shot a bank guard, and forced Bleak to marry her in order to keep him from testifying. Carbine gave the evidence that sent him to reform school so he could get his moll back, but she tries to destroy his happiness. Leave it to the Spirit to find out that she's the multiple-married Natchez Nellie, a.k.a. Rosie the Rock. (1/4/48; 1/11/48; 5/2/48; 5/9/48)

Feiffer, Jules: Joining Eisner's studio as a young artist in 1949, Feiffer soon showed the talent that would make him one of America's best known and most influential cartoonists, with his first book, *Tantrum* (1979), becoming a classic of American comic art. Beginning as an assistant, Feiffer was soon contributing his own story to *The Spirit*, a cartoony strip about the little boy named Clifford. Eisner would cast himself in *The Spirit* from time to time, and in a memorable story he cast Feiffer as well (12/31/50): Because Eisner is unable to meet a New Year's deadline, Feiffer comes in and kills him and substitutes Clifford in the role of the Spirit for the main feature. Eisner wakes up at the end, because it was all a dream—a dream occasioned by the fact that the real New Year's strip was in fact late. It ran the next week. (1/7/51)

Ferguson, Abel: In one of Eisner's tributes to mystery fiction and to radio drama, Ferguson is a retired steel magnate who is shot to death in a locked room. Ferguson bore a heavy burden of guilt. In 1906 his partner, John Dailey, fell or was pushed into a vat of molten steel in their mill, and though Ferguson was acquitted, he retired and lived in seclusion with his collection of unusual guns and his loving wife Elsie. In the end, it seems that Dailey took his revenge. (6/6/48)

Fine, Lou: Lou Fine was one of the assistants in Eisner's studio who

JULES FEIFFER

worked on *The Spirit*, playing a particularly prominent role as artist and, for many of the stories while Eisner was in the army from 1942 to 1945, sometimes writing as well. Fine's classically beautiful comic book work included such super heroes as the Condor and the Ray, and his work on the Fawcett comics featuring Captain Marvel, Jr. is widely considered some of his best.

Finnegan, Officer: Commissioner Dolan is assisted by a cop in a standard blue uniform until Finnegan, a patrolman, gets promoted to commissioner's go-for, wearing a black suit and derby hat. Less a character than a type, Finnegan appears in only a few episodes of *The Spirit*. (7/7/40; 9/29/40; 10/13/40)

Floss, Silken, M.D.: Despite her soft and feminine name, Silken Floss is an accomplished professional, a nuclear physicist and medical doctor. She first meets the Spirit when he rescues her from the lab of Dr. August Lateur, who has discovered the revolutionary Theory of Molecular Arrangement—which can change matter into any form. Unfortunately, his discovery has attracted the attention of the evil Victorian time traveler Dr. Ward Wilmore, who has learned of Lateur's work in his future home in the 24th century, and come back to steal it. Eisner designed Silken Floss as a foil to make the Spirit more human: "She represents something that is hidden in most men who like to think of themselves as worldly. She's a challenge, because you have to attain her, you have to be strong and you've got to be something worthwhile. It's not enough to be a loving man, you have to be something more." Medical doctor Floss sets out to save the world from the X-germ, a bacteriological weapon invented by the Nazis, but first she tricks the Spirit into a sham marriage so he'll have legal control of the deadly bug if her antidote doesn't work. It does, of course, but she discovers that it won't make her new-found love for the Spirit go away. Ebony knows her secret, and when the Spirit is blinded in a battle with the Octopus, the able assistant brings Floss's one true love to her for a cure. (3/2/47; 3/9/47; 9/14/47; 9/23/51)

Goople, Zoltan B.: Goople's Cream Corporation is the putative sponsor of a series of ads that appeared in the story of firebug Arson Pyre (4/25/48). Zoltan B. Goople is president of the cosmetic manufacturer that makes Goople's miraculous cream, touted in five ads in the story's seven pages. The ads claim that it will "grow back two hairs for every one you lose." The cream even has its own jingle: "Goople's, Goople's hits the spot/Where your hair *was* now is not/Twice as much as you had before/Keep ol' Goople's in y'r bureau drawer/Goople, Goople, Goople..." This bit of doggerel satirizes the best-known Pepsi Cola jingle of the time, "Pepsi Cola hits the spot, twelve full ounces, that's a lot." The whole structure of the story is based on old-time radio suspense shows like *Inner Sanctum* and, well, *Suspense*. "Radio was a very important part of our culture in 1948," Eisner said, and he even included a satirical station identification (called a "newspaper identification"): "This is your local Sunday paper, operating on a frequency of 250 newsboys and 40 bicycles." Another *Spirit* story is written like a crime radio drama, *Stop the Plot*, with the Octopus as the villain (12/5/48). Several different radio shows are parodied in "Young Dr. Ebony" (5/29/49), including *Young Dr. Malone* and *This Is Your F.B.I.*

Goran, Ogre: A bootlegger, Ogre Goran wanted to leave his wife Olga for the lovely Mary Cowan. He's sent up the river, but when he escapes, he goes after Mary, who sets him on fire, disfiguring him horribly. Wrapped in bandages, he returns and kidnaps her, but the Spirit saves her in a dramatic confrontation in the Harbor Point Lighthouse. (10/20/40)

LT. OREN GREY

Grey, Lt. Oren: The solid police detective of Albin Village, a town about fifty miles upstate from Central City, Grey is introduced to the Spirit (and the readers) by the chief of police as "one of our keenest and most able detectives." Eisner created this character because, after World War II, "people were becoming conscious of what is now called civil rights. I had strong feelings about the matter myself, so I introduced Lt. Grey. As far as I know, he was the first black man in popular fiction who spoke without a Southern drawl, and was a man accepted in the community." Grey returns to Central City when Serene Mayhem, a spoiled brat, demands he find her missing dog. Since her dad is political boss Ballot Mayhem, Chief Blotter puts him on the case. Oren finds the dog, but also gets the goods on Ballot's vote-buying. (3/16/47; 2/29/48)

Hanash Ben Adim, "Hot Rock": Hanash is the son of the late Sheik Abu Ben Adim, who ran a hash house on Central City's Third Avenue. When P'Gell finds out that Hanash stands to inherit oil-rich lands in the Middle East, she adds him to her list of husbands. Unfortunately, Hanash's criminal record arouses the Spirit's suspicions. The masked

detective follows Hanash back to the Middle East. When Hemisphere Oil offers a fortune for the lands, Hanash murders his brother Ali with their father's dagger, but dies in the desert before he can sell out and get rich. (6/15/47)

Handy, Jim: Ellen Dolan goes undercover to break up a phony salvage ring run by Clawson P. Grasp, head of the Sunken Salvage Company. She poses as Grasp's secretary, fighting off his advances to get the goods on his scams. F.B.I. Agent Handy, who's more interested in dates and smooches, ignores diver Claw Bends as he loots tommy guns from the Liberty Ship Peaceway, preferring to make passes at Ellen. The Spirit ends up in the ship's hold, decking Bends and stopping the crime. Liberty ships were cargo carriers used before and during World War II to send military supplies to the Allies. The bends is the potentially fatal build-up of nitrogen in the blood of divers who surface too fast. (7/28/46)

Healey, Ward: A "ward heeler" was a small-time politi-cal operative who canvassed the election precincts or wards for the bosses in big-city machines like New York's famous Tammany Hall. Healey is a Central City political boss who masterminded the murder of the newly elected dogcatcher, Jim Twitch, so his own patronage appointee, Mr. Bowser, could continue as the canine enforcer. Healey used Bowser to train wayward strays for use as messen-gers for his payoffs. Later he hires Firebug Butts to burn down a school so he can get the contract to rebuild it. His biggest operation is forcing Mayor Blast to withdraw from his reelection bid, and then putting up his own reluctant frontman, Cadaver Bonehead, in a contest with reform candidate Patrolman Klink. The two candidates surprise everyone by tying in the election, and then deferring to write-in candidate Mr. Bowser. When Healey gets the con-tract for the North River Tunnel, there's only one problem: Honest John Sliderule is the city engineer. Healey has him offed and replaces Sliderule with his own Happy Times

Political Club hack, Transit O'Plumb. When the heat gets turned on by the Spirit and Dolan, Healey bricks Transit into his own tunnel, but Transit escapes by tunneling right into Dolan's office. Romance finds Healey, much to Dolan's dismay, when Widow Walker falls for him instead of Dolan. (9/7/47; 10/26/47; 11/9/47; 3/21/48; 3/28/48; 7/11/48; 3/13/49; 11/12/50)

Hildie: The blonde-haired daughter of femme fatale Sylvia "Silk" Satin and Nazi sympathizer Ivan Tovaroff, Hildie was held hostage in Nazi Germany by Adolf Hitler until Silk could rescue her. Silk's interna-tional adventuring, whether as a secret agent or an insurance investi-gator working for Croyd's of Glasgow (a play on Lloyd's of London), makes it hard for her to give Hildie everything she wants to, and leads her into getting engaged to a rich scoundrel, British Lord Elbey. Of course the Spirit saves Satin from marrying him, and Hildie from hav-ing a scoundrel stepdad. (1/20/46; 10/12/47; 5/30/48; 1/14/51)

HILDIE

Hoagy the Yogi: A schemer, a grifter, and a fraud whose only mag-ical power is getting marks to believe in the product of no known use that only he knows how to make, called Floz. Long before dot-coms, Hoagy entices a gang of hustlers, including the butler of Skinny Flint, to invest in his mysterious Floz. Eisner

regarded Floz as almost a hypnotic product, one that is whatever the customer wants it to be. Skinny Flint is a hustler who's raised the art of the deadbeat to the point where it's made him a millionaire, but the Spirit catches up with him and inadvertently ends the investment scheme. Hoagy has hooked up with Ebony, who's fled when he believes the Spirit has married Silken Floss, and ends up on a trip through the Middle East and China, where Hoagy finally gets a pasha to invest in Floz. In the end, Ebony takes his share of the investment back to Central City, only to find that in the debased currency his share is one buck. (3/16/47; 3/23/47)

Hollyer, Hangly and Hubert: The Hollyer brothers' mansion is discovered by the Central City police and the Spirit after a murder-suicide, but only Ebony knows the true story. The brothers were both in love with Sarah, but each was too polite to go first in asking for her hand. Finally, she tried to kill one by putting sand in the tank of his biplane, only to have him emerge a cripple. During the years of waiting for him to die, the brothers filled their mansion with newspapers, junk, and booby traps. The story is based on the infamous Collyer brothers, whose New York apartment also had thousands and thousands of dollars hidden away in shoeboxes. Ebony and Pierpont pick up a picture off the street, starting to collect found objects just like the Hollyer brothers. They are stopped by a lady in Victorian garb who tells them the whole cautionary tale, only to melt away when she is revealed as the ghost of Sarah. (6/22/47)

Horse, Charlie: Anyone who grew up reading comic books from the 1940s through the 1960s remembers the ads for Charles Atlas's body-building course. Charlie Horse, "The Strongest, Toughest Man in the Whole World," offered his own course, and the wonderful ad (with its own facsimile comic strip, natch) boasted to readers "Don't let the other guys who read this ad get the drop on you. Make sure it's you who does the beating up of all the other weak, helpless little kids on your block!" In "Just One Word Made Me a Man" (1/18/48), the Spirit's slight assistant Ebony signs up, and instead of being the hero of the sandlot baseball diamond, ends up so stiff he can't move, giving "musclebound" a whole new meaning.

X-ray specs are perhaps the most famous product advertised in comics. The glasses in comics didn't actually work, but Ebony develops X-ray vision after accidental exposure to an experiment in the Spirit's lab. His new sight is depicted through fabulous visual effects, recalling the hallucination scenes in many 1940s Hollywood films. Ebony also realizes one of the fondest daydreams of many boys who grew up reading those ads in the comics. (9/15/40)

Hubert the Duck: Although he ends up on Commissioner Dolan's holiday dinner table, Hubert is a duck with personality who engineers his own escape from a poultry truck and then casts confusion among criminals when he swallows the

HUBERT
THE DUCK

Hobe Diamond. Parelli, the best diamond cutter in Central City (and a ringer for Charlie Chaplin), has been captured by criminals to split the gem. When the law intervenes, Parelli ends up making the cut for the Spirit and insurance investigator Sylvia "Silk" Satin. (12/29/46)

Hugo: A small-time crook, Hugo meets his end at Mouser's hands, a gory execution on Denny Colt's headstone. Hugo is based on Udo, Richard Widmark's debut role as a psychotic killer in the film *Kiss of Death* (1947), which was scripted by *Front Page* writer Ben Hecht. "This is a shameless caricature," Eisner said. He was probably impressed not only by Widmark's over-the-top performance, but also by the grittily authentic New York City locations used to shoot the film. Hugo engineers the death of his own murderer, Mouser, and the capture of his moll, Powder Pouf, from beyond the grave, in a scene inspired by famous French artist and engraver Gustave Doré. (12/7/47)

Hush, Mr.: Only Eisner could have created a supervillain so clearly and poetically rooted in human frailty. Mr. Hush, the Whisperer, is gossip personified, and his appearance is worthy of one of the Seven Deadly Sins. In his first caper, Mr. Hush nearly ruins Commissioner Dolan by spreading the rumor that "Dolan's going to kill the mayor," and makes Mayor Aldrich so paranoid that he shoots Dolan during their weekly checker game. The Spirit says, "The lowest...the most vicious form of human crime is rumor mongering," and then he turns the tables on Hush, branding him a squealer in the underworld. (3/8/42)

MR. HUSH

Jaxon, Hobo: With his partner Hijack Malone, this bad guy terrorizes the natives of a South Pacific island in his search for uranium with the help of con artist Professor Slack. The witch doctor pleads with the sky god Oga to deliver Goona Island from the oppressors, and the Spirit flies in for the same purpose. Who should he and Ebony find but Fraternization H. Shack, the African-American airman who is married to Goona's Queen!? In the happily ever after ending, Shack flies them off the island just in advance of an immense tidal wave that ends the suffering of the island's inhabitants. (6/2/46)

Kalkov, Serge: Creator of the Kalkov Formula of Prolonged Life in 1640, his assistant Emil meets the Spirit, P'Gell, and the end of his prolonged life in Istanbul in P'Gell's first appearance. Fez-wearing crime boss Picar kills Emil, but not before the Renaissance scientist has repented of his long life of crime and shared the formula with the Spirit, who returns to Central City and gives it to Dr. Cardiac. Perhaps this is why the Spirit is still such a vibrant character today! (10/6/46)

Kampf, Emil: Robots were a staple of film and comics in the 1930s and 1940s, from the sympathetic robot of director Fritz Lang's *Metropolis* (1926) to writer Jerry Siegel and artist Joe Shuster's Superman—most notably the 1940 robot story "The Bandit Robots of Metropolis," reprinted by DC Comics and Kitchen Sink Press in 1999 in *Superman: The Sunday Classics* and originally published at exactly the same time the Spirit destroyed the robotic Soldiers of Tomorrow. Arms scientist Yagor steals this invention from the Battle Arms Co. after murdering Kalin, its inventor, and sets out to sell it to European arms dealer Kampf. Although Nazis are never mentioned, the salesman takes his name from dictator Adolf Hitler's manifesto *Mein Kampf*, and the idea of invincible "Soldiers of Tomorrow" clearly has Nazi overtones. (8/4/40; 10/13/40)

Klink, Sam, Patrolman 3rd Class: Most of the cops on the Central City force are just members of the Greek chorus in the Spirit, generically named Mulligan or O'Brien (although a derby-hatted cop named Finnegan appears at Dolan's side before the war, he never develops a real personality). New recruit Klink, however-er, faces some of the Spirit's toughest opponents. First, he has a run-in with P'Gell. She's harboring Toothpaste, a thief and counterfeiter, to raise the money for the mortgage on her girls' boarding school. Klink soon has the crooks in the clink, but he falls under P'Gell's spell and protects her from the law and the Spirit because he can't believe an innocent widow and her daughter could do any wrong. The patrolman then joins the Spirit in a multipart battle royal with the Octopus. Klink shows he can take a Spirit-style beating, but then lets Gasher, the brutal henchman, escape from the station house. The rookie redeems himself in "Octopus Back in the U.S.A." (2/11/51) by stepping in when the Spirit is out of action, blinded by a flash from the Octopus's gun when rescuing Dolan from the Big-Three Mob. Klink clobbers these scam artists who've been fleecing discharged GIs by taking deposits for apartments in a building that will never go up. When Klink runs for mayor, it turns out he is a veteran himself. (8/3/47; 8/10/47; 8/17/47; 8/24/47; 8/31/47; 10/5/47; 10/19/47; 11/9/47; 7/11/48; 11/21/48; 11/28/48; 12/12/48; 8/7/49; 2/11/51; 3/25/51)

KRETCHMA

Kretchma: An Eastern European darling, Kretchma fell for no-good army deserter and small-time crook Homacyde. In "War Brides" (3/14/48), Homacyde is back in Central City, giving the F.B.I. a run for its money. The Spirit is on the case when his lovely war bride shows up. Unfortunately, Kretchma finds Homacyde's kisses weren't all she remembered. She's sorry she left the tractor factory in the Balkans until she kisses the Spirit, who's all tied up with Ellen Dolan in Homacyde's digs, and decides that he's the man to marry—until Ellen gets loose and sends her packing. (3/14/48)

Law, John: Detective John Law was one of several characters that Eisner tried to launch in independent newsstand comic books in 1948. *Baseball* and *Kewpies* comics were published by Eisner's own company but were not successful. *Pirate Comics* and *John Law* were completed but were never published. The John Law stories were later recycled into *The Spirit*, most notably the two-part Spirit story that features the first appearance of Sand Saref. The John Law stories in their original form were eventually printed by Eclipse Books in 1983. Writer/artist Gary Chaloner recently began creating a new John Law on-line adventure strip, approved by Eisner. They have been collected by IDW Publishing under the title *Will Eisner's John Law: Dead Man Walking*. (1/8/50; 1/15/50)

Links Robbery: The infamous Brink's robbery took place in Boston on January 17, 1950, netting the well-organized gang well over $2 million. The gang members disguised themselves with Halloween masks, including the super heroes Captain Marvel and Captain Marvel Jr. The story migrated to *The Spirit*, although it was translated to a safety deposit company located a ferry ride away from Central City, transparently called Beantown. Sammy is fascinated with the idea of what he'd do with his share of the $2 million take. When he invites a stranger he meets to stay in the Spirit's digs while the detective is away, it turns out that Thumbs is one of the robbers, and Sammy helps apprehend him. Big Arky gets farther away, taking his money to Egypt. It was Mona who put him up to it, and it's Mona who comes with him. But as Sammy had said, the safe way to go is to wait to spend the money. Arky follows this route, but Mona loses patience and Arky loses his life. (5/14/50; 5/21/50)

Lolo: Lolo is a lovely Inuit maiden who comes to visit Central City and captures Ebony's heart when he goes on one of his jaunts to try to establish himself as an independent figure, with a life apart from the Spirit. Lolo manages, by accident, to help the Spirit catch the Filch Crew jewel thieves, but the real catch she's aiming for is Ebony. But he's too young, by his own reckoning, and Lolo heads back north. (1/16/49)

Macbeth, Hazel P.: She's a fourteenth-generation witch, whose Salem branch of the family was famous. But witches get no respect these days, and she lives a lonely, impoverished life on Cauldron Hill in Central City. Her last name is a reference to the witches who appear in the opening scene of Shakespeare's *Macbeth*, and of course her first name is an astringent pun on witch hazel. The kids from P.S. 43 come to hear her stories, but even this turns sour one day when Hubert Loophole, the shyster lawyer's son, says he doesn't believe in witches and taunts her into burning down P.S. 43. She's put on trial before the Committee of UN-Natural Activities, and is almost convicted until the Spirit shows that corrupt politician Ward Healey had the school burned down to get a construction contract.

Hazel was part of Eisner's use of seasonal elements for *The Spirit*'s newspaper readers, but this story also is a very early reference to witch hunts by the U.S. Congress, led by Senator Joseph R. McCarthy (for whom McCarthyism was named) and by the members of the House Un-American Activities Committee (HUAC). Later, Hazel P. Macbeth is subjected to an inquisition by the prim old maids of the D.A.W.H., the Descendants of American Witch Hunters (which combines the prim Daughters of the American Revolution with HUAC). Hazel returns to Central City each year when a mysterious rock rises from a swamp, and on her second visit the Octopus tries to rope her into a scheme to steal valuable documents on witchcraft. She finds him "handsome in an ugly sort of way," and starts to go along until she realizes he's just using her. In "Elect Miss Rhinemaiden of 1950" (10/29/50), Hazel uses magic to get herself chosen as a soft drink spokesgal, a reference to the Rheingold Beer girls whose pictures used to decorate the subways and sidewalks of New York each year. (10/26/41; 10/26/47; 10/31/48; 10/30/49; 10/29/50)

Mad Moes River: Lizard is a desert rat who doesn't want to see his beloved river dammed. While he can't stop progress, he can slow it down with the help of Central City

MAD MOES RIVER

refugee gambler Stud Sharpe and his gal Queeny. Lizard's riverside shack becomes a den of iniquity that distracts the workers until the Spirit shows up. (2/9/47)

Madman Mike: In 1947, Eisner produced a reflexive story about himself and his studio, and what would happen if they missed a deadline for producing *The Spirit* section. In a very early example of an openly self-referential comic book, Eisner is unable to finish the story, and the Spirit and Ebony come to investigate. They discover that Eisner has created a monstrous character for the strip, Madman Mike, who has come to life and killed the cartoonist. The character was based on Eisner's assistant, artist Abe Kaenegson. (6/8/47)

Magoo, Charles "Chuck": After the United States entered World War II in December of 1941, *The Spirit* moved beyond stories about saboteurs (clearly Nazis, but usually not specifically identified as such) to actual stories about U.S. soldiers, particularly in a series called "Army Operas" (12/21/41; 5/10/42; 5/31/42). In the first "Opera," the Spirit gets Charles Magoo into the army to save him from a life of crime, but he experiences prejudice when the other soldiers find out about his past. When saboteurs try to corrupt him, Magoo shows what he's really made of. This story is an interesting foreshadowing of prejudice in the army which Eisner deals with in autobiographical fashion in his graphic novel *To the Heart of the Storm*.

Manitou: The Spirit is called to the Catskills, location of resort hotels that for decades were the playgrounds of the middle and working classes of New York (the setting for such films as *Dirty Dancing*). Manitou, one of the last Indians living in these mountains, is accompanied only by his faithful servant Iroquois. New York sharpie Solomon Grundy is trying to force him to give up his home for a resort. Manitou was never a personal name but a deity of the Iroquois—using it in this story makes "The Legend" (7/21/46) a metaphor for stealing land from Native Americans.

Marsten, Johnny: He should have been a rich man, but his father gambled it all away. When Marsten's wife is dying, the doctor says that to save her, he has take the woman to a dry climate, like Arizona. The only way Marsten knows how to raise the dough is to gamble. Lady luck is with him, until gambler Tony Morgan does him in so he can't keep his winnings, and dumps him in Wildwood Cemetery. Fortunately, the hood has botched the job, and the Spirit saves Marsten and his lovely wife while cleaning up the gambling joints of New York City. (6/30/40; 10/13/40)

Mayors: When the city where the Spirit operates was still openly identified as New York, in the first stories of the crime fighter's career, Mayor Hardy is the man who occupies city hall. He's a real blowhard, spouting off about the good work of the Anti-Crime Commission, which is of course headed by a mobster, Van Gaunt. All mayors must look alike, because in the story of the suicide of Eldas Thayer (7/21/40), which makes the Spirit into a fugitive, an identical character is called Mayor Aldrich. When Mr. Hush tries to engineer the murder of Dolan by Aldrich, he gets both Dolan and Aldrich wounded and it looks like Nero Blast will win unopposed. That is until the Good Old Days Party nominates Dolan, and he sweeps into office. But he really doesn't want to be mayor, and defers to Blast as long as he can keep his position. Maybe it's revenge of a sort, but when Dolan's Aunt Mathilda is widowed once again, she manages to pull in Blast with "marriage technique #5": hit them over the head and drag them to the justice of the peace! When the Spirit's home becomes Central City, Mayor Blast is still in charge. He has a run-in with a political boss, and withdraws from his re-election campaign after Ward Healey nearly kills him, and then forces him to call it a suicide attempt. The Spirit himself is tricked into a run for mayor by wheeling and dealing political operative Monica Veto. When the crooks from the opposition Prosperity Party kidnap the Spirit to get him out of the election, Dolan saves him and Monica decides that he's her man. Dolan runs for mayor again in "For Mayor: Dolan" (3/15/42)—a story with no mention of his earlier campaign. Dolan wins, but Monica manages to manipulate him until the Spirit comes up with a plan. Charlie White Cloud appears bearing a treaty with the Cloudfeet Indians that shows the city owes millions in back rent. Monica and her crew take a powder rather than face the fiscal music, and Dolan happily resigns to return to the commissioner's job.

The most famous mayor in Central City history is, of course, Miss Ellen Dolan. When Ellen appears on TV (on *Leave It to the Ladies*—this was when ladies organizations did public-interest activities), she makes a stirring statement about the struggle of women for equality: "Most men practice equality like a little boy practicing on the piano, one hour a day and then FORGET all about it!" Then TV's Milton (clearly Milton "Uncle Miltie" Berle) says she could win a mayoral election, and she's off. In "Ellen Dolan for Mayor" (11/12/50), the Spirit orders her to quit and, when she won't, he campaigns for Mike Poltax of the Prosperity Party. When Poltax kidnaps Ellen, naturally the Spirit has to intervene, and she wins by a landslide. (7/21/40; 9/22/40; 11/24/40; 1/19/41; 7/13/41; 3/8/42; 3/15/42; 4/19/42; 11/1/42; 11/22/42; 12/6/42; 6/23/46; 11/9/47; 8/21/49; 8/28/49; 11/12/50)

Maywee, Maurice: The Spanish Civil War (1936–39) was a rehearsal for World War II, with the Nazis supporting the Fascists who fought the Loyalists, supported by the Soviet Union and by many foreign fighters, including the Abraham Lincoln Brigade from the U.S. In "Journeys into the Bizarre No. 1: The Case of the Inner Voice" (8/11/46), Maywee (a pun on the French interjection *Mais oui!*, but yes) and Andre Bouchard are two adventurers who pretend to be Loyalists but loot the homes of the rich and bury their treasure. Maywee betrays Bouchard and becomes a double agent in the war. When he is wounded, a Nazi doctor saves him with a blood transfusion from a slave laborer—Andre! The Spirit finds Maywee on the Lower East Side after the war, haunted by Andre's voice which leads Maywee to his death.

McDool, Detective: Although private investigator McDool's first case for Croyd's of Glasgow (a pun on the famous Lloyd's of London), involving the Van Gaull Diamonds, is solved by Sylvia "Silk" Satin rather than by the Scotsman's efforts, Eisner had hopes for this character: "I envisioned him in a series of his own. He wasn't a typical hero, but he could solve cases with his brain and cunning. He was kind of funny-looking—he looked inept—but he was very competent. And of course, I liked working with his accent." When Soho Sander insures

DETECTIVE MCDOOL

blackmail papers with Croyd's, Silk again is the key to the case. But the papers involve her fiancé, Lord Elbey, and the Spirit has to save her. (12/15/46; 2/2/47; 10/12/47)

McNobby, Killer: A hardened killer, McNobby followed a life of crime, and enjoyed it so much that he decided to commit a murder each day. Naturally, this attracted the Spirit, and they had a showdown in a fenced yard, with the entire Central City underworld as audience for the their titanic battle, which lasted all night long. Eisner told their story in verse, adopting the meter and structure of poet Henry Wadsworth Longfellow's "Midnight Ride of Paul Revere." Eisner later used the meter of Robert Service's "The Face on the Barroom Floor" to tell the story of the Spirit's battle with Musclehead McSneer. (6/1/41; 2/15/48)

ROBERT MERRILL

Merrill, Robert: The star of the Metropolitan Opera in New York, later particularly well-known to the public for singing the national anthem at Yankee home baseball games, made an appearance as himself in *The Spirit* singing "Every Little Bug." This came about, Eisner noted, when "I got a letter from a publicist for Merrill. The publicist was a friend of mine, and he said it would make Merrill very happy to be caricatured in *The Spirit*." Merrill gets kidnapped by some "Halies" who don't want him to sing their school drinking song, the "Whiffenpoof Song," for a radio broadcast, because it will mean sharing it with the "peasants." "Whiffenpoof" is a real drinking song that memorializes a tavern near Yale University, and was a hit for the swing band orchestra of Fred Waring and His Pennsylvanians in 1947. (6/29/47)

Minx, Madame: She "always gets what she wants...ALWAYS!" and that's why the Squid recruits her to help destroy the Spirit so the Nazi agent can proceed with his sabotage unhindered. Minx picks up the ocean-soaked Spirit and Satin after a hijacked tanker is blown up, and the femme fatale falls for him. When he spurns her, she knifes him and Satin attacks her in a homicidal fury: "You killed the only man I cared a hoot for in this whole world!" The Spirit and Satin escape on a Coast Guard boat, but Minx is not so lucky when the Squid learns of her failure. (2/15/42)

MADAME MINX

Minyan, Philly: The head of a meat-hijacking operation, specializing in black market sales of this still-rationed commodity in 1946, Philly throws his pursuers off the scent when he slugs a federal agent with a meat-trademarking stamp that looks like a lipstick imprint. (Of course his name is derived from a fine cut of steak, filet mignon.) Soon cops all over town are kissing girls to see if they can find a match! But it's Ellen who solves the case, tracking down the meat truckers after she's tricked the Spirit into letting her tie him up. When she returns to set him free, he's covered with kisses himself, the handiwork of Nylon Rose. (4/7/46)

Miss Vitriola's School for Girls: When European adventuress P'Gell inherits this strictly upper crust school from one of her many late husbands, she renames it P'Gell's

School for Girls. It becomes her new base for marrying and money-making schemes, and here she finds a new ally in her long-lost daughter, teenage Saree Raymond. (1/19/47)

MISS VITRIOLA'S SCHOOL FOR GIRLS

Molloy, "Mayhem" Mike: As a young beat patrolman, Commissioner Dolan's first arrest was Mike "Mayhem" Molloy. This thug had killed and beheaded another hoodlum, and the body turned up in his hideout. Dolan found the head the night before Mayhem's trial, but when he mislaid it, Molloy beat murder one and got off with thirty years for manslaughter. Dolan advanced in the department anyway, and when Molloy finally got out on parole twenty-eight years after the 1918 pinch, the commissioner remembered that he had put the head in an old rolltop desk in the department. Molloy stole the desk but lost it—and his life—in a car chase with the Spirit and Dolan. Mike Mayhem, a different criminal with a similar name, dies in the electric chair in a later story. (5/5/46; 11/2/47)

Montabaldo: This exotic-sounding name is a remarkable conflation of the title of Mussorgsky's "Night on Bald Mountain," whose dramatic music was brought to life in Disney's animated film *Fantasia* (1940), and the name of the Pre-Columbian Mexican city of Monte Alban (the capi-

MONTABALDO

tal of the Mixtec Kingdom). In *The Spirit*, Montabaldo is a mysterious island that emerges briefly from the ocean, like a rising Atlantis, to reveal a mysterious Inca city that the Octopus manages to loot. (1/25/48)

Morger, Black: Revenge is sweeter, at least in mystery fiction, when it's delayed. The four Morger Boys swear to their mother that on the twenty-fifth anniversary of the day their criminal father, Black Morger (a pun on morgue) died on the gallows, they'll avenge his execution. Handily for their scheme (and for the atmospheric design of their *Spirit* story), they've grown up to be identical bald men in hound's-tooth jackets. Naturally, the Spirit sends them to jail, and one more lovely girl, a certain Miss Stuart (daughter of the now-deceased hanging judge), falls madly for the masked man. (8/18/40; 10/13/40)

Moxel, the Rebel: A freedom fighter from an unnamed European country who has brought the royal jewels to Central City during World War II, Moxel is captured by Cardox and his henchmen who want not only the jewels, but also to bring chaos to their homeland. However, the real and accidental hero of this story is a street vendor who sells wind-up Spirit toys and magnifying spectacles. His merchandise saves the Spirit when Cardox accidentally sights a Spirit toy through the spectacles and blows it away instead of the real thing. The story is a tour de force of optical effects, with giant eyes, monstrous bugs, and tiny humans, and a fun romp for bystander P.S. Smith. (5/26/46)

Murdoch, Ellis: International crime is easier when you're married to a shipping magnate, and dumpy, mustachioed, and rich Ellis fits the bill when exotic adventuress P'Gell makes him her seventh husband. The S.S. P'Gell takes to the high seas to deliver 300 contraband atomic rifles to peninsular warlord Kwang King, as well as a luxury getaway car for her. The Spirit scuttles P'Gell's scheme and her ship, and she loses her husband as well—but as usual she rides away in style. (5/20/51)

Murmansk, Manny: Before the fractured syntax of Al Capp's Lower Slobbovians invaded the funny papers in "Li'l Abner," Eisner created a tough and rollicking Russian detective who comes to Central City seeking a treasure map hidden in a Siberian Dagger that had been collected by local mobster "Morgue" Mason. Manny races rival detective Niechevo, the Great Siberian Sleuth, to get the dagger for his one true love, Orcha Chornya

MANNY MURMANSK

of the Soviet Secret Service. Like Rasputin, Manny survives gangland gunshots to bring the dagger back to his fur-hatted Russian sweetie—in his back, where she had buried it! These Laurel and Hardy–like detectives, who get their strength from eating lots of onions (which is why they belch a lot) return on a mission from the country of Greppsany ("*grepps*" being Yiddish for "belch") to deliver the "cosmic answer," a scientific discovery to equal the atom bomb. Of course, the formula turns out to be more slapstick than earth shattering. With these funny characters, Eisner said that, "I was trying to appeal to a wider audience. *The Spirit* had a Sunday newspaper following: parents, kids, and so forth. I really had to go on and develop peripheral characters, characters that had some real cartoon humor about them." (1/27/46; 2/2/47)

Mutton, Glut: The Edward G. Robinsonesque gangster who's affianced to Commissioner Dolan's much-married sister Mathilda, Glut Mutton is a combo of various Hollywood types. He tells his piano player (à la Humprey Bogart in *Casablanca*) to "Play it, Gam! Play it... Dis is me weddin' day," but the song he is referring to is "Every Little Bug," not "As Time Goes By." He tells Skinny Bones, his Lauren Bacall look-alike girlfriend, to "Go 'way...ya bodder me!!" accompanied by a Cagneyesque slap. Of course, the Spirit sees to it he ends up in jail, not at the altar. (6/9/46)

Nazis: Nazis always make good opponents for detective and comic book heroes, and the Spirit gets involved in several Nazi-related cases before the war. Ex-Nazis also make trouble for him and for some of his lady friends after the war is over. Before the war, the Spirit assists Dr. Prince von Kalm, deposed president of Slavia when the Dracham, the secret

police, are sent after him by the evil Karl Axtrol. The Spirit goes to Slavia to protect Kalm and his daughter Magda, and brings the secret World Domination Document back to the U.S., revealing the plans of Axtrol and his "Master Race" to conquer all democratic countries. The Good Neighbor Policy, promulgated by President Franklin D. Roosevelt in 1940, was designed to keep the countries of Latin America from embracing the Nazis. When Nargoff and his henchmen land on an island off the coast of Mexico to take over the Americas, the Spirit is soon "waging a one-man defense of America."

In one of the many *Spirit* stories dealing with radio, a hugely important element in American life in the 1940s, traitorous Fifth Columnists try to take over radio station WLXK to fill the airwaves with fascist propaganda. The most memorable Nazi-related story, "The Tale of the Dictator's Reform" (6/22/41), shows a war-mongering dictator, clearly a portrait of Adolf Hitler, as a puppet of the secret police, the army, and technocrats—what President Dwight Eisenhower identified as the military-industrial complex in the valedictory speech of his presidency. The Squid is a saboteur who appears in America to destroy its defense capability on behalf of the Fatherland, but the Spirit and Satin manage to defeat this representative of the Master Race. After the war, Mussolini's treasure is sought by P'Gell when she comes across a map leading to it. The Octopus is a European criminal who flourished under the fascists, and had to reconstitute his criminal enterprises after the Allied victory. A Nazi rocket, accidentally shot into space in 1946, returns to Earth with a group of rockets coming in to Yellow Sands Proving Grounds. It carries Artemus Peep and Nazi scientist Adolphe Link. Less related to Nazis than to Eisner's stories featuring characters lost in time, the story also

On the morning of the 27th, the city with military precision moved huge equipment into the streets and began the million-dollar job of snow removal ... life began to regain its tempo, and things long buried under the drifts began to melt....

SNIFF....
AAAHHHH...
AT LAST !

NEW YORK CITY

refers to the U.S. Government's transport of Nazi rockets and scientists from Peenemünde, Germany, to White Sands, New Mexico, after World War II in a program called Operation Paperclip, which paved the way for the U.S. space program. In his first nonfiction graphic novel *The Plot* (2005), Eisner exposed a forged anti-Semitic document that played a key role in Nazi propaganda (see page 168). (11/17/40; 12/29/40; 2/16/41; 6/22/41; 1/18/42; 4/22/42; 5/25/47; 5/22/49)

New York City: Although Central City's name could suggest a location in the cornfields of the Midwest (certainly a large part of the target market of Sunday papers for *The Spirit* section), it is clear that the city is mostly made up of Eisner's birthplace and residence for most of his life, New York City. When *The Spirit* section began on June 2, 1940, the locale was specifically identified as New York. The police chase the Spirit, a wanted man in one sequence, through the intersection of 42nd Street and Broadway—Times Square. Although later the city is renamed, the geography against which the stories are played out is clearly that of the Big Apple. Central City Harbor is a frequent location for boat chases and lowlife antics along the waterfront. In *The Spirit* stories from after World War II, Central City is a place of postwar intrigue, a magnet for the good and the bad from Europe, much as New York was at this time. In "Journeys into the Bizarre No. 1: The Case of the Inner Voice" (8/11/46), the Spirit finds one of these scoundrels in the famous neighborhood in lower Manhattan that housed generations of Irish, Italian, Jewish, and other immigrants, the Lower East Side. Ellen Dolan's involvement in international intrigue leads her to attend a meeting of the U.N. Security Council, an organization whose headquarters is on the east side of midtown Manhattan. The murder of "Tattler" Jeeks in the top-security precincts of the police headquarters courtyard sends the Spirit on an odyssey into the sewers where Worm, the murderer, and other criminals hide from the law. "It always intrigued me that cities, particularly New York City, had miles and miles of catacombs under the streets," Eisner said in discussing the setting of this story. (8/11/46; 2/2/47; 2/22/48)

O'March, Ides: The Scottish undertaker who goes to the seaside dive the Bucket o' Blood, looking for business, O'March finds himself in the middle of a brawl between the Spirit and a pack of wharf rats over a mysterious green anthropomorphic charm that promises, "Whosoever owns this shall have immunity from death itself." Sure enough, this "thing" seems to confer invulnerability on whoever has it, but when Ides ends up with it at the end of the fight's musical chairs, he sells it to the barkeep because he hadn't managed to drum up any other business, and he is a "proctical mon." (6/16/46)

O'Shea, Darling: There's something about a temperamental heiress that inspires fiction writers, from Shakespeare's *Taming of the Shrew* to any number of Katharine Hepburn films. Darling O'Shea is strong-willed, mysterious—and maybe all of seven years old. On a sea voyage on the *Imperial*, a passenger-cargo ship, her governess hires the Spirit as her bodyguard, but the haunted vessel itself is out to get her. Darling takes on the ship and wins when she seizes control of the wheel herself. (The Spirit had also taken on a ship with a mind of its own, the *Raven*, in two prewar adventures, and the *Raven* also shows up at Hiroshima when the atom bomb is dropped.)

Darling is another *Spirit* orphan, the only daughter of the late marriage of Oklahoma oilman Tydeland O'Shea. Imagine her surprise when con man Barnaby O'Lyme shows up from London claiming to be her long-lost uncle. Darling can take care of herself, and she takes care of him too, helping Barnaby out, or maybe along is the right word, when he has a little coronary problem. Only one person ever reaches Darling's heart, and that's Santa Claus himself in a really heartwarming *Spirit* Christmas story. Darling didn't know anything about Santa since he'd never brought her any gifts, and when she finds out, she wants him sued for defaming her character, then puts out a contract on him with her guards. The jolly old fellow himself shows up and gives her the gifts he never could deliver before because there were too many bodyguards around. As he leaves, shots ring out—but her guards

have missed, intentionally. Even the Octopus is no match for Darling. When she buys the Lonesome Islands in the middle of the Everglades for a vacation spot (Miami is just "too plebeian"), she finds the Spirit chasing Oc through the swamps. The Spirit gets put to work landscaping, and when Oc falls into quicksand, she unmasks the criminal and turns him over to the Spirit. (4/20/41; 4/12/42; 7/9/50; 10/8/50; 12/10/50; 1/14/51; 3/18/51)

O'Toole, Titmouse J.: After the United States entered World War II in December 1941, *The Spirit* moved beyond stories about saboteurs (clearly Nazis, but usually not specifically identified as such) to actual stories about U.S. soldiers, particularly in a series called "Army Operas." In "Army Operas No. 2" (5/10/42), the well-meaning Titmouse J. O'Toole takes his orders too literally, and can't seem to stay out of trouble. When the Spirit finds O'Toole on patrol in Wildwood Cemetery, the masked crime fighter takes an interest in the GI. When Titmouse is captured by saboteurs, radioing information to U-boats along the Atlantic Coast, the Spirit springs him and lets him take credit for the intelligence information that results in the submarine being blasted out of the water. In "Army Operas No. 3" (5/31/42), poor Sgt. Guff pours out all his frustration in letters to his mom as he tries to discipline O'Toole. But the Spirit helps out O'Toole again, and he gets O'Toole and Guff to join forces in destroying another U-boat. (12/21/41; 5/10/42; 5/31/42)

Octopus, the: This purple-gloved evil mastermind is the major nemesis faced by the Spirit, Eisner's own version of Sherlock Holmes's Professor Moriarty. The Octopus was the head of a vast worldwide criminal ring before World War II, but his syndicate was dealt a setback by the Allied victory. "Octopussie" is Dulcet Tone's mocking pet name for him, over two decades before Ian Fleming's James Bond novel with a similar title, *Octopussy*, was published. The Octopus first revealed himself to the Spirit in 1946, when Silk Satin shanghaied our hero to Germany to help her fight the Doc (reformed, she's now a U.N. agent), but in a later and revised version of the Spirit's origin, it turns out that, unbeknownst to Denny Colt, the Octopus had assisted Dr. Cobra in the plot to poison Central City's water supply that helped turn the detective into the Spirit. The Octopus snatches the Portier fortune from under P'Gell's nose after she's gone to all the trouble to marry and be left widowed by the heir, Waldo, and later the Octopus snatches an improved atomic bomb formula and its inventor, Mortimer J. Titmouse, from under the Spirit's nose.

The Octopus is one of the most violent criminals the Spirit has ever encountered. In the stunning sequence that opens a three-issue story arc (8/10/42, 8/17/42, 8/24/42), the Spirit is pounded to a pulp repeatedly with fists, baseball bat, and a crowbar, by Octopus and his psychotic henchman Gasher (also called Crusher), like William Bendix's brutal beating of Alan Ladd in the film version of Dashiell Hammett's *The Glass Key* (1942). With Gasher captured, a peaceful picnic forms the quiet center of a trilogy of alternating dark, light, and dark stories. In the final movement, Gasher escapes and the Spirit trails him. The Spirit uses his tormenter as bait to lure the Octopus into a trap. A battle in the dark, the brutal execution-style slaying of the henchman by his boss, and a suicidal explosion that may or may not have killed the Octopus complete the sequence with the Spirit left blind by a revolver's flash. The Octopus's European crime connections lead him to show himself still alive when Baron Von Schlozz tries to retrieve black market jewels in army surplus umbrellas, and the mastermind cuts himself in for part of the loot. Schlozz and his henchman Sapper Sam were modeled on GIs Eisner had known in the army. When the Octopus returns to Central City in "Octopus Back in the U.S.A." (2/11/51), it seems as though he's at last revealed his face, until it turns out that he's wearing multiple masks. He joins up with gang leaders, captures the Spirit, and begins cleaning out the police files on himself and other criminals by wearing a Spirit mask when the crooks mistake him for the actual Spirit and blast him. (7/14/46; 7/6/47; 8/10/47; 8/17/47; 8/24/47; 12/28/47; 1/25/48; 8/1/48; 10/31/48; 12/5/48; 2/4/51; 2/11/51; 3/18/51)

Oldest Man in the World, the: In 2941 AD, two archaeologists in the western United States discover a *Spirit* section. The section becomes a story-within-a-story, or a strip-within-a-strip (like Li'l Adam, Eisner's satire of Al Capp's Li'l Abner). The Spirit and Ebony stop the Oldest Man from acting like the Pied Piper of Hamelin and leading all the children of the world to drown in the ocean. The Oldest Man wants to reduce the number of people in the world to give himself more room to roam. At the end of the story, the Oldest Man murders the archaeologists. Like the stories of Abraham Pewter and other long-lived characters, the Oldest Man is lost in time. "The Oldest Man in the World" features some of the most famous experimental coloring in *The Spirit*, using pink and blue without a black plate for the opening and closing bookends of the story, showing events take place in the future. (10/19/41)

Orang, the Ape Man: Eisner has credited the masters of the American short story with being influential on his work, including

ORANG, THE APE MAN

Ambrose Bierce, O. Henry, and of course Edgar Allan Poe. In the story of Orang (9/1/40), in which Dr. Egel of Vienna uses brain surgery and training to give an orangutan a human mind, *The Spirit* pays homage to Poe's "The Murders in the Rue Morgue." The twist here is that he's turned Helen, the daughter of his friend Dr. Fredrich Hoyd, into an ape-woman, reversing evolution. Like Frankenstein's monster, Orang turns on his creator, then kidnaps Ellen to return to Sumatra as his mate. In "The Return of Orang, the Ape that Is Human!" (9/8/10), the Spirit gets to take a Tarzan-like turn as he rescues her. Orang, however, loses his life to the alpha male, Aaka.

Orange, "As Ever": Many a woman has come between two men, but there's probably nothing in American fiction quite like the breakup of Denny Colt and Ebony White brought about by "As Ever" Orange (2/10/46). When Eisner makes his first move to drop the black sidekick Ebony from *The Spirit*, it's characteristic that he should do so in a story featuring a femme fatale. But it's part of Eisner's unique ability to grow throughout his career that the character of "As Ever" Orange should not only be the catalyst for removing Ebony, but also become the focus for a meditation on the depiction of black speech and characters. Miss Orange is a beautifully spoken, wealthy, social-climbing teenager, not unlike some of Eisner's other femmes fatales. She falls for an Army Air Corps pilot with a British accent who is unmasked as a scoundrel by Ebony and his own squadron commander, Major Jones, who speaks perfect standard English. Orange ultimately rejects Ebony because he "sounds like a Civil War minstrel man," to the disgust of Major Jones, who tells her, "It's no disgrace to talk with a Southern drawl." With the Spirit's help, Ebony leaves Central City to get a real education and learn to speak with a "Northern drawl." Interestingly, Ebony is silent in his next appearance in the strip (3/31/46), afflicted by laryngitis.

Orange's name is a play on a potboiler bestseller (filmed by Otto Preminger in 1947), *Forever Amber* by Kathleen Windsor, but there's no real relation between this Restoration costumer and the character in *The Spirit*. Ebony's first girlfriend, Scarlett Brown, similarly had a colorful name, although the reference there is to Scarlett O'Hara, the heroine of Margaret Mitchell's novel and the film made from it, *Gone With the Wind*. (4/6/41; 9/21/41; 3/29/42; 2/10/46; 3/31/46).

Orphans: Eisner's stories featuring orphans usually have the atmosphere of the Dead End Kids films and their successor, the Bowery Boys. Sidney Kingsley's powerful Broadway play was the source of the original film that launched these series, *Dead End* (1937), directed by William Wyler with a screenplay by Lillian Hellman. Portraying tenement kids growing up into hoodlums, the film series often featured "scared straight" stories, that showed the boys avoiding their fate through the intervention of a priest, social worker, or other well-meaning adult. When "Gangster" Barney Jones and Billy "The Hood" Baker escape from an orphanage, the Spirit takes them along as he breaks up Ripper Reagan's mob to show them what "yellow rats" criminals are. He and Ebony save the unbelievably cute Sawbuck Brown from a similar fate. Only Pinhead, the orphan who finds fulfillment as a cartoonist, is left to rot in jail—drawing comics! One of the cutest orphans in *The Spirit* is Willum Waif, whose story is recycled from a character Eisner created in an unsuccessful attempt to sell a syndicated newspaper comic strip, "Nubbin the Newsboy." Small-time embezzler the Baron has fraudulently won custody of the orphan, but the Spirit per-suades the crook that he's a bad influence and he lets Willum go. Willum also stars in "The Song of Little Willum" (11/26/50), a satire based on Longfellow's poem "The Song of Hiawatha." (Eisner's refrain,

"By the Shores of Central City," doesn't make real geographic sense, but the town has no famous river name like Gitche Gumee associated with it.) Willum's new, better life with the Spirit includes a trip to summer camp with the masked crime fighter's sidekick, Sammy. (8/25/40; 4/6/47; 11/2/47; 6/18/50; 8/27/50; 11/26/50; 12/17/50)

PALYACHI

Palyachi: Palyachi is a clown, deranged by love for his fellow circus performer, the lovely dark-haired Marka. In "Palyachi, the Killer Clown" (7/28/40), the harlequin first kills Flipo the trapeze artist to fulfill a passing whim of Marka's, then murders a bank teller in a scheme to enrich her. The clown's name comes from Ruggero Leoncavallo's opera *I Pagliacci* (1892), while the story has the emotional tone of Marlene Dietrich's breakout role in the film *The Blue Angel* (1930).

Paraffin, Mrs.: Waxel Paraffin was the stereotypical mad scientist, a molecular physicist who was literally insane and confined to his country house, tended by his long-suffering wife. In one of the Spirit's strangest cases, Waxel invents a compound that can completely destroy organic matter. When Dr. Paraffin proposes a suicide pact, his wife manages to destroy him first. Mrs. Paraffin turns herself in and wants to be charged and convicted. This is difficult without a body, so she enlists the Spirit to help prove her guilt. The title "The Strange Case of Mrs. Paraffin" (3/7/48) comes from the Alfred Hitchcock film *The Paradine Case* (1948), but there the similarities end. The real parallel is with voiceover narration in films, since the story is told with the Spirit's notecards from the case alternating with panels.

Pewter, Abraham: Like animator Chuck Jones's Michigan J. Frog from the famous Warner Bros. cartoon, or the ghosts who haunt the structure demolished in Eisner's own 1987 graphic novel *The Building*, Abe Pewter is a figure from the past who briefly haunts the present. A Continental army veteran who fled the chaos of 1786 America by digging a hole and pulling it in after him, a still-living Pewter is discovered in 1946 by banker Fiduciary P. Smith, who is equally disgusted until he sees the modern world through Pewter's eyes and decides it isn't so bad, especially given the ladies! When Pewter hears a radio broadcast about postwar shortages and the atomic bomb, he flees back to his hole in the ground. (4/28/46)

P'Gell: She's an international woman of mystery. She's beautiful and deadly. She's been married many times (eight and counting) but her first love is cold, hard cash. She was born in the slums of Paris, and she's used her beauty and her wiles to become an international adventuress, traveling the world from Istanbul to Arabia to the South Pacific. But there's only one man who's ever really won her heart, Central City's crime fighter in a blue mask. She's P'Gell, named for the Place Pigalle, the Paris red light district that won the hearts (and wallets) of so many GIs after World War II. She first appeared in *The Spirit* on October 6, 1946, when the Spirit meets her in exotic Istanbul where he's seeking the Kalkov Formula of Prolonged Life, and she becomes smitten with him. Though he calls her "nature's gift to elemental man," he's able to resist her charms.

Her wealthy husbands had an unfortunate habit of meeting untimely ends, but the charming P'Gell was never without male companionship for very long. She always looked smashing in widow's weeds, and the next rich catch was never very far behind. "She's an image of all fantasy; a slim Mae West, with all the sexiness and mystery of a cobra," is how Eisner described her. A marriage to Central City millionaire Waldo Portier leads to her first visit to the Spirit's hometown when she comes to collect her inheritance after his mysterious death. Unfortunately, the Octopus makes off with her dough and nearly frames her for murder.

P'Gell was a woman of many talents, and she sometimes found herself on the right side of the law. In 1948, her help proved invaluable to Commissioner Dolan in capturing Don Carlos and recovering the Central City Museum's Spanish jewel collection, and she even devoted herself to education, as headmistress of the exclusive Miss Vitriola's School for Girls, and later as a French teacher for Central City's Riverbend University.

One of her best pupils was her stepdaughter, Saree, who learned more than French from her devoted stepmom. A precocious teenager at Miss Vitriola's, Saree soon begins to attract the attention of the men who swoon over P'Gell, leading P'Gell to say "Honey...I see in you the beginnings of some keen competition."

But her two greatest passions were money—"It brings out my artistic side"— and the handsome Spirit. Although she had an unfortunate tendency to whack him on the head when he tried to make her follow the straight and narrow, she fell for him big time and really was never happier than when he'd give in and kiss her. But despite many offers to fly away with her to exotic locales and live the life of luxury, the Spirit always remained true to his crime-fighting mission and the lovely Ellen. Even when they're cast away together on a desert isle after P'Gell is downed in the South Pacific during a scheme to double-cross political refugees, the Spirit manages to resist her charms. But, oh those kisses... (10/6/46; 12/1/46; 1/12/47; 1/19/47; 5/18/47; 5/25/47; 6/15/47; 8/3/47; 11/23/47; 5/23/48; 9/10/50; 1/14/51; 5/20/51; 7/1/51; 7/8/51; 5/4/52; 5/11/52)

Picar: Crime boss of Istanbul, Picar tries to get a formula for prolonging human life but loses out to the Spirit. His consolation prize is marriage to the lovely P'Gell, but then she moves, ending up a couple of husbands later as the owner of Miss Vitriola's School for Girls, bequeathed to her by John (also referred to as Roger) Raymond. When she's about to lose the school to mortgage holder Lady Macbeth, whose son Algy Beeker is yet another of P'Gell's mysteriously dying husbands, Picar shows up with enough contraband diamonds to save the day. (10/6/46; 5/18/47)

PICAR

Pickens, Slim: Not a country western music star but a hoodlum who falls into his role as a boss almost by accident. Slim tells his story to cellmate Johnny Beaver—a cautionary tale, like those that get the orphans in *The Spirit* stories to go straight. Slim's career begins when he kills Abel Kane, the man who gave him an honest job as a grocery clerk. The Spirit pins the rap on him after he's become a million-dollar boss by finding the jack handle with his prints on it that laid Kane down. Of course, the biblical story of Cain and his brother Abel is the inspiration for this fable. In the end, Johnny Beaver vows to go straight: "I'm gonna get me a job...*an honest job!!*" he promises the warden. (12/15/40)

Pierpont: A friend of Ebony White, Pierpont is also an African-American boy who is somewhat more sophisticated in the ways of the world. Pierpont introduces Ebony to various aspects of city living, including the racetrack tout Fat Louie, who shows the boys his stuff as he tries to scam the bettors at the track, only to end up getting scammed himself by insiders like the owners and trainers. (10/12/41; 10/26/41; 11/16/41; 1/4/42; 2/16/47)

Pinch, Lizzie: Unlucky in love is Commissioner Dolan. Ace McCase, master crook, has just settled down to a cushy retirement in a vine-covered cottage when one of the mugs he's framed plugs him. When Commissioner Dolan tries to take possession of the house to locate the loot, he finds it's already been rented by Rubenesque Lizzie, and his heart skips a beat or two. But when some crooks move in on her to get the dough, Dolan takes them out. His reward is a smooch, and then the brushoff, because Lizzie is really a policewoman from Eagle County, with all the right warrants, and Dolan's just done all the work for her pinch. (9/26/48)

Pinhead: Long before Bill Griffith's comic strip "Zippy," Eisner created a character who is physically unusual, but whose only desire is to express himself. Orphaned at birth in the Tennessee hills, Pinhead is raised in inhuman conditions by a professor who wants to study him. Pinhead grows up and escapes to Central City where he finds a career as a fighter. Pinhead is hired by the femme fatale Sylvie Vault, and ends up behind bars where he finds what he's looking for: he draws comics for "self-expression." Eisner has said, "That's a comment on the cartoonist's life. Working in this field is a very, not lonely, but *solitary* life. We could still turn out comics in jail, and our lives would not be a hell of a lot different." (4/6/47)

Plaster of Paris: Like Lorelei Rox, Plaster is a one-off femme fatale, but she's such a powerful character she belongs in the gallery of the best of *The Spirit* dames. She's the toast of Montmartre, the famous artists' quarter of Paris, and her fiery dagger dance makes all men's hearts beat faster. She's engaged to Inspector Guillotine, but her heart belongs to the criminal Don Macabre. When the Spirit comes to help his friend Guillotine capture the international thief, Plaster nearly kills him, but ends up sacrificing herself instead. Eisner remains fond of her: "She portrays the kind of woman who has always interested me. Slender. Neurotic. Plaster is reminiscent of [actress] Lizabeth Scott, who always looked out through a wisp of hair over her eyes." (11/7/48)

Pool's Toadstool Facial Cream: "Plucked from the heath at the fleeting moment of a maddening midnight moon," the cosmetic endorsed by Commissioner Dolan's sister Mathilda appeared in a *Spirit* splash page that satirized a contemporary print campaign for Pond's Cold Cream. In the magazines, the ad's headline read, "She's lovely... She's engaged... She Uses Pond's Facial Cream..."; Eisner's version ran, "She's Ugly! She's Engaged! She uses Pool's Toadstool Facial Cream." (6/9/46)

Pouf, Powder: A villainess in the tradition of P'Gell, Powder snatches up Bleaker Moore, a rudderless bystander, on his first day out of the reformatory, and drags him along on a jewelry heist. Powder becomes an agent of fate, leading him on: "Some men are like flies...without a plan—without direction," and Eisner drapes her and the backgrounds in real and metaphorical webs. Bleak eventually resists her wiles when he falls big time for Powder's cellmate, Sparrow Fallon, who's gone to jail to take the rap for her embezzling father. (11/7/47; 1/4/48; 1/11/48)

Psychology and psychiatrists: "The mind of man is not unlike a rubber band! It can be twisted this way or that—stretched and stretched and s-t-r-e-t-c-h-e-d! Until at last..." said Commissioner Dolan, when he was ready to snap under public pressure to solve a crime. The metaphor of the human mind as a rubber band is extended when two other characters undergo breakdowns. The wealthy Vannest snaps and commits suicide when accused of murder, and the evil Grumly—who forged Vannest's will and

POWDER POUF

faked his own death to drive Vannest insane—snaps under the Spirit's relentless pursuit and confesses his crimes (6/23/46). Before the war, a psychologist named Professor Pinx had advocated this model of the brain's inner workings, but Eisner has said he did not realize when he created the second story years later that he was reusing the metaphor (8/2/42). Psychobabble is parodied by the girls at Miss Vitriola's school, when P'Gell's stepdaughter Saree Raymond is warned that she might develop a neurosis from living with the femme fatale, and would-be boyfriend Inchly the 3rd is dismissed as a paranoiac introvert, who is also not good criminal material since he isn't egocentric enough to kidnap the Spirit (1/19/47). In one prescient story, "The Deadly Comic Book" (2/27/49), Eisner paints a portrait of an innocent music teacher driven to violent thoughts by a comic book. His school's psychologist is Dr. Wolfgang Worry, who burns comic books to protect children. This is a satire of psychiatrist Dr. Fredric Wertham, whose 1954 book, *Seduction of the Innocent*, helped launch a nationwide crusade against comic books.

QUIRTE

Quirte: A card shark and a criminal, Quirte wants to take over the mysterious town of Boot Camp, the former hideout of Sam Chapparell and his gang. The healthful air here would make it perfect for the children's hospital the commissioner's daughter, Ellen Dolan, wants to build, but Quirte wants the old bandit's loot, and he'll burn it to the ground to get it. The Spirit puts Quirte to flight into the Rockies, where he waits for his chance to return. When he's helped by an old Indian, Little Fox Hermit, Quirte is ungrateful and steals his food. It's Thanksgiving, and the Spirit, Ellen, and some kids are celebrating in the ruins of Boot Camp as best they can, while Quirte is abusing the Indian who tries to help him. The Indian's curse works, and Quirte dies of hunger and thirst just before he makes his way back to town. (11/14/48; 11/21/48)

Ramadan, Dr.: Ramadan is the holiest month of the Muslim calendar. Dr. Ramadan is actually Faroud El Rhamid, an Egyptian scientist who's wanted for murder. He drags Bleaker Moore into his web of evil when the former criminal answers his classified ad, wanting to go straight. Rhamid has custodianship of Jack Frye, a 372-year-old man who is the product of an experiment in 1590 by a court physician. Bleak is about to get an operation to remove from a gland in the back of his brain the necessary ingredient for endlessly prolonged life, when the Spirit saves him. Another long-lived individual appeared in the earlier *Spirit* story "The Oldest Man in the World." (10/19/41; 5/9/48)

Raven's Point: The end of the line for the late-night Central City trolley called "The 29 Car," and the end of the line for a trio of criminals in one of Eisner's most macabre *Spirit* stories. Head-teller Crauley has engineered the robbery of his own bank, and tipped off the Spirit and the police without letting them know he was involved. When the Spirit cops to the scam, Crauley shoots him, and heads home on the trolley. There he finds a newspaper headlined, "The Spirit Murdered, Body Missing." Then he spots what appears to be the Spirit's body (actually a dummy), and his two co-conspirators, "Killer" Conch and "Bottles" McTopp. Crauley's soliloquy spills the beans to his former co-conspirators, who turn out to be corpses placed there by the Spirit, who also planted the newspaper story and is disguised as the conductor. The name Raven's Point is based on Hunt's Point Terminal in the Bronx. (3/24/46)

Raymond, Saree: The stepdaughter of unrepentant femme fatale P'Gell, Saree marries Roger Raymond, a former convict gone straight. She sets up Miss Vitriola to commit suicide, exploiting Vitriola's disappointment that Saree's dad is marrying P'Gell instead of the school marm, and plans to kill P'Gell until she finds out that they're sisters under the skin. When P'Gell decides her next husband will be Dr. Bigelow, the history teacher on whom Saree has a schoolgirl crush, the teenager flees the boarding school for a life of crime, joining the Rattler's gang. When the Spirit rescues Saree, she finds a new love—the Spirit. One of his favorite characters, Eisner later described Saree as follows: "She had a dancer's rhythm and was a good actress. She had the subtlety of character that I like to use in a

SAREE RAYMOND

comic strip. You got the feeling that underneath the teenager was a growing woman with explosive potential." (1/12/47; 1/19/47; 5/18/47)

Robin, Cox: With a name taken from the nursery rhyme "Cock Robin," the Spirit (and the reader) are given a puzzle to solve: all the clues to the crime are contained in a single, black and white photograph of a woman's hand, a gun, an ashtray, and a ring. Cox was the widow of gossip columnist Nosey Noonan, and her body was found in the apartment of hood Killer Quigly. Deduction is the order of the day as the Spirit uses the fact that Robin had bumped off her husband in '42 and then used his files to blackmail actors, plus visual clues available to the Spirit and readers, to "tie" down the solution to the crime of "Who Killed Cox Robin?" (8/4/46).

COX ROBIN

Roger: Animals are rarely lead players in *Spirit* stories, but Roger, the dog who was accused of murder, does several star turns. He almost takes a murder rap for Ward Healey, until Mr. Bowser, the dogcatcher, clears him through his Dr. Doolittle-like ability to talk to animals. He's auctioned off to Serene Mayhem, the spoiled rich little daughter of political boss Ballot Mayhem, but he had bonded with Ebony and escapes to return to him, leading to an all-out custody battle. Eisner loves music and adopted a title from an actual musical piece from French composer Jacques Offenbach's opera *The Tales of Hoffman*, "Barkarolle," for the last Roger story (7/18/48).

"When I was a little kid, my mother bought me a violin. I had some lessons. I played this piece endlessly—I remember it to this day," he has recalled. (In Eisner's hands, the opera becomes *Tales of Arfmann* by Jacques Arfenbark in its canine incarnation.) Roger is led astray by Sven Galli, whose role in corrupting dogs comes from Charles Dickens's Fagin (from *Oliver Twist*), and whose name comes from the hypnotic mastermind Svengali who corrupts artist's model Trilby in the 1894 novel of the same name by George du Maurier. (9/7/47; 2/29/48; 7/18/48)

NYLON ROSE

Rose, Nylon: Perhaps with a prescient nod to the developing American consumer economy, Eisner's first postwar femme fatale was named after the ladies' garment that was much-desired but rarely available in the days of Rosie the Riveter—nylon stockings. The lovely, beret-wearing Miss Rose falls bigtime for the Spirit when she first meets him. "Woof! Woof! *Who* is that gor-r-r-geous hunk o' man?" she asks the commissioner's daughter, Ellen Dolan. Nylon is a federal agent posing as a crook who cracks a scheme to smuggle counterfeit U.S. bills into France. The bills were wrapped in the bandages of fake patients who sail on ocean liners. In her next case, she finds the Spirit tied up and ignores the meat highjackers she's supposed to be tracking for the Feds, smothering the boy in kisses. (3/17/46; 4/7/46)

Rox, Lorelei: Of the many femmes fatales the Spirit encountered, Lorelei is one of the most mysterious. Lorelei (of Odyssey Road, a reference to the sirens who try to lure sailors like Odysseus to his death on the rocks), returns to Central City as a war bride. Like the Lorelei of the Romantic poem by Clemens Brentano, who lures sailors on the Rhine to their destruction, the Spirit's Lorelei lures truck drivers to their doom at the roadhouse owned by her husband, Blacky Marquett. (It's on Odyssey Road as well.) Although only appearing in one story, Lorelei is one of *The Spirit*'s most famous bad girls, in part because of the powerful, film noir splash page that opens the story, the surreal effects panels that depict the dizzied truck drivers, and the beauty of the design of her character. (9/19/48)

Rubber Lips: One of the more physically grotesque thugs encountered by the Spirit, Rubber Lips is the enforcer for Murder McCoy of the Big-Three Mob. Their racket is to scam ex-GIs out of deposits in a phony apartment-construction scheme. The struggle of returning GIs to find housing in New York after World War II, and the building of new housing in the city, provides the realistic backdrop for this scam. (8/31/47)

LORELEI ROX

Sally of the Islands: In an extended adventure in the South Seas in "the islands beyond the Marquesas" called the Peligros (Spanish for "danger"), spunky heroine Sally finds herself in the clutches of criminal Kragg. The Spirit rescues her, but in disguise as the anonymous Mr. Smith. Sally turns down the colonial governor's proposal of marriage because the Spirit has won her heart. While the Spirit's gone, Ellen hires Willie Ankle, Private Eye, to find this mysterious man. In a cute turnabout, the private eye falls for Ellen and dresses up as the Spirit to win her affections by showing he can be a hero too. Before the Spirit leaves the South Pacific, he and his assistant, Sammy, help Governor Baptiste win reelection on Monabau over the corrupt Baby Manuelo thanks to Sammy's baseball-playing prowess. (The reference here is really to the Caribbean and the island of Haiti, where the

BUT NOT ME! EVERYTHING I TOUCH, I DESTROY...ALL MY LIFE HAS BEEN A...A NIGHTMARE HELD TOGETHER BY A HOPE OF A BETTER DAY...BUT NOW I KNOW I'VE BEEN WASTING MY DREAMS...

SALLY OF THE ISLANDS

corrupt Duvalier family, including "Baby Doc," ruled for many years.) Also in the Peligros is Matua, an island that began life as a volcano and turns into a monster. When the Spirit and Sammy come seeking a couple of scalawags named Ace and Cutter, they witness the taming of the monster by a Tan-Gau, a native religious practitioner. (7/17/49; 7/24/49; 7/31/49; 8/7/49)

Sammy: After several years of growing concern on Eisner's part that the character of Ebony White would be perceived as demeaning to African-Americans, and after many—and most would agree successful—efforts to grow the character into a boy with professional ambitions and accomplishments, Eisner finally decided it was time to simply give the Spirit another sidekick. Enter Sammy, who first appears as a baseball-playing wonder kid who helps the Spirit keep democracy and American ideals alive on the South Seas Island of Monabau. Sammy's first star turn comes via a satire of another type of comic book, "Lurid Love, Sickening Stories about Other Peoples' Misery & Heartache" (9/18/49), featuring an advice column by Wanda Lust (wanderlust). Sammy develops a schoolboy crush on Ellen, and in the overheated prose of imagined romance comics, he narrates the story of his lovesick heart, as well as the crime tale of Seth Passifik and Ugly Mary, criminals who hole up in the Dolan home. This section includes several satires of the ads that used to appear in comics for weight loss and weight gain products, magic tricks, and of course, "Be A Cartoonist!" Sammy's best-known role is the one he played out with femme fatale Autumn Mews (10/9/49), who tricks him into helping her blackmail the Spirit to get her boyfriend, Virgil Gunbelt, sprung. The splash page depicting the Spirit is one of Eisner's best, and the dark ending, with Mews and her boy gunned down after Sammy springs him, is equally memorable. (7/31/49; 8/7/49; 9/18/49; 10/9/49; 12/11/49; 1/22/50; 2/12/50; 3/5/50; 5/14/50)

SAMMY

Sampson, Squire: The rackets always need a respectable front man, and the Squire suits the bill. When Salty Peters captures Ebony and puts his foot in a torture device—the Chinese Boot—it looks like the Spirit's going to have to give in to a frame-up that will end his racket busting. That is until Ebony shows that he's resourceful enough to give the mobsters the boot. When Central City is chosen as a test community for trying out blackouts, the mayor and Dolan are embarrassed before the whole country when the darkness is used by Sampson as a cover for stealing police cars. (During the war, blackout meant dousing all the illumination in a community so that enemy bombers would be unable locate their targets.) (11/24/40; 7/13/41)

DARLING!

SAND SAREF

Saree (see **Raymond, Saree**).

Saref, Sand: She was never meant to be in *The Spirit* at all. Her heart belonged to the Eisner character who never saw the light of day until decades later when Eclipse Comics published the comic book *John Law, Detective*. Originally she was called Sand Blue, and the dark settings and conflicted emotions of her tale make her name perhaps more appropriate than her final denotation. (The name's a pun on sans serif, meaning a typeface without serifs, the small lines that finish the top and bottoms of the main strokes of letters. Sans serif fonts are considered uncomplicated and easy to read, quite the opposite of Ms. Serif.) Sand and Denny Colt (in the revised story) grew up together in a tough neighborhood, and Sands' dad was a cop killed by Denny's uncle, a petty thief who never meant to hurt him. But it made her hard.

During World War II, Sand became an international adventuress. When they meet again in Central City, she's at the middle of a plot to buy a deadly virus from Dr. Vitriol. The Spirit breaks it up, but for old times' sake, he lets Sand flee. When the Spirit heads to the Middle East to track the Jewel of Gizeh, he finds both Sand and Mr. Carrion (with his

SAND SAREF

ever-faithful and loving buzzard Julia, of course) aboard his tramp steamer, and they all end up marooned on a tropical island together. Here they find criminal Archie Flye, who's joined by a U-boat full of Nazis, all looking for the jewel. But the Spirit and Sand manage a nice hole-in-one, collecting all the bad guys. When they return, Ellen is jealous, and Sand cries bitter tears.

Sand provides the occasion for one of the Spirit's rare forays into television. Radio drama provided a background and source for many *Spirit* stories, but since television only emerged as a mass medium toward the end of *The Spirit*'s run, few episodes deal with it. But Eisner casts an episode in the form of a TV show because "They got color television...now! We are not going to take this new competition lying down." The *Spirit* story involves Sand smuggling diamonds in dolls, cast in the form a TV program with Dolan being interviewed by Bert Smirk (Bert Parks, TV show host and long the emcee of *The Miss America Pageant*), complete with ads for "Gunny Sack Tobacco" and "Contour Blades! The Rubberized Razor Blade Made to Fit Your Face!" (1/8/50; 1/15/50; 3/12/50; 3/19/50; 3/26/50; 4/9/50; 12/10/50; 1/14/51; 8/12/51)

Satin, Sylvia "Silk": The femmes fatales in *The Spirit* were like the glamour goddesses of Hollywood, and sometimes specifically modeled on these gorgeous and charismatic gals. Skinny Bones was based on Lauren Bacall, and Silk Satin was born from brainy Academy Award–winning actress Katharine Hepburn, especially her cross-dressing role in director George Cukor's *Sylvia Scarlet* (1935). An underworld character when the Spirit first encountered her before the war, it was later revealed that Satin was married to Nazi Ivan

Tovaroff. Her criminal activities and her later career as an international agent, first with the Nazis and then with British intelligence, were motivated only by her desire to rescue Hildie, the daughter she had had with Tovaroff, from the clutches of the Nazis.

Silk's first caper brings her to the Spirit's home town with two other European super criminals to steal the Malbro Medal from Count Gazoff. When the Spirit interferes, she soon has him hanging from a beam. One kiss and she falls in love with him, and he's impressed, too: "You're really a nice girl...too bad you've got a criminal mind!" They next meet when Silk saves the Spirit and Ellen after the freighter they are sailing to Europe is sunk by a U-boat and they are among the prisoners taken to occupied France. Sylvia appears to be cooperating with the Nazis, but her deeply hidden maternal instincts are forced to the fore when she and the Spirit get custody of King Zenix II, ex-ruler of Balkslavania, when the Nazis try to kill him to end all resistance to their conquest of his country.

After the war, it turns out that she never wanted to be a criminal or a Nazi: she had married Ivan Tovaroff, who joined up with Hitler's Brownshirts and kept their daughter Hildie hostage to secure her services. She and the Spirit rescue Hildie, and Silk brings her skills to the newly formed United Nations, enlisting the Spirit's assistance in tracking down European criminals. Then she brings her secret agent skills to a new position with the famous insurance company Croyd's of Glasgow.

In the caper of the Hobe Diamond, she saves a set of European crown jewels for the insurance company, but like the old Silk she manages to literally cut herself in for a share. Insurance is also the key to her brief romance with the rich British noble scoundrel Lord Elbey. When Soho Sander uses Croyd's to insure incriminating blackmail papers, Elbey

offers to marry Silk if she'll retrieve them but puts her in a frame only the Spirit can spring her from. Silk had only agreed to marry Elbey to provide for Hildie, and she's glad to get back to work for Croyd's. She next heads to India to retrieve the stolen Emerald of Rajahpur. The Spirit follows, and finds Elbey is involved, so he engineers the imprisonment and torture of Elbey to make sure he can never marry Silk and to get revenge for her.

Eisner was fond of Silk as well: "I enjoyed her," he explains. "She wasn't an obvious female type. I felt she had more dimension than most women portrayed in comics. She is the Spirit's equal, and in fact I regarded her as the female Spirit." Although set on the fictitious island of Puerto Que near Barbados, one of the best Silk Satin stories (11/13/49) partakes of the atmosphere of South Seas romances like the Dorothy Lamour movie vehicle *Typhoon* (1940) and many others. This is also one of the best *Spirit* love triangles. The romance plays out entirely in subtle undercurrents as the Spirit, Hildie, Silk, and her new husband, the weak importer, Kurt Van Breck, face a hurricane. Kurt dies, and the Spirit hides the man's cowardice from Silk. She returns the favor by finding Dr. Anschluss, believed to have died in Dachau, who is the only medical expert who can save the Spirit when bullet wounds in his legs become infected. (3/16/41; 6/8/41; 7/6/41; 10/5/41; 1/18/42; 6/7/42; 6/21/42; 8/23/42; 1/20/46; 7/14/46; 12/29/46; 10/12/47; 5/30/48; 11/13/49; 1/14/51)

Scallopini, Joe "Heel": A victim of political corruption, Scallopini was a precinct worker for the Prosperity Party, beaten to death by the hoodlums of the Reform Party. The corruption of big city politics is indicted along with the hoods after the Spirit enters the case, and the masked detective even gets the aptly named alderman Julius Caesar to truly reform. (3/2/47)

Scarr, Max: A haunting character, Scarr was the head of the German branch of the international banking firm The House of Minter. The Spirit and Dolan are invited by Mr. Minter to come to his home for the unveiling of a map in a time-release vault that will show where the European branches of the bank hid their riches from the Nazis. Max Scarr was the head of the German branch, and Minter believes he's dead at the hands of the Nazis. It is revealed that Scarr has survived the concentration camp, horribly changed, and is now Minter's butler! The party is filled with former Gestapo agents searching for the map, whom Scarr poisons before revealing that it's tattooed on his chest. (4/14/46)

Seasonal stories: The Spirit often featured stories about holidays. The most famous are the Christmas stories, which were featured in an anthology called *The Christmas Spirit*, published by Kitchen Sink Press in 1987. Other regular seasonal features were the Halloween stories, for which Eisner created a funny and misunderstood witch, Hazel P. Macbeth, who miraculously appeared each year in Central City. Thanksgiving stories appeared from time to time, as did the occasional baseball or football stories. The Christmas, Halloween, and other seasonal stories were part of Eisner's efforts to keep in mind the syndicate that circulated *The Spirit* section to newspapers and the editors of the individual papers. "When you dish out comics on a weekly basis, you have to keep track of the seasons," he observes. "It's a springboard; it helps make the strip *au courant* with life. You insinuate the strip into the reader's life."

Shack, Fraternization H.: As lucky as Disney cartoonist's Carl Barks's Gladstone Gander in the Donald Duck comics, "Frat" has a way with slot machines and a suave British accent. He first appears as Ebony White's rival for the affections of the lovely "As Ever" Orange. Unfortunately, Shack has fraternized with a civilian, and in fact married Princess Polywogg of Muddgonia in 1944. Thanks to the intervention of his commander, Major Jones, the couple are reunited and return to her home, much to Shack's dismay. The Spirit and Ebony encounter him again on the South Pacific island where he and his bride had gone (although the island is now referred to as Goona), and the henpecked Shack is more than happy to fly with the crime fighters away from the island—and his wife!—before it's destroyed by a tidal wave.

Unfortunately, his princess is rescued by the Coast Guard. Weeks later she is working as a scrub woman when she finds him, much to his dismay. He later moves to South America, and gives the Spirit a ride to the mysterious island of Montabaldo on his Volar la Noche (that is, Fly by Night) Airlines. (2/10/46; 6/2/46; 1/25/48).

Shnobble, Gerhard: Although he only appeared once, this diminutive character in a bowler hat has become one of the best-known of Eisner's *Spirit* characters. An otherwise unremarkable individual who dies in a hail of bullets as an innocent bystander, Gerhard Shnobble had one unusual talent: he could fly. And his flight was achieved not through any magic or mysterious technology, but through his own belief that he could do so, even though he was completely ordinary in every other way. This story of the unassuming individual whose dream and belief in himself makes the impossible come true has been reprinted more often than any other *Spirit* story. Eisner's portrait of an everyman transformed by a dream is not only a fine short story in the American tradition of O. Henry and Raymond Carver, but also a subtle and—appropriately for *The Spirit*—pointed commentary on the super hero mythos itself (9/5/48).

This Eisner character has been translated into other media as well. In 1994, Brazilian film student Bruno Vianna made a short cinematic version of Eisner's story, set in the slums of Rio de Janeiro. "Geraldo Voador" (Gerhard the Flyer) is a poor slum kid. He flies once, but is punished by his mother for it and swears never to fly again. He becomes a lookout for a drug gang, one of the kids who sends up a kite to warn them if the cops are coming. He decides to quit and run away. When he's chased, he flies once more, but is shot down and dies. The Spirit does not appear in this prize-winning, poetic black and white short.

In 1996, Eisner was one of five artists invited by the city of Copenhagen, Denmark, to design murals to be painted on the sides of historic buildings in the city. Eisner created a two-foot-high original painting, not a scene from the story. It was translated into a full-color mural showing Shnobble flying past a dozen workmen on ladders and ledges on the side of the building. Eisner's painting was also reproduced as a limited-edition print. [See color section for a reprint of the complete "Gerhard Shnobble" story.]

Signs: One of the hallmarks of *The Spirit* series, and one of the most influential on comics ever afterward, was Eisner's use of signs: as logos for the weekly comics, as architecture, as panels, and as dialogue in the strip. From an eye chart with the Spirit's name in smaller and smaller letters, to signs and billboards across a cityscape, signs were often the inventive logos of the weekly *Spirit* sections. Cityscapes were festooned with posters, from those advertising wanted criminals like Rocco Ayjiss pasted to a hoarding, to campaign posters for Ellen Dolan's mayoral run, including one featuring the dour and disapproving face of the Spirit himself. Transparent surfaces come to life in Eisner's work, especially office doors with lettering on them, sometimes towering threateningly over characters engaged in skullduggery, or becoming entire panels unto themselves. At the moment when Walker Evans was turning America's signs into gallery art through his photographs, and Stuart Davis was making the neon of America's cityscapes into the architecture of his jazz-inspired paintings, Eisner was making signs into a new and innovative element in America's native art form, the comics. Speaking of his famous splash pages, Eisner has said, "To me, lettering is as much a part of the art as anything else. As the borders, as the panels, lettering has a visual impact, it has a storytelling effect."

Skinch, Joshua: The dark partnership of Skinch and Joe Dawes is the most cynical portrayal of business in *The Spirit*. Bespectacled and mustachioed, the very portrait of respectability, Skinch parlays his wealth into a run for alderman, but it all goes down when the framed Dawes returns from prison. The Spirit has been digging into the dirt, and gets shot and left for dead by Skinch's henchmen, but even he didn't suspect that Skinch's accountant was the dirtiest of them all. "The violence gave me the chance to create some drama," Eisner has said. "I was trying for a great deal of emotion," and in the ironic finale to their partnership, Skinch's henchmen kill their boss and the accountant takes out Dawes. (1/26/47)

Smith, P. S.: He's a little kid in an aviator's helmet, and he never has a word to say for himself, but he appears as a wide-eyed witness to humorous events in some of the Spirit's more interesting cases. He's sometimes shown as a drooling toddler and appears as a silent partner to Ebony, although he manages to get the better of him when he makes off with Roger, the dog Ebony's lost his heart to, by being first to get a license for him. He wears a yellow nightshirt, and sometimes sucks a candy cane as though it's a cigar, an homage to R. F. Outcault's stogie-smoking Yellow Kid, the star of the very first comic strip beginning in 1895. Smith's trademark candy gave him his nickname, Peppermint Sticks. He got another nickname, the "Unknown Terror," when he won the benefit Pennyweight Championship boxing match. It was then revealed that his real name was Algernon. Since this moniker was too "sissy" for his fighting career, Ebony broke the fourth wall to ask readers for suggestions for a new name: "We'll use the best one in a future story." Response must have been underwhelming, since no new name ever appeared.

P.S. SMITH

In a story inspired by *Alice in Wonderland*, P. S. Smith takes on the title role when he falls down a rabbit hole while on a picnic with the Spirit gang at the beach (8/8/48). When the Spirit goes to rescue him, they find themselves in an underwater wonderland full of beauty and danger. The story was conceived by Eisner as a tribute to two adventure illustrators he admired, John R. Neill (of *The Wizard of Oz* fame) and William Robinson Leigh. As New York's Thomas E. Dewey battled Harry S. Truman for the presidency in the summer of 1948, P. S. ran for president in Central City's junior elections against the bookmaker's son Scratchy Parlay (8/15/48). When dad tries to fix the election, the kids learn a valuable lesson about fair play. (6/22/41; 7/27/41; 10/12/41; 5/26/46; 9/15/46; 9/29/46; 2/29/48; 8/8/48; 8/15/48; 1/9/49; 2/27/49; 4/10/49; 11/20/49; 12/25/49; 1/22/50)

Smudge, Simon: When old Donjon Prison is torn down, a mysterious prisoner surfaces from under the portion of the prison that burned to the ground in 1911. Like Abraham Pewter, Smudge wants to stay away from the world. He was framed thirty-seven years before by his lawyers, Redtape & Snarl, but he likes being in prison because it gives him lots of time to practice his harmonica. (8/29/48)

SINGAPORE SMYTH

Smyth, Singapore: A male model featuring a Continental sophisticate's white, wavy hair and moustache and goatee— the spokesmodel for Borschtbelt's Buttermilk. Smyth and his down-on-his-luck friend Pixie Powers (whose name is derived from the slang adjective pixilated or drunk) exchange places in society. Ebony and the Spirit get on their tails when one tries a stock scam, but the two friends only find happiness when they're down and out and riding the rails together again. (8/18/46)

Spanking: It only happened once, but it's become an indelible image for *Spirit* fans, one of the most often reproduced splash pages. Young Ellen Dolan is a student at State, and her girls' dorm needs one thing—the Spirit. She gets a premed student to lend her a corpse, and sends out an SOS for the Spirit. When her hapless helper spills the beans, the Spirit turns her over his knee. But then he saves the girls from a real menace, the insane Prof. Van Verikt, who has murdered Dean Cross and is ready to kill anyone who "crosses" his path. In the end, the Spirit is rewarded with the kisses of dozens of coeds. (12/1/40)

Spirit, the: Denny Colt is the Spirit, a crime fighter like no other. On June 2, 1940, Denny was presented with an unusual opportunity: he had dedicated his life to fighting crime as a private detective, but after a gun battle with the criminal mastermind Dr. Cobra, during which he was sloshed with mysterious chemicals that left him in a state of suspended animation, the world presumed him to be dead. Reports of his death were, however, greatly exaggerated, and he took up residence in Central City's Wildwood Cemetery, where his underground apartment is equipped with all the modern conveniences a bachelor and crime fighter needs. Of course he has a fully equipped laboratory for scientific and forensic work, and in the prewar stories he has a garage where he parks a romantic red autoplane. The autoplane, a Tom Swift sort of device in the form of a classic roadster that could sprout wings and fly when the Spirit was in hot pursuit of criminals, was quietly dropped in Eisner's postwar stories.

Denny Colt hides his identity behind a simple blue eye mask. Since the world presumes him to be dead, he doesn't need an elaborate disguise. But the mask also emphasizes the human qualities of the Spirit—he doesn't need a costume, like the super heroes found in newsstand comic books. Instead, he wears a suit and a tie, blue gloves, plain brown shoes like any other detective, and a neatly blocked hat. The only costume he needs is his mask, which emphasizes rather than hides his eyes. Clear blue, they see the plight of the citizens of Central City, and guide the Spirit as he helps them when they're in need.

His unusual living conditions make it a bit difficult for Denny to entertain lady friends, but that never kept the Spirit from having a full, if somewhat complicated, love life. The good girl who's most likely in the end to win his heart is Ellen, the daughter of his friend and ally in fighting crime, Police Commissioner Dolan. Ellen was the American ideal of the girl next door, and Denny was ever true to her. But he couldn't help but occasionally find himself in the clinches with bad girls, who also couldn't help themselves when they threw themselves at him. It was hard to resist sultry temptresses like Silk Satin, Sand Saref, and the dreamiest of all, P'Gell, but the Spirit (despite the occasional lipstick traces) never really fell for anyone but Ellen. Although the Spirit was tricked or manipulated into popping the question to Ellen a couple of times during the course of the strip, unlike other famous comics creators like Al Capp, who reaped huge promotional and publicity opportunities from the wedding of Li'l Abner and

Daisy Mae, Eisner never let Denny and Ellen marry. One of the great charms of the strips was the bad girls who threw themselves at the Spirit, and these episodes would have had a very different tenor if the Spirit were not a bachelor.

The Spirit was adept at crime solving, and the "evil doers" usually found themselves at the end of the long arm of the law (although first-class villains like Dr. Cobra might escape to plague him another day). But Denny Colt was also a fine observer of human

nature, and some of the most memorable Spirit stories find him simply marveling at the Eisner characters who may best exemplify the human spirit, including poor little rich girl Darling O'Shea, spunky orphans like Willum Waif and Sawbuck Brown, and ordinary souls who transcend their humble lives like Gerhard Shnobble.

In addition to Dr. Cobra, the Spirit faced several other criminal masterminds of the highest order in his career. The Octopus was one of the most devious and powerful—the master of a worldwide criminal ring, and the Spirit's adversary who is closest in "spirit" to the evil mastermind of the Sherlock Holmes stories, Professor Moriarty. The Octopus's face is never revealed, only his striped gloves, and he seeks what we now call "weapons of mass destruction," as when he gets a hapless janitor to hand over the secrets of atomic weapons. Like the battle at Reichenbach Falls, the Spirit engages in a duel to the death with the Octopus, but the Spirit emerges blinded, while the Octopus apparently has died by his own hand in a grenade blast. (Not to worry: The Spirit's sight was later restored and, of course, the Octopus was heard from again as well.)

The blind Spirit becomes a litmus test of responses from those who care for him, and the Spirit himself feels inadequate and vulnerable: "Blind...shut in...a big case brewing and I stumble about like a fool! Blind...Blind...BLIND!" But with some unobtrusive help from his ever-faithful assistant, Ebony, the Spirit does capture Rubber Lips, the toughest crook in town. Eisner had considered using the blindness episodes to do away with the Spirit's mask (8/10, 8/17 and 8/24/48). "But I was reminded that I'd have a trademark problem if we did that, so he went back to a mask instead," Eisner later recalled.

In fact, Eisner never wanted to use a mask at all, or any kind of costume, because he didn't want the Spirit to be a costumed super hero. The mask was a compromise with his business partner, Everett Arnold, who was responding to pressure from newspaper editors, who felt if they were going to buy a comic book for their newspapers, didn't it have to have a super hero, like the successful comics featuring Superman and Batman? Eisner gave his character enough to keep everyone happy—a mask, an origin story, a secret identity, and a romantic name—clearing the way to create stories that featured action and adventure, but also pushed the aesthetic boundaries of the comics medium, exploring the psychology of his characters and the meaning of the human condition.

Spirit Section: Will Eisner's *The Spirit* was only one—although the lead and eponymous feature—of three different stories featured each week in *The Spirit* section. An innovation of Eisner and his partner Everett Arnold, putting a comic book in the Sunday newspaper probably would not have been as successful in attracting subscribers if there had been only one long story about a single character. Like the earliest comic books with original material such as *More Fun*, *The Spirit* section featured multiple action and humor strips. Also like comic books, but unlike the comic strips that appeared in other sections of the paper, the stories in *The Spirit* supplement were all complete in each issue, never continuing or serialized. Various features appeared in *The Spirit* supplement over the years. Besides *The Spirit*, the other features in the supplement included *Lady Luck*, *Mr. Mystic*, *Intellectual Amos*, *Flatfoot Burns*, and *Wendy the Waitress*.

Splash panels: No one had ever done anything like it before. Everyone who has come after has tried to equal it, but few have succeeded. The splash pages of *The Spirit* were the

solution to a practical problem: How do you create a cover for a comic book that's never going to be on a newsstand? *The Spirit* section was included in the Sunday newspaper, just like the funnies or any other magazine supplement. The trick wasn't to get readers to buy it—they already had. The problem was to get them to read it, and keep reading it, week after week. A fabulous image, or the opening of a story with a strong hook, could catch the interest of the casual reader. However, *The Spirit* section had constraints other comics didn't. Like the funny papers, but unlike most newsstand comics, *The Spirit* section was all newsprint, with no glossy paper for the cover; in industry parlance, it was self-covering. And it was short, especially compared to a 64-page comic book: just sixteen (and later eight) pages. Therefore it made sense to start the story immediately on the first page, and with the biggest bang possible. Thus Eisner created the splash pages that open each *Spirit* story, changing comics forever.

Eisner is the kind of restless, innovative creator who will always take a challenge and make it an opportunity. And, as if it weren't enough to have to overcome the constraints of the format, Eisner had to up his own ante by deciding not to create a standard logo, but to instead reconceive the title lettering week after week. Eisner has said, "My partner, Everett Arnold, didn't like it. There wasn't a standard logo that could be copyrighted." But Eisner knew that it was more important to grab readers by the collar and pull them into the story. And with his characteristic combination of waste not, want not economy and soaring imagination, Eisner made the logo a part of the story. Sometimes the word "Spirit" became a building in the urban background, a hidden-picture puzzle for the reader to solve. Sometimes it became a poster, or a newspaper headline, or another written or printed image that both identified the section and advanced the story. What it never became was a dead, repetitive, copyrightable block of text. Instead, Eisner had the whole canvas of the front page to introduce a striking character like Mr. Hush or a femme fatale like P'Gell, to show the Spirit in action, or to turn into a page from another kind of book, like one of the fairy tales twisted and updated in *The Spirit*.

The role of the splash page, however, didn't end with *The Spirit*. When Eisner returned to the comics field in 1978 with his groundbreaking graphic novel *A Contract with God*, the splash was incorporated into Eisner's storytelling innovations. Using the edge of the page as a panel border, or making the lettering a part of the story, was one aspect of the innovative sequential art Eisner employed to tell his autobiographical stories. As a result, the storytelling techniques he pioneered during his *Spirit* years helped fuel the development of a visual language for this new medium, the graphic novel.

Squid, The: A Nazi agent who shows up in America to destroy the nation's defense capability, the Squid wears a green hood and goggles. His face is never shown, like that other mysterious super villain also named after an ocean-dweller, the Octopus. In his first caper, the Squid tries to destroy the great power dam at West Armsville (no doubt an important source of power for the munitions industry). It takes both the Spirit and Silk Satin to prevent the blowing up of the dam. The next target of the Squid is the city's reservoir, and he attacks it using dirigibles. The Octopus, too, had targeted the reservoir, and was attempting to poison it when he paralyzed Denny Colt, leading to the birth of the Spirit. (1/18/42; 2/15/42; 4/5/42)

Stone, Rockhead: One of Central City's most wanted criminals, Stone is addicted to radio contests but is too big a bonehead to ever win a quiz. The efforts of the Central City police to capture him are complicated by his doppelgänger, DeWit Fan Pook, and hapless Captain Mulligan keeps getting the wrong man. Meanwhile, Stone kidnaps Spirit's sidekick Blubber Wales when he realizes the diminutive Arctic native is a quiz master extraordinaire, and finally realizes his dream of winning a quiz—but only after Blubber has helped the Spirit park him in the slammer. (2/24/46)

Strand, Thorne: A strong, smart woman with a dark streaked widow's peak, Thorne Strand takes over her husband's business and suggests he retire. Her friend Roxie Haven makes sure he does, though they call it suicide. Roxie's a fight promoter who wants the Strand arena, but Thorne's the real brains who cooks the books. When the Spirit assigns himself to be her bodyguard, the attraction is so thick you can cut it with a knife. He's just trying to get the goods on her, but Ellen gets jealous, and rightly so. Then Thorne kidnaps the Spirit and takes him to the Vortex, a ship whose all-female crew is led by Long Jane

Silver, master smuggler. Thorne and the other girls love having the Spirit as their prisoner, and though he may have to break up the smuggling ring, the Spirit is not above letting the ladies escape. Eisner himself liked Thorne Strand: "She was a kind of independent woman of her own, not necessarily part of the earlier image of the clinging symbol who had to be protected. She's the kind of woman I've always found interesting." (1/23/49; 1/30/49)

Sunday Supplements: Although *The Spirit* stories are reprinted in collections like DC Comics' *The Spirit Archives* (begun in 2000), it can be easy to forget that they originally

THORNE STRAND

appeared in Sunday newspapers. Each *Spirit* story was headed "Comic Book Section," because *The Spirit* sections were circulated to newspapers to be included in Sunday newspapers, just like the comic strip sections, Sunday magazines like *Parade* or the Sunday *New York Times Magazine*, or the book review section. *The Spirit* section was a new way to distribute comic books, and while it never appeared in more than fifty papers, it remains a unique and innovative solution to the problem of selling comic books. Eisner and his partner Everett "Busy" Arnold were following in the tradition of Pulitzer and Hearst, who first added Sunday supplements to the newspapers. Pulitzer added a Sunday magazine to the *New York World* in 1893, the progenitor of all Sunday newspaper magazines, and shortly thereafter followed it with a humor supplement, which was soon dominated by the strip "The Yellow Kid," the first and most important comic strip in America. Eisner continued his incredible record of innovation in comic formats in his two decades of work on the educational military magazine *P*S, The Preventive Maintenance Monthly*, and in his triumphant publication of *A Contract with God* in 1978, marking the era of the graphic novel.

Suremoney, Cousin: Ebony White's scheming cousin, Suremoney is always coming up with a way to flimflam customers out of their dough. Suremoney sells everyone under the sun pens that write underwater (and that can "spell, subtract, and can be used as a flashlight, radio, glasscutter, and positively will not leak in high altitudes"). The Eisnerian irony is that they actually work, and the pen Ebony sells to flimflam man Carrier Jones is actually used in an underwater salvage scam. This satirizes a silly but long-running real comic book ad campaign for a pen that supposedly wrote underwater, although why that was a virtue remains anyone's guess. (7/28/46)

Talking Animals: *The Spirit* stories are influenced by many sources, including fables, and talking animals show up in a few of them. Hubert the Duck communicates in an almost-human fashion, and the downfall of tout Fat Looie is pronounced by a racehorse. Pancho de Bool tells his own story of how he was raised to fight Pepin de la Mancha, who would be a great matador in Mexico. Eisner recycled the name "Pancho de Bool" from an earlier story, but in that one it's the name of a criminal. (1/19/41; 12/29/46; 2/16/47; 10/24/48)

"Ten Minutes": Ten minutes can change—or end—a life, according to one of the most famous Spirit stories (9/11/49). It's also the amount of time this story takes to read, according to the introduction, and for its events to unfold, with the minutes counted down page-by-page on a pocket watch.

Freddy was a good kid from downtown, but he wanted to escape. He kills Max in his mom-and-pop soda shop for chump change. When the Spirit and Dolan come to investigate, Freddy is killed at the 13th Street subway station as he tries to escape. A second time-keeping device in the story is a little girl bouncing a ball with an alphabet rhyme, who goes from A to R. A similar device, counting down the minutes, appears in a much more lighthearted story, "The First Man" (8/20/50). Herkimer Zither, with no other accomplishments, must be the first one through the new Garrison-to-Brookville Tunnel. He is first, but then mysteriously disappears—an ironic counterpoint to his search for a small bit of fame.

Thayer, Eldas: A skinflint with no heart, Eldas Thayer refuses to help pay for an operation for his niece Mary when the Spirit visits to let him know she'll die without it. The Spirit not only pays for Mary's operation by the famous surgeon Dr. Marka, but donates his own rare type A-1 blood to Mary to make sure she pulls through. Thayer had been told by his coronary specialist, Dr. Clay, that he was about to die. Using a Rube Goldberg–type contraption that stabs him, Thayer commits suicide and sets up the scene so the rap is pinned on the Spirit (7/21/40). Thayer's plot leaves the Spirit a wanted man, an outlaw, for several months of continuity, until "The Spirit: Who Is He?" (10/13/40), where reporter Demon Bealy returns from Europe and by digging into the Spirit's identity, sets in motion a series of events that clears his name.

Titmouse, Mortimer J.: Named after a small gray bird,  Mortimer J. Titmouse is a retiring and diminutive man of no importance. Although he feels insignificant and incompetent, in order to contribute to the war effort, he goes to work as a janitor in an atomic plant during World War II. The plant is part of the Knickerbocker Project, Eisner's takeoff on the Manhattan Project, which developed the atom bomb. (In addition, the Dutch settlers of New Amsterdam, which is now New York, were called Knickerbockers.) Titmouse studies the trash, pretends to develop an atomic bomb, and then almost by accident does come up with the formula for an improved atomic bomb! The Octopus ends up with Mortimer and the secret, and the Spirit is powerless to prevent it. (7/6/47)

Tone, Dulcet: A slinky, gorgeous brunette crime mistress, Dulcet hooks up with Skinny Bones to take over the rackets of imprisoned mobster Glut Mutton. Although her name suggests a singer with an oh-so-sweet voice, her appreciation of music extends only to ordering Glut's piano player, Gam, to play it and play it again. Before Ellen became mayor, Eisner penned an almost protofeminist fable about female crime lords who use their feminine wiles, of course, but also use the skim from the bookies to "provide us with enough capital to buy controlling stock in Scarcity Distributing Company!" These women also prove to be speedboat-racing brawlers, and finally end up in mortal combat in Central City's harbor, where Skinny tries to off Dulcet with a shiv. Surviving the attack, Dulcet not only lends a helping hand to the Octopus in restarting his criminal organization, but also tries to get Skinny locked up for assault with intent to kill. (7/7/46; 7/14/46)

Tovaroff, Ivan: A peanut cartel magnate and owner of Continental Peanut, Ivan Tovaroff was secretly the husband of Spirit femme fatale Silk Satin. Ivan is revealed as the father of Silk's daughter Hildie in a great murder-go-round story: Tovaroff is killed by Van Gilt, who gets killed by Silk, and then Silk, the Spirit, Ellen, and Hildie get captured by Prince Glenko and his thug "Bones" Granet. Hildie unties Silk's bonds and she does in their captors, allowing all to escape. Silk had left Tovaroff when he signed up with the Nazis in 1939. Her career as an underworld criminal and later service as a British intelligence agent were both a means to a single noble end—the rescue of her blonde daughter, who'd been held as Hitler's hostage. (1/20/46)

Twitch, Nazel B.: Florence, the car, can't talk, but Nazel B. Twitch believes she has a soul, and loves her more than anything else. When he loses his job, his wife sells his 1929 Flash. Nazel goes and hangs around the lot until the dealer sells it to some crooks. They hire Nazel to drive what they call the "jalopy," and he's happy to do so because he thinks they're insurance inspectors. In a reference to conditions after World War II, when the consumer economy was heating up after years of shortages and controls, the wife sells the car for $500, and its price is $5,000 when the crooks get it from the sleazy used car dealer. (10/17/48)

Two Bottles of Ink Story: A type of story that depends on mood and atmosphere for its powerful effects, developed through the use of heavy shading and dark shadows. "For me, the colors of black and white are, in effect, my sound track. It's the only thing one has to work with in this medium that goes beyond what's on the paper," Eisner has said of this type of tale. The dark atmosphere indicates that the story will deal with a serious subject, and creates an air of menace. This kind of atmosphere can be conveyed immediately to the reader when Eisner uses one of his famous opening splash pages to set the tone of the story. (2/23/47)

TWO BOTTLES OF INK STORY

Vault, Sylvie: Like Barbara Stanwyck in the film noir classic *Double Indemnity* (1944), the beautiful Sylvie engineers the murder of her husband Avery by his partner Roger Deficit. Their plot is helped along by an obituary written by a scurrilous reporter named Byline—an obituary that appears before her husband is dead. The obit draws the Spirit in, and it turns out to have been an April Fools' joke. The joke ends up being on Sylvie when she engineers the death of a blackmailer, enabling the Spirit to finally get the goods on her. (3/30/47; 4/6/47)

Wales, Blubber: After the first departure of Ebony White, who gets sent off to school, the Spirit was briefly joined by a new sidekick of a different ethnicity, Blubber Wales. Blubber is an Inuit teenager (usually, and offensively, called Eskimo) whom the Spirit met in the Arctic while chasing a whale-killing pirate (2/17/46). Like Ebony, he is loyal, quick-thinking, and ready to make fun of the Spirit at any moment, but his perfect diction indicates he is well-educated, turning the tables on the linguistic stereotype of the ethnic sidekick. Blubber demonstrates his wide-ranging education by winning radio quizzes, leading to his kidnapping by bad guy Rockhead Stone (2/24/46). Blubber also collaborates with Ebony in the capture of Public Defacer Zoltan P. Yafodder by staging an art exhibition (3/31/46). The teenager returns to the North Pole when Ebony returns from his educational experience at Mr. Carter's School to resume his role as the Spirit's sidekick. (2/17/46; 2/24/46; 3/3/46; 3/31/46; 4/21/46; 5/12/46)

Walker, Widow: She's a lady of ample proportions and a certain age, but she makes Commissioner Dolan's heart beat faster. She's not a hit with Ellen when she tells her, "A new hairdo, take off a *teensy* bit of weight, and you'll be breathtaking." Dolan's feelings for the Widow Walker present an opportunity in the mind of Stuffer Balot, the politico who wants boss Ward Healey to give him Dolan's job. Stuffer kidnaps the merry widow, but Healey ends up saving her to save his own skin. Healey knew Dolan would pin the rap on

WIDOW WALKER

him if the widow wasn't returned, but he gets a different kind of sentence when Widow Walker falls for him. (7/11/48)

Watts, "Ampy": This electrically gifted killer makes the Spirit late for Ebony's welcome home party from Mr. Carter's school when he fails to give himself up by the nine o'clock deadline the Spirit has imposed. The Spirit does finally bring him in, but it's too late for him and Ebony, the guest of honor, to join the festivities. (5/12/46)

Weaver, Flaxen: She's not the kind of girl who'll be sitting at home weaving flax or anything else, but Flaxen Weaver's hair may shine like the finest flax. She's a top-notch skier who helps Matty Luger and some other hoods fence gold across the Canadian border. But when he turns on Flaxen and wings her, she doesn't shed a tear, and the Spirit can't help but admire her. Flaxen's a smooth European with a charming accent, and the next time they meet she's become the Baron La Planche, at least till she and Blink can steal Lord Clayborn's peace medallion from the World Unity Society. When the gang picks her to shoot the Spirit, bound and helpless, she kisses him instead, and the gang dies at her hands when she drives them all into the river. (12/4/49; 12/11/49)

FLAXEN WEAVER

Wellman, Manly Wade: Wellman was a science fiction and supernatural short story writer and novelist whose work appeared in many magazines, including *Weird Tales*, *Astounding*, and *Galaxy*. *Twice in Time* (1958), featuring Leonardo da Vinci, is one of his best science fiction novels. Wellman wrote many comic book scripts, notably crafting adventures for Fawcett Publishing's super hero Captain Marvel. He was an assistant in Eisner's studio and did much of the writing of the *Spirit* series while Eisner was in the army between 1942 and 1945.

White, Ebony: The African-American sidekick and assistant to the Spirit, the character of Ebony is a legitimate source of controversy. Stereotypes of black characters are part of American popular arts, from minstrel shows through old-time radio, films, and television. Introduced as an adult of small stature, a Central City cabbie, Ebony was always an intelligent and astute partner in Eisner's own *Spirit* stories. Eisner later made Ebony into a kid sidekick, a common feature of 1940s Joe Simon and Jack Kirby super hero comic books, like Captain America's Bucky Barnes. But Ebony always spoke in the minstrelsy- and vaudeville-derived phrases that passed for African-American speech in popular culture of the time. The character was certainly never intended by Eisner as a slur, and qualifies as one of the better black-stereotype characters in popular fiction, comparable to Eddie "Rochester" Anderson who was truly a costar with Jack Benny in the comedian's radio and television programs.

The Spirit met Ebony near the beginning of his career. It seems that every cab he hails in his first adventures is driven by Ebony, the fastest cabbie in what was originally referred to as New York. The most stereotyped depictions of Ebony appear in the World War II–era stories created by Eisner's shop in his absence, those written by Manly Wade Wellman and

Bill Woolfolk. A few months after Eisner returned from his World War II service, he removed Ebony from the comic for a while by sending him off to school. As Ebony prepares to leave, the characters in this story engage in a discussion of Ebony's accent, defending it as Southern speech with historical roots (3/31/46). This discussion, and Eisner's decision to send Ebony to school, might be linked to the artist's experience of prejudice in the army, so movingly depicted in his 1991 graphic novel *To the Heart of the Storm*.

After Ebony returns from school, the Spirit decides that he will be Ebony's private tutor so he can continue his education. In the story "The Lost Fortnight" (6/30/46), Ebony directs a film satire of the Billy Wilder film *The Lost Weekend* (1945). Ebony casts himself in the Academy Award-winning Ray Milland role, though he's addicted to soda pop, not alcohol. Ebony has a whole series of careers after this, sometimes providing satire of contemporary popular culture, but for the most part these pursuits actually functioned as they were intended, making Ebony a more rounded and diverse character (9/15/46; 2/16/47). Eisner finally brought in a new sidekick for the Spirit, an orphaned white boy named Sammy (7/31/49). Sammy appeared regularly in *The Spirit* stories after his introduction, but Eisner never formally marked Ebony's departure from the Spirit's side. Eisner allowed Ebony White to reappear from time to time in the strip after much of the work was taken over by studio assistants, as in a late story featuring a kid gang. (6/24/51)

Whittler, Dick: When the Spirit investigates the case of orphan Willum Waif, Whittler gives him the lowdown on the Baron, who's unjustly taken custody of the tyke. Whittler is

the law of Riverbend, a town of 3,000 folks sixty miles south of Central City. The Spirit solves the Baron case, and then Whittler brings the Spirit down to help with the murder of visitor "Joseph Smith." The only clue is that the deceased sent some letters to the Central City police department. When it turns out that the victim was Michael O'Dolan, murdered by his wife, Whittler figures that the Spirit beat him up before he was murdered. The Spirit takes it on the lam, and Dick picks him up in a diner—but not before brotherly murder between Eddie the owner and his mad sibling Woody, who didn't keep the diner clean enough! When the governor set Hamilton Curdle on a political witch hunt for corruption, one of his first targets is Commissioner Dolan, whom he has an old grudge against. Dolan's half brother Michael decides to make a little hay, and sends blackmailing letters. The Spirit investigates, but wants to keep the full story from Whittler to protect the commissioner. In the end, Whittler destroys the letters and lets the Spirit go. Whittler's name is a pun on *The Whistler*, a mystery fiction radio drama of the 1940s. (6/18/50; 7/30/50)

Wilder, Rice: A runaway bride, Rice Wilder is a poor little rich girl who feels like a prisoner of her class, so she hooks up with crook Mike Caliban and starts her own life of crime. When she finds out he's betrayed her too, he only wants her family's ransom money, and when the Spirit shows up she makes a break for it and dies by Caliban's gun. With her dying breath she tells the Spirit, "Now I know I'll be free." (4/4/48)

Wildwood Cemetery: When Denny Colt apparently dies at the hands of the criminal mastermind Dr. Cobra, he's interred under a simply carved but large headstone in Wildwood Cemetery. This tomb, enlarged to make a great bachelor pad and house his laboratory, becomes the base of operations for the Spirit.

Winklenod, Horton J.: Wealthy and diminutive department store magnate Winklenod is crushed one Christmas to discover that there is no Santa Claus—and that the Santas in his stores are actors hired from the Acme Santa Claus Company. Winklenod loses himself in the frozen winter landscape, where he's discovered by "Soups," a criminal who wants to go straight, hoping the ransom he can collect for the businessman will allow him to do it. Winklenod is rescued by not one, but two Santas. This Laurel and Hardy pair, one tall, one short, encourage Horton to leave the money Soups needs to reform in his stocking, and then visit Bugsy, one of the department store Santas, leaving him money and a pardon. Winklenod's faith in Santa is restored by the two Yuletide costumed crime fighters—the Spirit and Ebony. (12/19/48)

Worry, Dr. Wolfgang: Eisner has identified Dr. Wolfgang Worry, school psychologist, as a satire of Dr. Fredric Wertham. Wertham was a respected, European-born psychiatrist, a social activist who founded the La Farge free clinic in Harlem and was the therapist for the sons of Julius and Ethel Rosenberg after their parents were executed as atomic spies in the 1950s. Wertham was friends with the leading artists and intellectuals of his day, and although he personally opposed censorship, his book *Seduction of the Innocent* (1954) led to the Comics Code and ultimately to the rejection of comics as an adult artistic and literary medium in the United States.

In the story "The Deadly Comic Book," the Spirit meets a high school music teacher who reads a crime comic that turns him into a trembling wreck, expecting criminal vengeance at every turn (2/27/49). Worry is the psychologist at the teacher's school, and the musician has attended one of Worry's weekly comic book burnings, "a simple, innocent affair." In addition to satirizing adult reactions to comics, in this story Dolan points out kids have been reading exciting, violent literature since he was a boy raised on penny dreadfuls, the predecessors of dime novels.

Yafodder, Zoltan P.: His name is one of Eisner's trademark punning names, as numerous and funny as those of Disney's master Donald Duck artist, Carl Barks, who created, along with many other characters, inventor Gyro Gearloose and oil magnate Petrolio Vasolino. Yafodder defaces public property by drawing moustaches on advertisements and paintings, but the real reason for his crime is to create the pun "Your father's moustache," a turn-of-the-century kid's insult that would have been known to Eisner's readers from vaudeville, movies, and popular fiction. Yafodder is foiled by Blubber and Ebony (the only time they work together), who stage a fake art exhibition featuring only bearded portraits, causing Yafodder to go crazy and give himself up. (3/31/46)

Yougian, Ahmed: Ahmed-the-Trader is a Middle Eastern smuggler who once had P'Gell in his harem (probably the only time she was married to someone who'd had more mates than she had!). In cahoots with Mr. Quinse of the Central City Building and Loan Co., Yougian is planning to take P'Gell's School for Girls and the pirate treasure hidden (unbeknownst to her) in the main house. Unfortunately, he remembered P'Gell's beauty but not her wiles, and in the end finds himself locked up by the Spirit, while she gets married yet again—to Mr. Quinse. (11/23/47)

Two Spirit origin stories appeared in the Sunday Comic Book Section: June 2, 1940 (reprinted in *The Spirit Archives,* Vol. 1) and January 13, 1946 (reprinted in *The Spirit Archives,* Vol. 12). Revived interest in the Spirit in the 1960s led Eisner to create a revised origin story for *The Spirit* no. 1 (Harvey Comics, October 1966). Here it's revealed that Dr. Cobra had help from another criminal mastermind, the Octopus, in his plot to take over Central City. This origin was later reprinted in *The Spirit Magazine* no. 10 (Warren Publishing, October 1975). The original story and art are by Eisner, with inking assists from Chuck Kramer; the all-new color for this story is by Mark Chiarello (based on the originals from American Visuals).

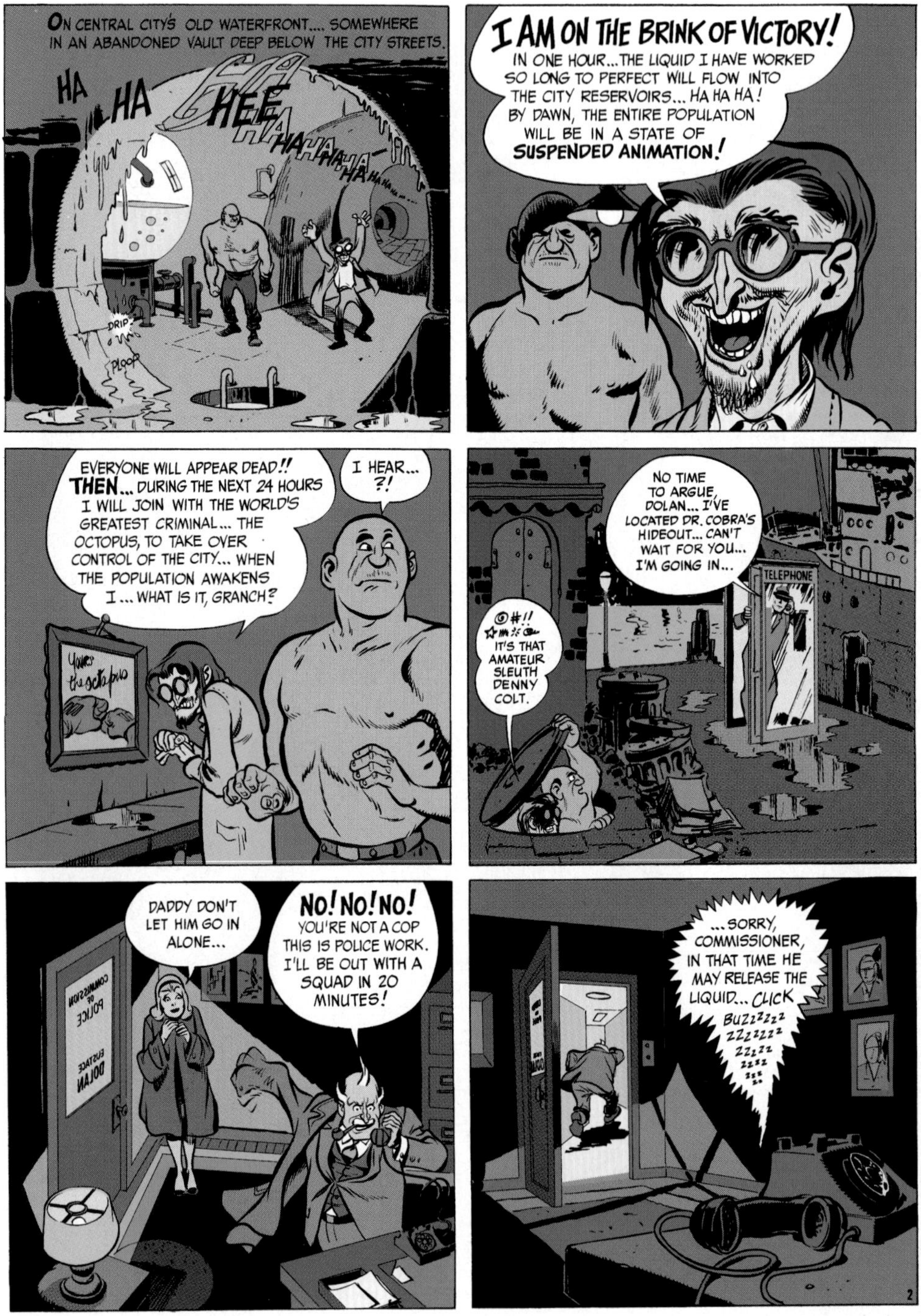

ON CENTRAL CITY'S OLD WATERFRONT.... SOMEWHERE IN AN ABANDONED VAULT DEEP BELOW THE CITY STREETS.
HA HA HA HEE HA HA HA HA HA HA
DRIP
PLOOP
I AM ON THE BRINK OF VICTORY! IN ONE HOUR...THE LIQUID I HAVE WORKED SO LONG TO PERFECT WILL FLOW INTO THE CITY RESERVOIRS... HA HA HA! BY DAWN, THE ENTIRE POPULATION WILL BE IN A STATE OF SUSPENDED ANIMATION!
EVERYONE WILL APPEAR DEAD!! THEN... DURING THE NEXT 24 HOURS I WILL JOIN WITH THE WORLD'S GREATEST CRIMINAL... THE OCTOPUS, TO TAKE OVER CONTROL OF THE CITY... WHEN THE POPULATION AWAKENS I... WHAT IS IT, GRANCH?
I HEAR... ?!
NO TIME TO ARGUE, DOLAN... I'VE LOCATED DR. COBRA'S HIDEOUT... CAN'T WAIT FOR YOU... I'M GOING IN...
TELEPHONE
IT'S THAT AMATEUR SLEUTH DENNY COLT.
DADDY DON'T LET HIM GO IN ALONE...
NO! NO! NO! YOU'RE NOT A COP THIS IS POLICE WORK. I'LL BE OUT WITH A SQUAD IN 20 MINUTES!
...SORRY, COMMISSIONER, IN THAT TIME HE MAY RELEASE THE LIQUID... CLICK
BUZZZZZZ ZZZZZZZ ZZZZZ ZZZZ ZZZ

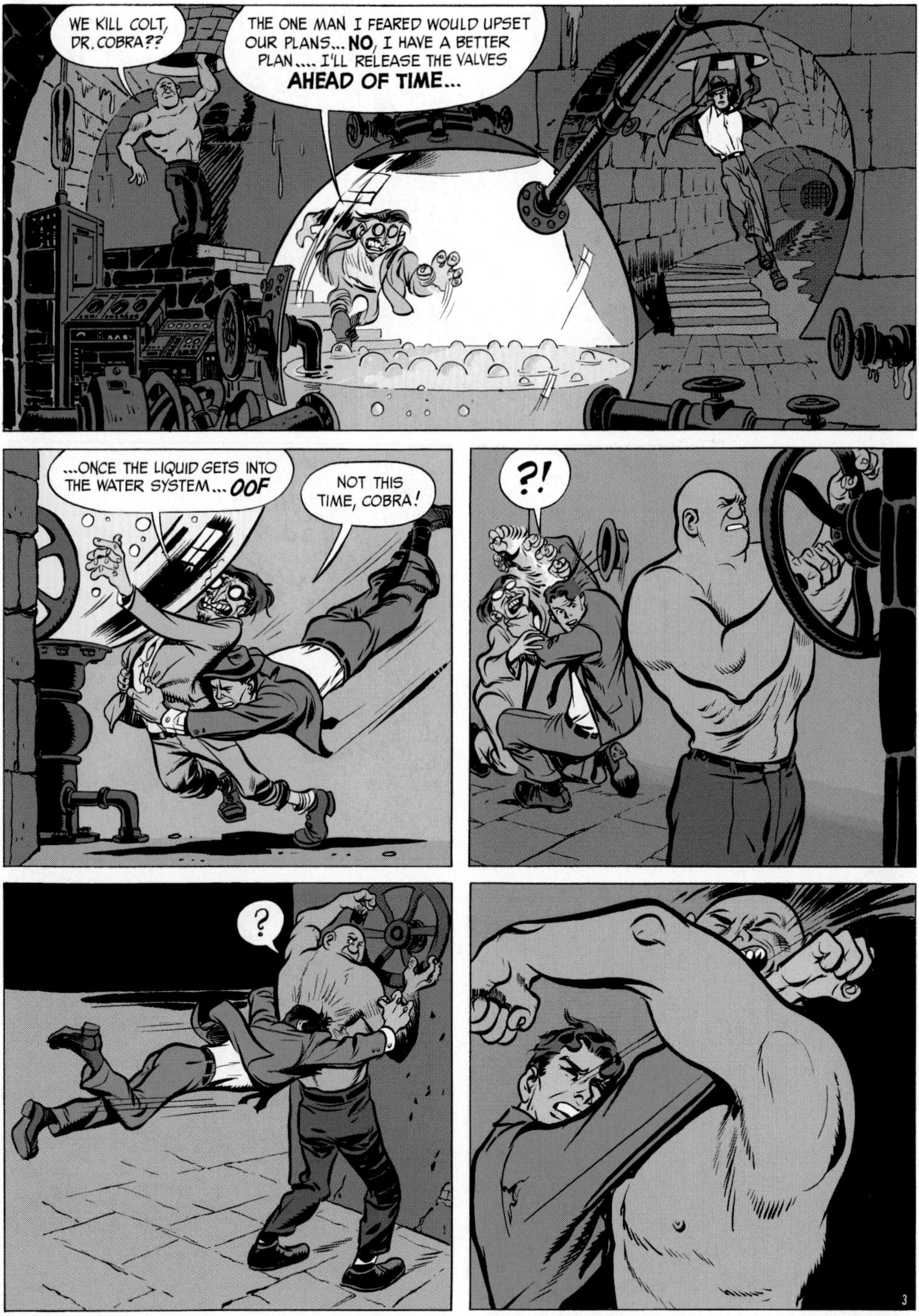
WE KILL COLT, DR. COBRA??
THE ONE MAN I FEARED WOULD UPSET OUR PLANS... NO, I HAVE A BETTER PLAN.... I'LL RELEASE THE VALVES AHEAD OF TIME...
...ONCE THE LIQUID GETS INTO THE WATER SYSTEM... OOF
NOT THIS TIME, COBRA!
?!
?

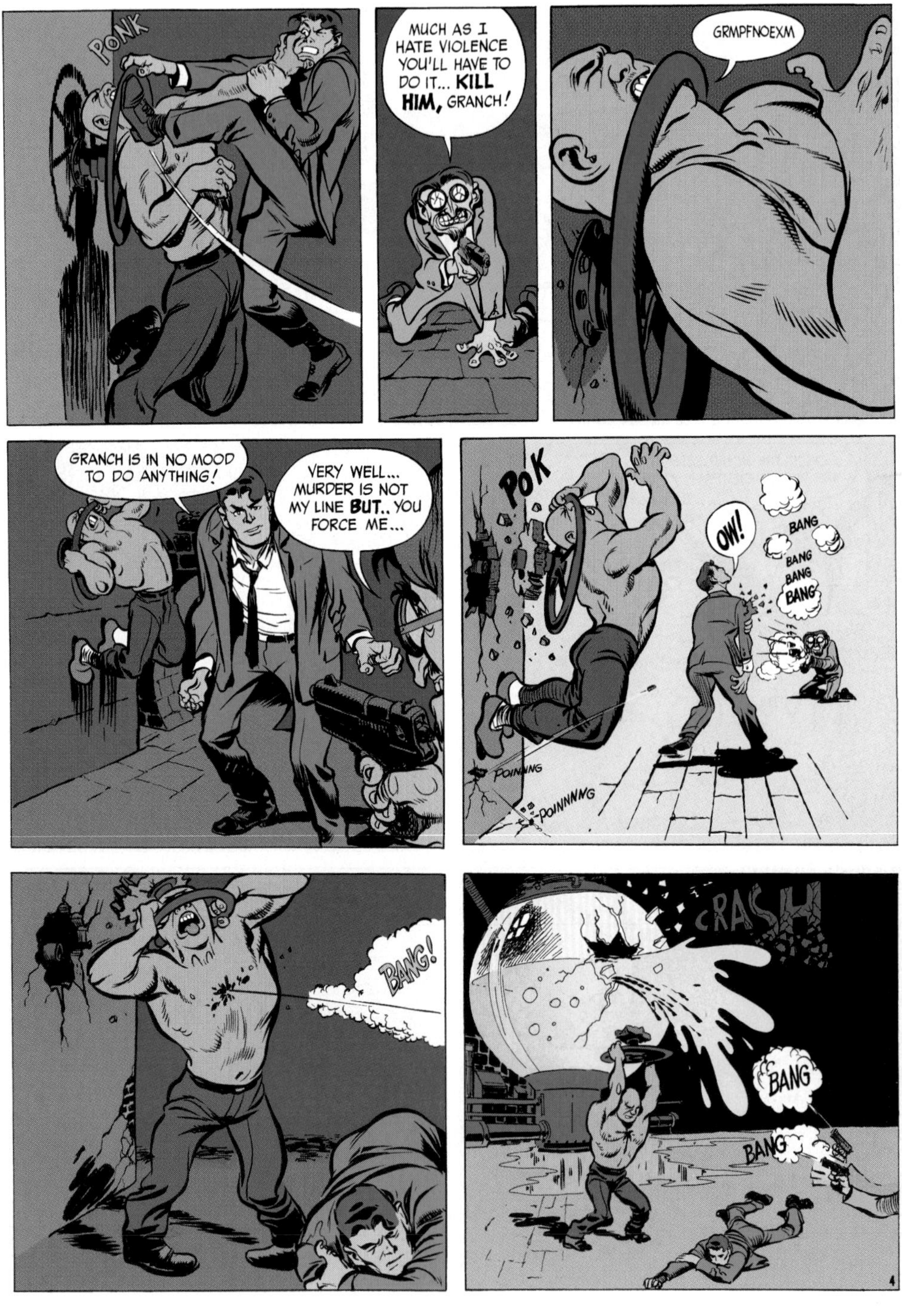
PONK
MUCH AS I HATE VIOLENCE YOU'LL HAVE TO DO IT... KILL HIM, GRANCH!
GRMPFNOEXM
GRANCH IS IN NO MOOD TO DO ANYTHING!
VERY WELL... MURDER IS NOT MY LINE BUT.. YOU FORCE ME...
POK
OW!
BANG
BANG
BANG
BANG
POINNNG
POINNNNG
BANG!
CRASH
BANG
BANG

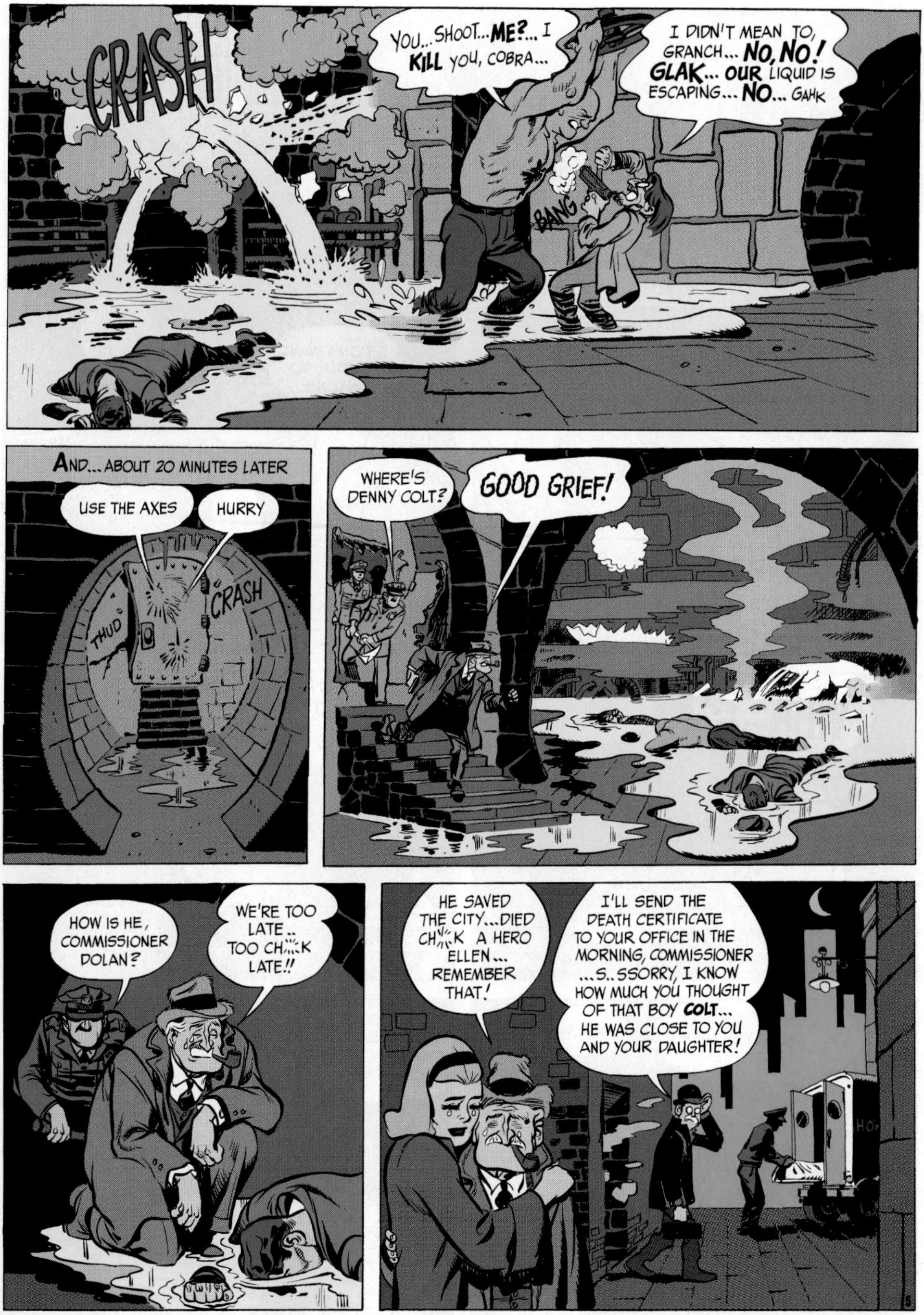
CRASH
YOU...SHOOT...ME?... I KILL YOU, COBRA...
I DIDN'T MEAN TO, GRANCH... NO, NO! GLAK... OUR LIQUID IS ESCAPING... NO... GAHK
BANG
AND... ABOUT 20 MINUTES LATER
USE THE AXES
HURRY
THUD
CRASH
WHERE'S DENNY COLT?
GOOD GRIEF!
HOW IS HE, COMMISSIONER DOLAN?
WE'RE TOO LATE.. TOO CH K LATE!!
HE SAVED THE CITY...DIED CH K A HERO ELLEN... REMEMBER THAT!
I'LL SEND THE DEATH CERTIFICATE TO YOUR OFFICE IN THE MORNING, COMMISSIONER ...S..SSORRY, I KNOW HOW MUCH YOU THOUGHT OF THAT BOY COLT... HE WAS CLOSE TO YOU AND YOUR DAUGHTER!

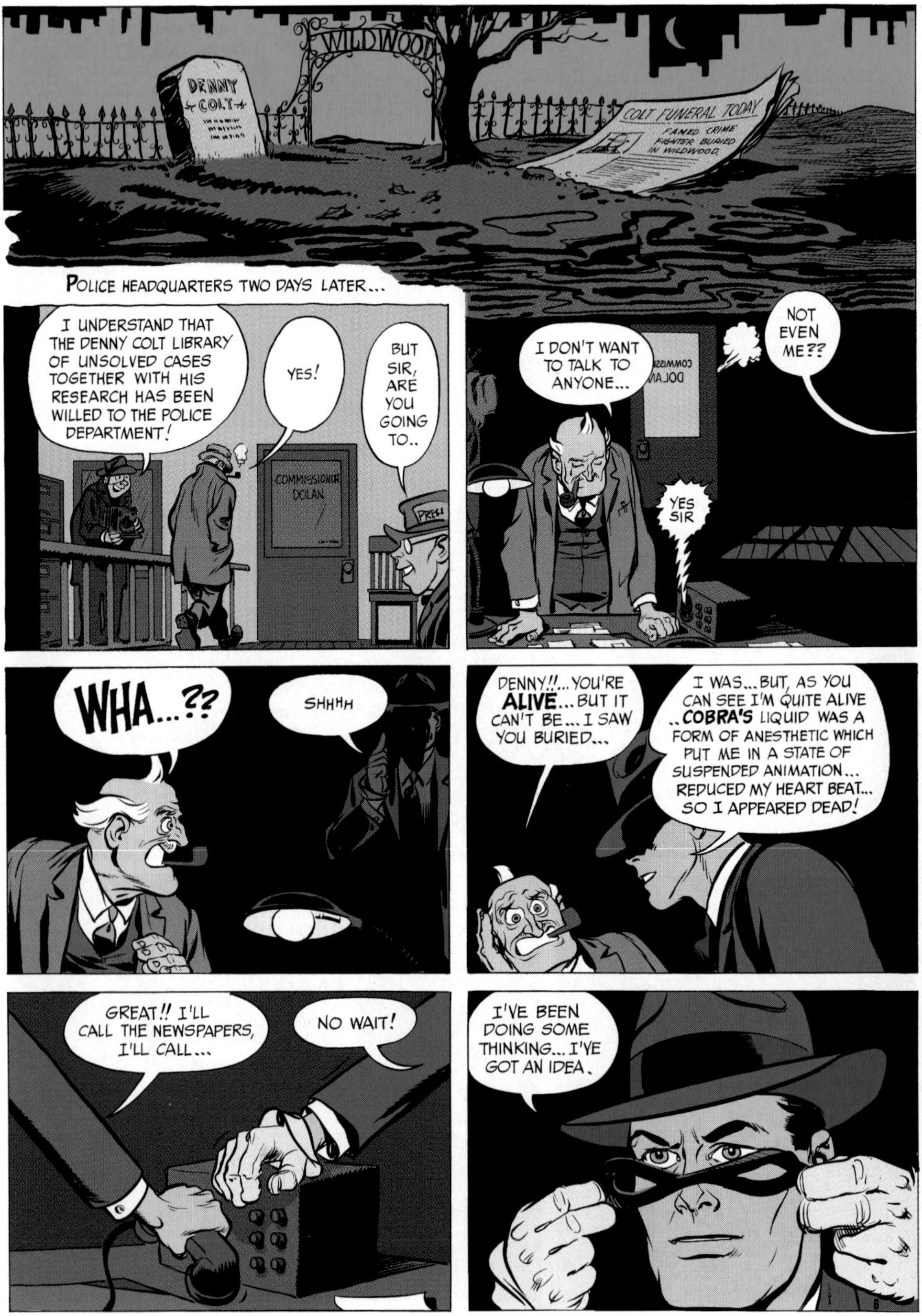
WILDWOOD
DENNY COLT
COLT FUNERAL TODAY
FAMED CRIME FIGHTER BURIED IN WILDWOOD.
POLICE HEADQUARTERS TWO DAYS LATER...
I UNDERSTAND THAT THE DENNY COLT LIBRARY OF UNSOLVED CASES TOGETHER WITH HIS RESEARCH HAS BEEN WILLED TO THE POLICE DEPARTMENT!
YES!
BUT SIR, ARE YOU GOING TO..
COMMISSIONER DOLAN
PRESS
I DON'T WANT TO TALK TO ANYONE...
NOT EVEN ME??
YES SIR
WHA...??
SHHHH
DENNY!!... YOU'RE ALIVE... BUT IT CAN'T BE... I SAW YOU BURIED...
I WAS... BUT, AS YOU CAN SEE I'M QUITE ALIVE ..COBRA'S LIQUID WAS A FORM OF ANESTHETIC WHICH PUT ME IN A STATE OF SUSPENDED ANIMATION... REDUCED MY HEART BEAT... SO I APPEARED DEAD!
GREAT!! I'LL CALL THE NEWSPAPERS, I'LL CALL...
NO WAIT!
I'VE BEEN DOING SOME THINKING... I'VE GOT AN IDEA.

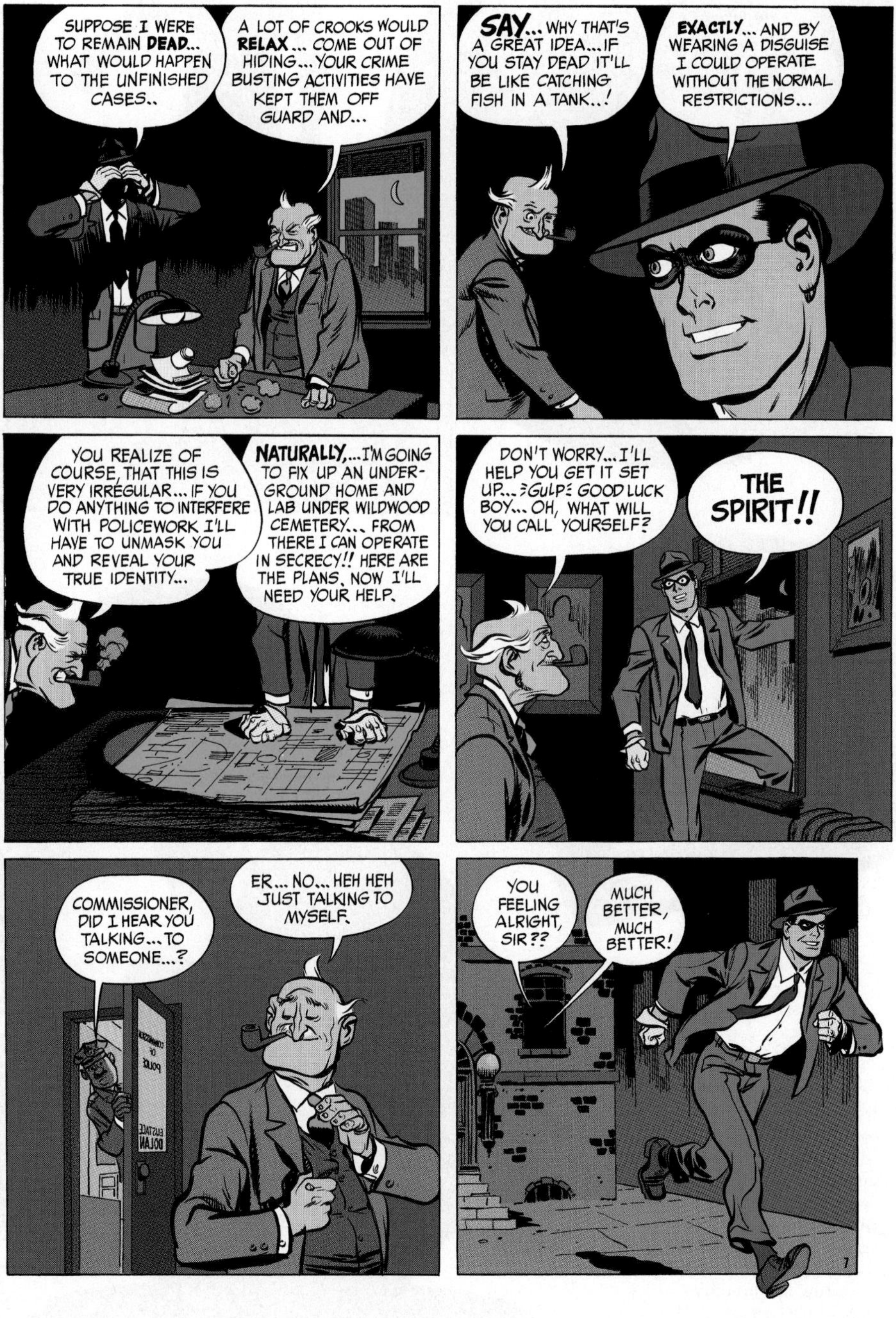
SUPPOSE I WERE TO REMAIN **DEAD**... WHAT WOULD HAPPEN TO THE UNFINISHED CASES..
A LOT OF CROOKS WOULD **RELAX**... COME OUT OF HIDING... YOUR CRIME BUSTING ACTIVITIES HAVE KEPT THEM OFF GUARD AND...
SAY... WHY THAT'S A GREAT IDEA... IF YOU STAY DEAD IT'LL BE LIKE CATCHING FISH IN A TANK..!
EXACTLY... AND BY WEARING A DISGUISE I COULD OPERATE WITHOUT THE NORMAL RESTRICTIONS...
YOU REALIZE OF COURSE, THAT THIS IS VERY IRREGULAR... IF YOU DO ANYTHING TO INTERFERE WITH POLICEWORK I'LL HAVE TO UNMASK YOU AND REVEAL YOUR TRUE IDENTITY...
NATURALLY,...I'M GOING TO FIX UP AN UNDER-GROUND HOME AND LAB UNDER WILDWOOD CEMETERY... FROM THERE I CAN OPERATE IN SECRECY!! HERE ARE THE PLANS. NOW I'LL NEED YOUR HELP.
DON'T WORRY... I'LL HELP YOU GET IT SET UP... ≡GULP≡ GOOD LUCK BOY... OH, WHAT WILL YOU CALL YOURSELF?
THE SPIRIT!!
COMMISSIONER, DID I HEAR YOU TALKING... TO SOMEONE...?
ER... NO... HEH HEH JUST TALKING TO MYSELF.
COMMISSIONER OF POLICE
EUSTACE DOLAN
YOU FEELING ALRIGHT, SIR??
MUCH BETTER, MUCH BETTER!

Spirit fans had to wait until the classic stories were reprinted for a whole new generation of readers before the masked hero was featured in merchandise. The Spirit now regularly appears in classy collectibles such as the 12-inch Spirit Picture Disk featuring "Ev'ry Little Bug" (Kitchen Sink Press, 1987; top left); The Spirit Statue, sculpted by William Paquet (DC Direct, 2001; top right); The Spirit Bust, sculpted by James Shoop (DC Direct, 2002; bottom right); and The Spirit Lunchbox (Dark Horse Comics, 2001).

Originally published September 5, 1948, this slightly reworked version is from *The Spirit* no. 1 (Harvey Comics, October 1966). Modified colors by Mark Chiarello.

The Story of GERHARD SHNOBBLE

ACTION Mystery ADVENTURE

THE SPIRIT

BY Will Eisner

EFORE WE BEGIN THIS STORY WE WANT TO MAKE ONE POINT VERY CLEAR ..

THIS IS NOT A FUNNY STORY!!

WE MEAN TO GIVE YOU A SIMPLE ACCOUNT OF GERHARD SHNOBBLE... BEGINNING AT THE POINT WHEN HE FIRST DISCOVERED HE COULD **FLY**.

PLEASE .... NO LAUGHTER ....

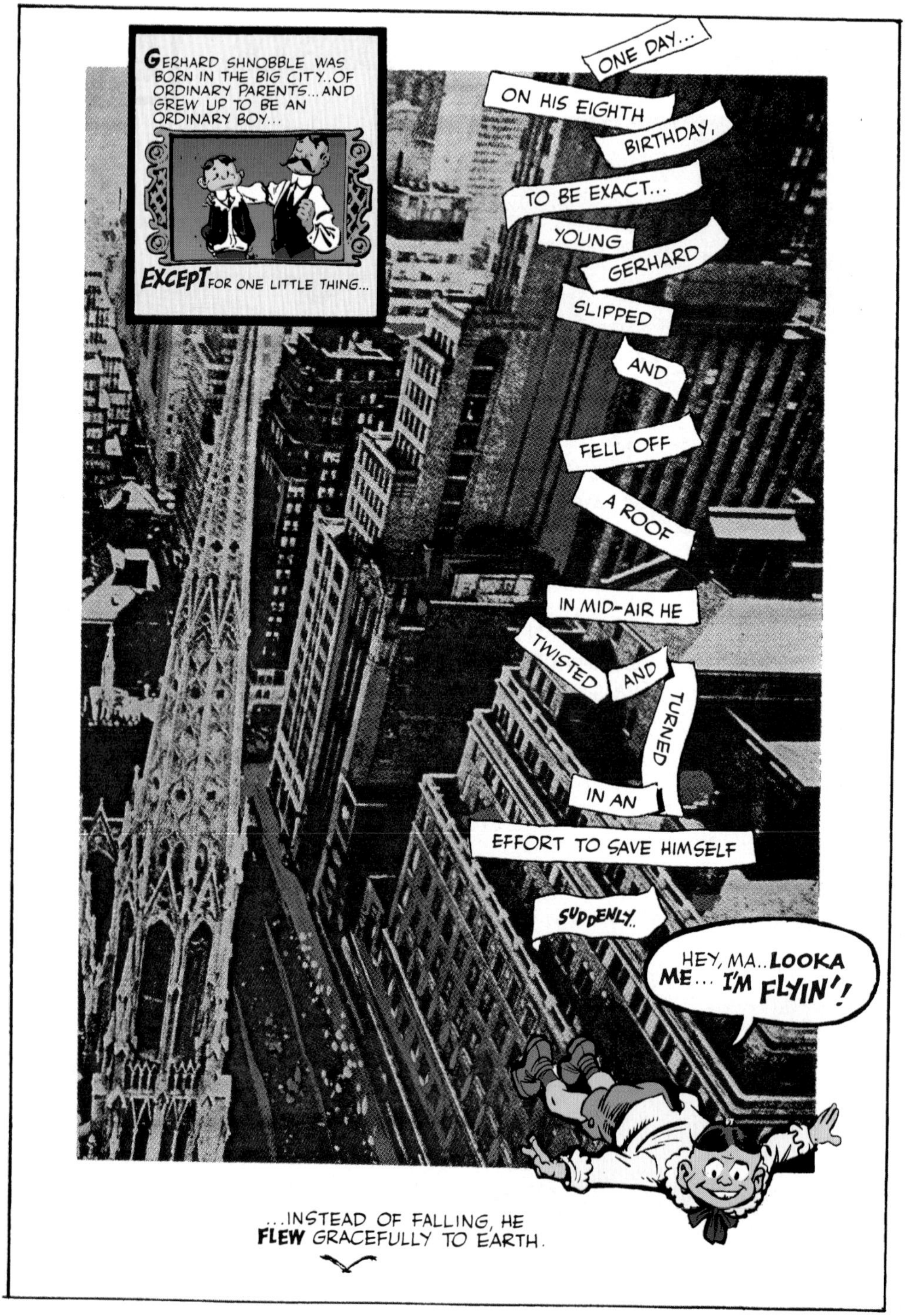
GERHARD SHNOBBLE WAS BORN IN THE BIG CITY..OF ORDINARY PARENTS...AND GREW UP TO BE AN ORDINARY BOY...
EXCEPT FOR ONE LITTLE THING...
ONE DAY...
ON HIS EIGHTH
BIRTHDAY,
TO BE EXACT...
YOUNG
GERHARD
SLIPPED
AND
FELL OFF
A ROOF
IN MID-AIR HE
TWISTED
AND
TURNED
IN AN
EFFORT TO SAVE HIMSELF
SUDDENLY..
HEY, MA.. LOOKA ME... I'M FLYIN'!
...INSTEAD OF FALLING, HE FLEW GRACEFULLY TO EARTH.

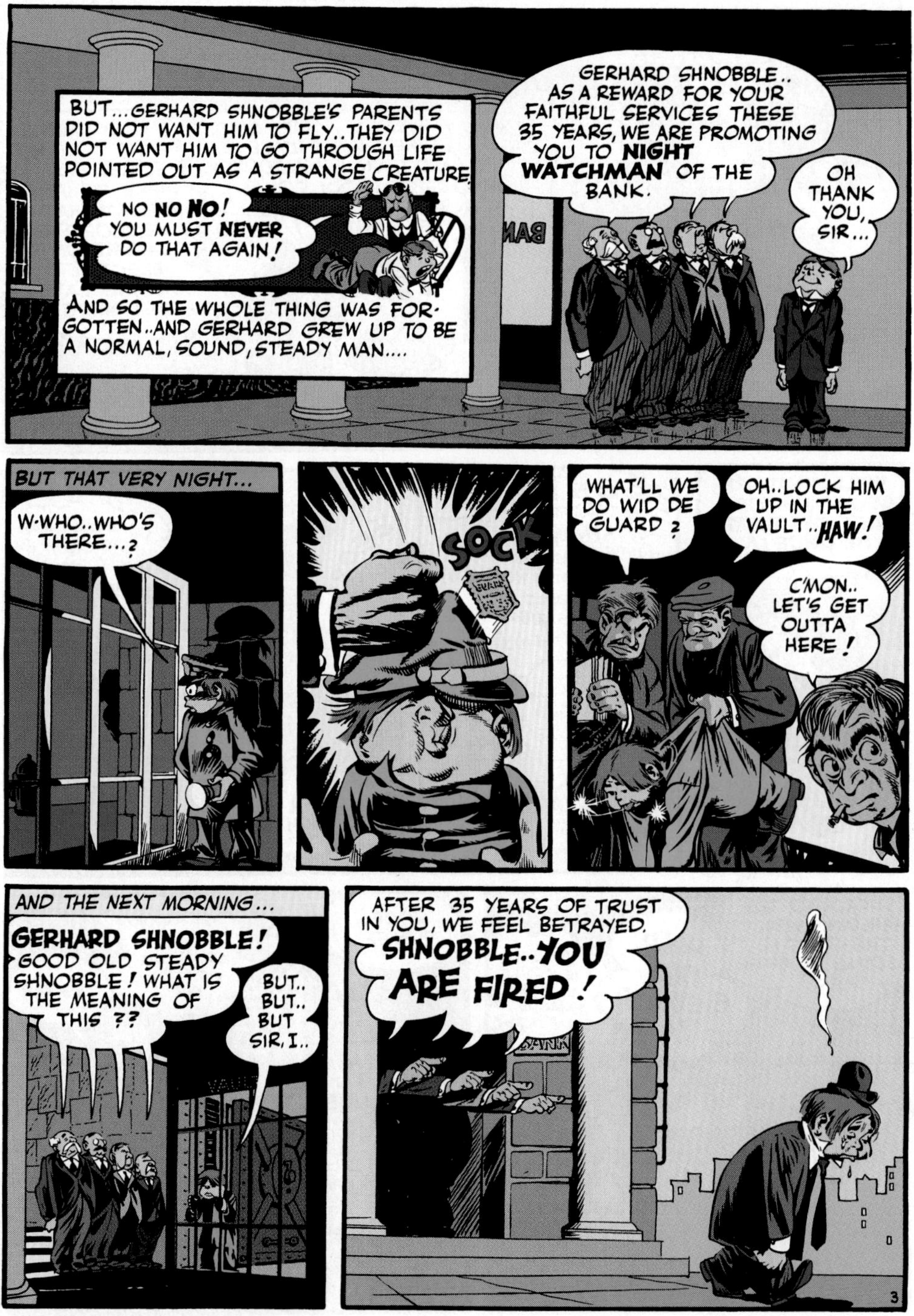

BUT...GERHARD SHNOBBLE'S PARENTS DID NOT WANT HIM TO FLY..THEY DID NOT WANT HIM TO GO THROUGH LIFE POINTED OUT AS A STRANGE CREATURE.
NO NO NO! YOU MUST NEVER DO THAT AGAIN!
AND SO THE WHOLE THING WAS FOR-GOTTEN..AND GERHARD GREW UP TO BE A NORMAL, SOUND, STEADY MAN....
GERHARD SHNOBBLE.. AS A REWARD FOR YOUR FAITHFUL SERVICES THESE 35 YEARS, WE ARE PROMOTING YOU TO NIGHT WATCHMAN OF THE BANK.
OH THANK YOU, SIR...
BUT THAT VERY NIGHT...
W-WHO..WHO'S THERE...?
SOCK
WHAT'LL WE DO WID DE GUARD ?
OH..LOCK HIM UP IN THE VAULT..HAW!
C'MON.. LET'S GET OUTTA HERE!
AND THE NEXT MORNING...
GERHARD SHNOBBLE! GOOD OLD STEADY SHNOBBLE! WHAT IS THE MEANING OF THIS ??
BUT.. BUT.. BUT SIR, I..
AFTER 35 YEARS OF TRUST IN YOU, WE FEEL BETRAYED.
SHNOBBLE..YOU ARE FIRED!

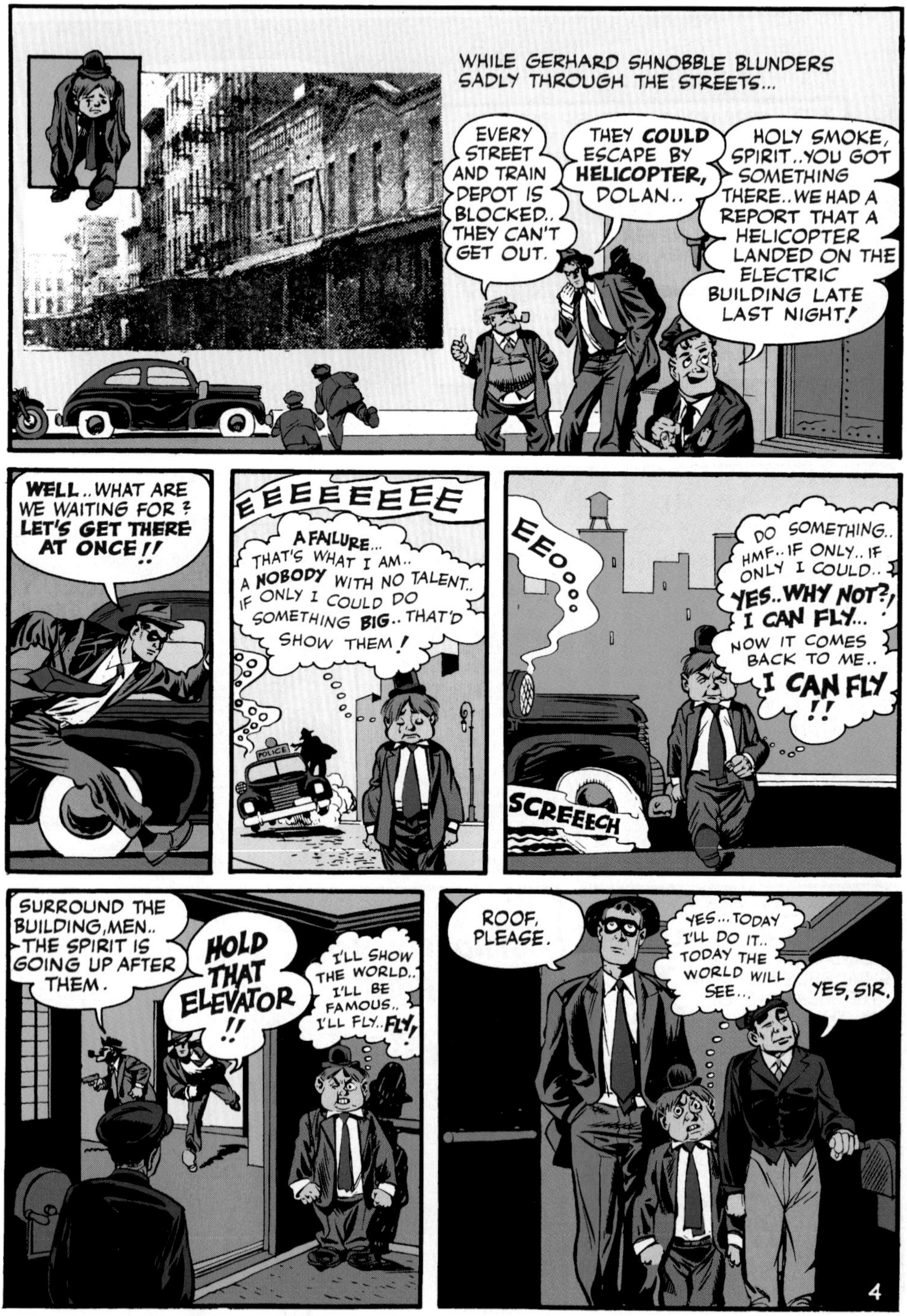
WHILE GERHARD SHNOBBLE BLUNDERS SADLY THROUGH THE STREETS...
EVERY STREET AND TRAIN DEPOT IS BLOCKED.. THEY CAN'T GET OUT.
THEY COULD ESCAPE BY HELICOPTER, DOLAN..
HOLY SMOKE, SPIRIT..YOU GOT SOMETHING THERE..WE HAD A REPORT THAT A HELICOPTER LANDED ON THE ELECTRIC BUILDING LATE LAST NIGHT!
WELL..WHAT ARE WE WAITING FOR? LET'S GET THERE AT ONCE!!
EEEEEEEEE
A FAILURE... THAT'S WHAT I AM.. A NOBODY WITH NO TALENT.. IF ONLY I COULD DO SOMETHING BIG.. THAT'D SHOW THEM!
POLICE
EEOooo
DO SOMETHING.. HMF..IF ONLY.. IF ONLY I COULD.. YES..WHY NOT?! I CAN FLY... NOW IT COMES BACK TO ME.. I CAN FLY!!
SCREEECH
SURROUND THE BUILDING,MEN.. THE SPIRIT IS GOING UP AFTER THEM.
HOLD THAT ELEVATOR!!
I'LL SHOW THE WORLD.. I'LL BE FAMOUS.. I'LL FLY..FLY!
ROOF, PLEASE.
YES...TODAY I'LL DO IT.. TODAY THE WORLD WILL SEE...
YES, SIR.
4

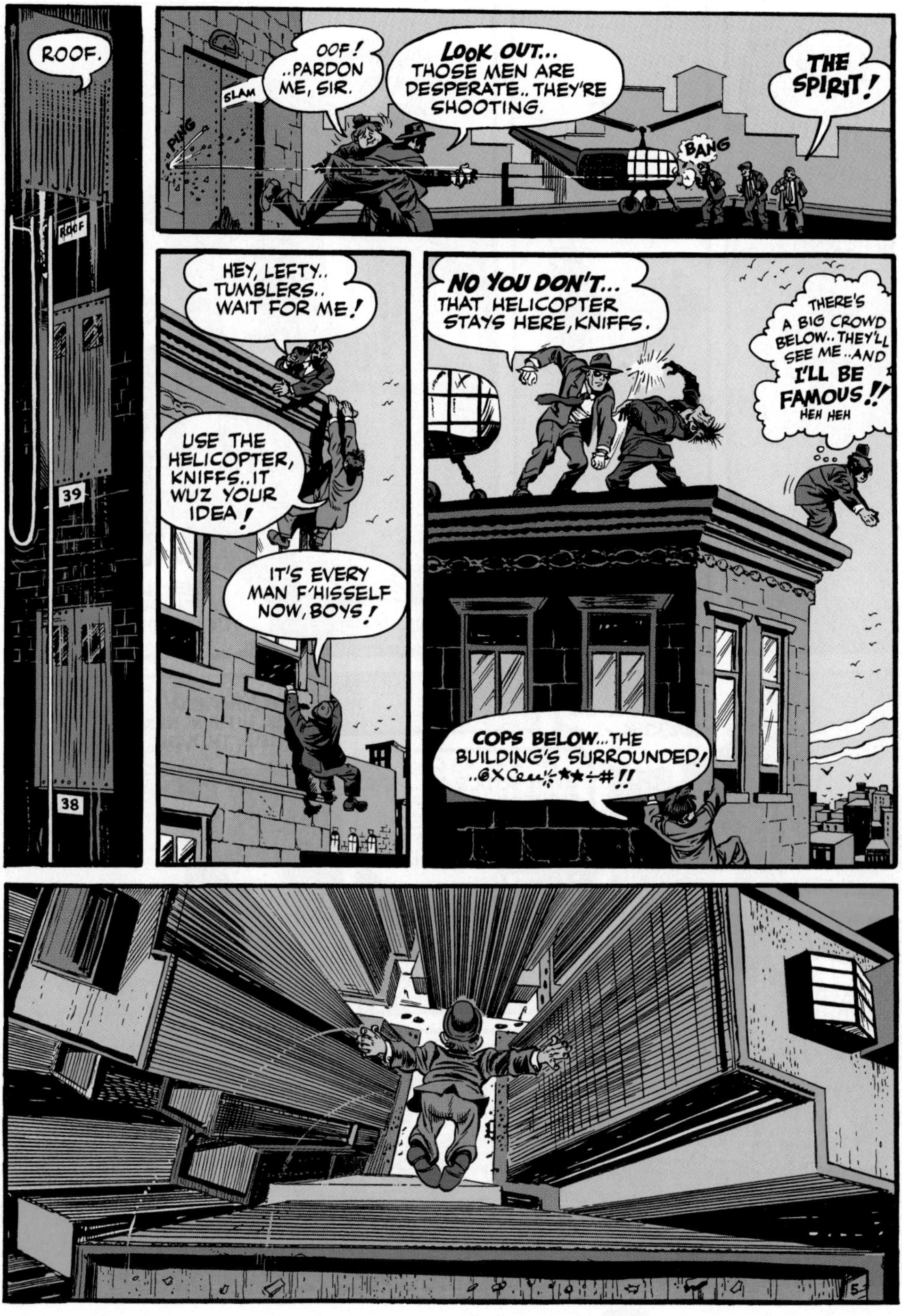
ROOF.
ROOF
39
38
SLAM
PING
OOF! ..PARDON ME, SIR.
LOOK OUT... THOSE MEN ARE DESPERATE.. THEY'RE SHOOTING.
BANG
THE SPIRIT!
HEY, LEFTY.. TUMBLERS.. WAIT FOR ME!
USE THE HELICOPTER, KNIFFS..IT WUZ YOUR IDEA!
IT'S EVERY MAN F'HISSELF NOW, BOYS!
NO YOU DON'T... THAT HELICOPTER STAYS HERE, KNIFFS.
THERE'S A BIG CROWD BELOW.. THEY'LL SEE ME ..AND I'LL BE FAMOUS!! HEH HEH
COPS BELOW... THE BUILDING'S SURROUNDED! ..@X Ceee*★★÷#!!
5

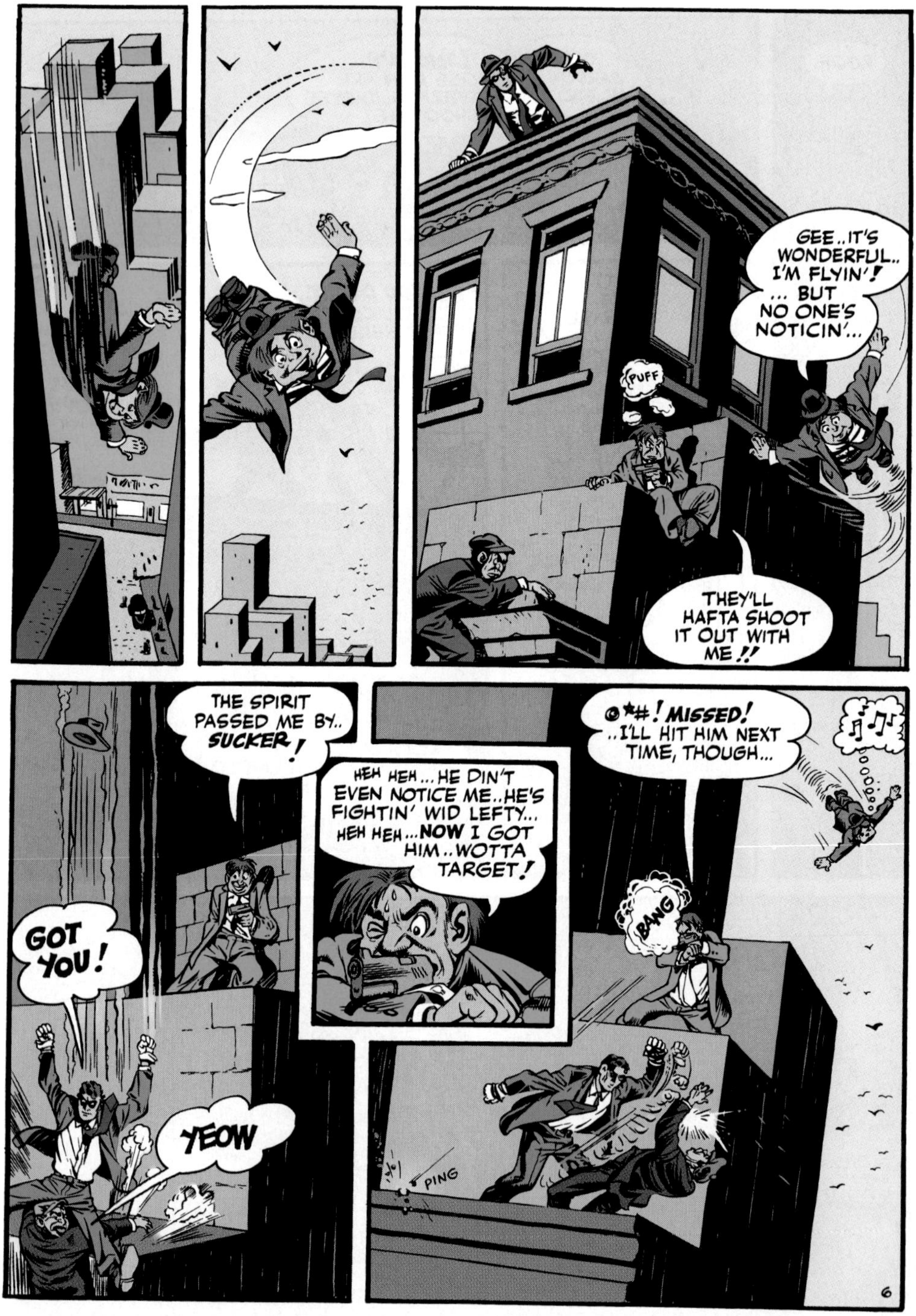

GEE..IT'S WONDERFUL.. I'M FLYIN'! ... BUT NO ONE'S NOTICIN'...
PUFF
THEY'LL HAFTA SHOOT IT OUT WITH ME!!
THE SPIRIT PASSED ME BY.. SUCKER!
HEH HEH... HE DIN'T EVEN NOTICE ME.. HE'S FIGHTIN' WID LEFTY... HEH HEH... NOW I GOT HIM.. WOTTA TARGET!
@*#! MISSED! ..I'LL HIT HIM NEXT TIME, THOUGH...
BANG
GOT YOU!
YEOW
PING

AND SO... LIFELESS...
GERHARD SHNOBBLE FLUTTERED
EARTHWARD.

BUT DO NOT WEEP
FOR SHNOBBLE...

RATHER SHED A TEAR
FOR ALL MANKIND...

FOR NOT ONE PERSON IN THE
ENTIRE CROWD THAT WATCHED
HIS BODY BEING CARTED AWAY...KNEW
OR EVEN SUSPECTED THAT
ON THIS DAY GERHARD SHNOBBLE
HAD **FLOWN**.

Will Eisner's covers each tell a story, with or without type.

Clockwise from right: *The Dreamer; To the Heart of the Storm; Invisible People; New York, the Big City;* and *A Contract with God.*

The child in us does not remember the adults we met as they actually were; he remembers them as archetypes— as caricatures, almost. He remembers them as Eisner draws them.

—Dennis O'Neil, from his introduction to
A Contract With God

.

PIONEER AND STORYTELLER:
THE GRAPHIC NOVELS OF WILL EISNER

by Stephen Weiner

I am not writing an autobiography in verse, my friends.
—John Berryman, *Love and Fame* (1971)

A compelling argument can be made that Will Eisner is among the greatest living writer-illustrators, and one who understands the wide potential of the graphic novel format better than any other practitioner.

Eisner has had a lifelong love of comics, and a career as an illustrator beginning in 1933. In 1940 he created the seminal detective, the Spirit, whose stories were laden with irony, humor, and given a super hero twist. When *The Spirit* ceased publication in 1952, Eisner made his living selling educational materials told in comic book format to the military and other industries. His return to the storytelling aspect of comics began when he appeared as an honored guest at a New York City comic book convention in 1971. At the conference, Eisner met Art Spiegelman as well as cartoonist/publisher Denis Kitchen.

The new environment fascinated the veteran illustrator. The "Underground" cartoonists, as they were called, received royalties on their published work, but even more important, these young artists were using the comics medium as Eisner had always hoped it might be used—as a vehicle for personal and political expression rather than an assembly line for producing regurgitated genre stories.

Inspired by this influx of energy, Eisner sold his publishing company, and in 1972, at age 55, rededicated himself to the field of comics. At this time, he'd been a professional artist for 36 years.

Eisner's new commitment was rooted in the belief that adults who'd grown up reading comics still liked them, but were bored with the genre stories most comic book publishing companies produced. With that in mind, he set out to create a story utilizing the cartoon format that would interest readers like himself—mature, educated, and open to the possibility of literate, longer comic book stories.

The experiment was successful. His first book, *A Contract with God and Other Tenement Stories* was brought out under the banner "a graphic novel" by Baronet Press in 1978. Eisner popularized the term "graphic novel" while trying to interest the editors at Bantam Books in the project a few years earlier. Bantam declined, but the label stuck.

Baronet was a trade house with little interest in promoting their books throughout the network of comic book stores that spread across the country in the 1970s. *A Contract with God*, a collection of four thematically related stories set at 55 Dropsie Avenue in the Bronx during the 1930s, was sold to bookstores, and except for the comics format it might be compared to Sherwood Anderson's novel *Winesburg, Ohio* or Henry Roth's *Call It Sleep*. But, because of its uniqueness, many booksellers didn't know what to do with the book. When

Baronet Press went out of business, *Contract* was picked up in 1985 by Kitchen Sink Press, led by Denis Kitchen, who had been reprinting Eisner's *Spirit* stories for the comic book reading audience.

By this time, Eisner was very interested in the long comic book format. His next effort was a spy thriller imbued with political satire, *Signal From Space* (later reprinted as *Life on Another Planet*). This book utilized many of the adventure elements found in his earlier work, only deepened, making it appealing to adults.

For his next book, Eisner created a "graphic novella" of an autobiographical nature. *The Dreamer* told the story of young Billy Eyron, a cartoonist/entrepreneur full of vision for the burgeoning comic book industry. When Billy is called to court in a copyright case, he is faced with a decision: If he tells the truth, his company will lose a client. Eyron does tell the truth and his company loses a major account. But the publicity generated by the legal proceedings draws interest in Billy from a major cartoon syndicate. *The Dreamer* exemplifies one recurring theme in the graphic novels of Will Eisner: If you remain true to your ideals and study your craft, you will be rewarded.

The Building, Eisner's next major graphic novel, took a format similar to *A Contract with God*, in which the lives of several characters intersect around the Hammond Building. One of Eisner's goals in this book was to explore the powerful effect a building might exert over ordinary lives.

His next book, *A Life Force*, contains multiple stories, but focuses on protagonist and senior citizen Jacob Shtarkah's struggle to build a meaningful life. Considered by many to be Eisner's finest work, it follows the structure of classic prose novels such as Dostoyevski's *Crime and Punishment*. Set in the mid-1930s, *A Life Force* is the story of lost love, wealth (both newfound and sudden monetary loss), homelessness, racketeering, union corruption, and intermarriage. Shtarkah is Will Eisner's everyman, one who tries to be kind, living day to day, while hoping to learn life's deeper meaning.

Almost as powerful, Eisner's next major work is an autobiographical graphic novel set against the backdrop of World War II. *To the Heart of the Storm* is the story of Willie, a child with artistic leanings. While growing up, Willie faces anti-Semitism from sources as close as his best friend. Willie somehow learns to assimilate, and the book concludes with the young artist enlisting in the armed forces, determined to defend a country where he has faced almost constant prejudice.

Eisner's next major effort, *Dropsie Avenue: The Neighborhood*, explores the upswing and decline of a fictional street, Dropsie Avenue, over a hundred-year period. This book expands on themes first seen in Eisner's *The Building*, where he depicts the effects of a skyscraper on human memories. In *Dropsie Avenue*, Eisner explores the collective memories of a

neighborhood as well. Another major theme exhibited in Dropsie Avenue is that the disabled heal one another, as wheelchair-bound protagonist Rowena Shepard marries a deafmute thief. The two live happily and prosperously, and as an old woman Shepard redevelops Dropsie Avenue with her acquired wealth.

Family Matter, Eisner's next book, was published in his eighty-first year, and is an examination of family ties. Grown siblings gather to celebrate the 90th birthday of their father Ben, only to decide in which nursing home he should be placed. Sickened by his children's attitudes, and haunted by the abuse he fostered on them, Ben purposely overdoses, demonstrating that the aged do not always go gently into the night.

Eisner's *The Name of the Game* chronicles the rise and fall of the powerful Arnheim family, and dissects the ways that families raise their social status through marriage. One aspect of this graphic novel that differs from his previous works is that *The Name of the Game* focuses on well-off Jewish families rather than newly arrived immigrants.

Will Eisner's most recent published work, *Fagin the Jew*, published in his sixty-seventh year as a practicing illustrator, retells the Charles Dickens classic *Oliver Twist*. But this time the protagonist is not Oliver, but Moses Fagin, reduced to the life of a petty thief as a result of anti-Semitism practiced in the London streets during the early nineteenth century.

Interspersed among Eisner's graphic novels are a handful of illustrated story collections: *New York, the Big City*, an examination of multifaceted metropolitan life; *City People Notebook*, a series of vignettes and graphic essays centered on an examination of three facets of city life: time, space, and smell; *The Will Eisner Reader*, contemporary tales of poignant reality, imaginative forays into fantasy, ruminations on the human condition, and lighthearted exercises in whimsy; *Invisible People*, which casts a compassionate eye on those anonymous faces in every crowd, the "invisible people" we pass with indifference each day of our lives; *The Last Day in Vietnam*, an example of comics journalism drawn from Eisner's memories and experiences in World War II, Korea, and Vietnam; and *Minor Miracles*, a book of apocryphal stories of outrageous fortune and unlucky coincidence that, like memories themselves, are subjective and often unreliable.

Eisner has also rounded out his later years of publishing with a series of literary classics for young readers starting with *The Princess and the Frog*; followed by *The Last Knight*, an adaptation of Miguel de Cervantes' epic novel *Don Quixote*; *Moby Dick*, based on the Herman Melville classic; and *Sundiata*, an African legend.

Several important themes recur in the body of Eisner's work. The predominant one is the story of Jewish assimilation into American culture. Secondary motifs include the temporary nature of wealth; the ability of the disabled to heal one another and make themselves whole; young, idealistic men seduced by older, more worldly women; the innate responsibility we all have to give back to our community; and dreamers rewarded by realizing their dreams. In Eisner's books several of these themes usually coalesce, giving the books a powerful resonance.

No discussion of Will Eisner's work would be complete without noting the graphics, which imbue the text with even greater meaning. Eisner's illustrative style is deceptively simple, and the artist ably expresses a range of characters, emotions, and ideas as well as internal conflict. Eisner is subtle, a rare quality in any medium, and his work evokes pathos.

Will Eisner's pioneering spirit has been a beacon for cartoonists worldwide. The courage to take chances that expand the range of the comics medium and his ability to succeed in these ventures makes him both a visionary and a world-class writer/artist. His inspiration is felt in a generation of younger artists as diverse as Robert Crumb, Frank Miller, Eric Drooker, and Scott McCloud, all of whom have expanded on different aspects of his work.

Eisner's influence isn't limited to the comics page. As a teacher at New York City's School of Visual Arts, he has produced two seminal books on the subject of illustration: *Comics & Sequential Art* (1985) and *Graphic Storytelling* (1996). In 1988, an annual award program for the best in comics excellence, the Eisner Awards, was inaugurated.

Yet through it all—after more than 70 years in the business—Will Eisner perseveres unfazed, his eyes focused on his next book, ready to dip into autobiography if necessary, or use satire and historical research to make a point clearly. Always ready to let the stories themselves guide his graphic novels, sometimes into uncharted territory, he continues to educate readers with the vast potential of words and pictures.

A CONTRACT WITH GOD AND OTHER TENEMENT STORIES

A Contract with God and Other Tenement Stories was originally published by Baronet Press in 1978. *Contract* is not a conventional novel, but consists of four short stories that form a continuous whole. The first story, "A Contract with God," recounts the life of Frimme

Hersh, a good man devastated by what he perceives as God's broken promise. The second story, "The Street Singer," offers a view of Depression-era life rarely seen. In the third story, "The Super," a young girl so humiliates an apartment manager that he shoots himself. The fourth story, "Cookalein," finds fifteen-year-old Willie learning about the joys and burdens of adulthood.

About *A Contract with God*, Will Eisner writes: "A person's obligation to a Deity is prescribed by the people who reveal the religion to him. All those who accept the existence of a God are bound by some sort of contract with it. In exchange for their observances of the ordained rules, commandments, or rituals, their God promises them rewards either in life or in the hereafter. My book *A Contract with God* is a result of my bemusement over the fact that it seems that neither party lives up to the terms of their agreement."

"A CONTRACT WITH GOD"

55 Dropsie Avenue: Protagonist Frimme Hersh buys his first tenement house located at 55 Dropsie Avenue, and during the story's climax donates the property to his synagogue. The same address figures prominently throughout Will Eisner's graphic novels, ranging from *The Building* to *A Life Force* to *Invisible People* as well as *Dropsie Avenue: The Neighborhood*. About *Dropsie Avenue,* Will Eisner writes: "Dropsie Avenue is a fictitious name. It is a composite fabricated from my memory of the kind of neighborhood in the Bronx that represents the environment typical of the period."

55 DROPSIE AVENUE

Hersh, Frimme: Hersh, the protagonist, was born in 1882. Frimme is a good man, lovingly called "Frimmeleh" by his peers. He is sent to the United States by the elders of his

small Russian village, Piske, because of his reputation for doing good works. Hersh was so well known that the villagers believed that he was a favorite, chosen by God.

While traveling, Hersh makes a contract with God, which he writes on a small stone tablet. After Hersh settles in New York City, an anonymous mother abandons an infant girl on the doorstep of his tenement house. Hersh believes it is a sign from God, and adopts the baby and names her Rachele, after his mother. Hersh is a devoted father, doting on Rachele. Then one day, in the "springtime of her life—Rachele fell ill. Suddenly and fatally." Following the girl's sudden death, Hersh feels that God has violated their agreement. In anger, he throws the stone tablet upon which he had etched the contract from his window. Immediately after Rachele's funeral, he begins purchasing tenements with funds embezzled from the synagogue treasury.

Hersh's first purchase is a tenement at 55 Dropsie Avenue. After making a small fortune buying and selling real estate, Hersh repays the synagogue the money he stole, and returns the tenement to the rabbis with interest, on the condition that they write him up a new contract between him and God. After much debate and deliberation, the rabbis agree to write Hersh a new contract. "Is not all religion a contract between man and God?" asks of the rabbis. "So what is Hersh asking, after all?...He is asking us to provide him with a guiding document—so that he might live in harmony with God...Can we truly deny him this??" The others agree. When presented with a new contract, Hersh is enlivened, and pledges to make a new life for himself, to do charitable work, and hopes to marry. "I shall have a daughter," he proclaims, "and I shall name her Rachele." The excitement of considering the possibility of having a second child causes Hersh to suffer a fatal heart attack.

Hersh is in some ways modeled on biblical heroes such as Jacob, who physically wrestled with God, and walked away wounded. Unlike Jacob, Hersh's experience was metaphysical and he did not survive the encounter.

Khreks, Shloime: Khreks, a young Hassidic Jew, saves three small children, and the widow, Missis Kelly, as a fire rages through Dropsie Avenue. Being new to the neighborhood, and different, Khreks is bullied. Defending himself by throwing stones at his attackers, Shloime comes across the same stone tablet on which Frimme Hersh had written his first contract with God. Hersh tried to destroy the tablet, believing that God had violated their contract by allowing his young daughter Rachele to die. That evening, Khreks discovers that he holds Hersh's contract. Continuing the tradition of a young man renowned for his selflessness, Shloime etches his own name on the stone, making it his contract with God.

SHLOIME KHREKS

Missis Kelly: Kelly is a tenant at 55 Dropsie Avenue who is very kind to Frimme Hersh and offers him a bowl of soup as he returns from his daughter's funeral. Hersh declines. As the story progresses, Hersh purchases the tenement house on Dropsie Avenue, but refuses to give tenant Kelly a discount on her rent although he is aware that

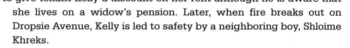

she lives on a widow's pension. Later, when fire breaks out on Dropsie Avenue, Kelly is led to safety by a neighboring boy, Shloime Khreks.

Rachele: The adopted daughter of Frimme Hershe, whom he finds abandoned on his doorstep as an infant. Hersh is completely devoted to Rachele, who dies mysteriously as a child, making Hersh believe that God has violated their contract. Rachele is also the name of the child Hersh hoped to father after entering into his second contract with God.

RACHELE

"THE STREET SINGER"

"The Street Singer," published as the second story in the graphic novel *A Contract with God and Other Tenement Stories*, represents a maturing of Eisner's illustration skills as well as his interest in crafting stories for adult readers.

Convincingly depicting "real life" during the Great Depression without relying on representation, Eisner evokes sympathy for both the protagonist, Eddie, and the aging diva by presenting an emotional reality brought on by the financial instability of the 1930s. Yet the real magic of the story happens offstage inside the reader's head, for we know before the characters do that the situation won't resolve happily. The emotions expressed through the illustrations, both bold and subtle, instantly characterize the desperate plight experienced by many during the 1930s.

As in other Depression-era literature such as John Steinbeck's *The Grapes of Wrath*, the characters are both defeated by—and accepting of—their fate simultaneously, the ultimate ironic resolution giving readers from any era an immediate point of identification.

SYLVIA SPEEGEL

Barry, Ronald: The inflated stage name of back alley singer Eddie, who had been employed as an accountant before the Depression. Performing outside stage diva Sylvia

Speegel's window, she invites Eddie into her apartment, informing him that she is the famous soprano "Marta Maria." Now past her prime, she intends to make Eddie her protégé, and renames him "Ronald Barry."

Speegel seduces Eddie, promising him a musical career, and gives him money to buy appropriate clothes. Instead Eddie buys whiskey with the money. When he returns to his own apartment and family, he and his wife Sophie argue violently and, in a drunken rage, Eddie tosses their young child aside.

Eddie's story concludes on a tragic note. The next afternoon, after Eddie and Sophie make amends, Eddie sets out to begin his training with Marta Maria, only to discover that he's forgotten which tenement house she lives in—and because he doesn't know her real name, has little hope of ever finding her again.

Speegel, Sylvia: Also known by her stage name as "Marta Maria," Sylvia Speegel is a pretentious diva who seduces Eddie, a young minstrel whom she hears from her window. Speegel has two motives for seducing Eddie: to feel young again, and to entice him into pursuing a musical career under her tutelage.

"THE SUPER"

Rosie: The ten-year-old niece of Mrs. Farfell, Rosie offers to show the building super-intendent, Mr. Scuggs, her private parts for a nickel. This sets off a chain of events that culminates with Scuggs shooting himself out of shame for accepting her offer, rage because she poisons his dog and steals his money, and humiliation because the police come to mistakenly arrest him.

Scuggs: When Mrs. Farfell complains to Mr. Scuggs, the tenement superintend-ent, that she has no hot water, the super goes upstairs to talk to her. Inside Farfell's apartment, Scuggs meets her ten-year-old niece, Rosie, who has a mis-chievous look on her face and is dressed in a towel. Mrs. Farfell informs Scuggs that Rosie can't finish her bath because there's no hot water. Uncomfortable, Scuggs returns to his own basement apartment, cranks up the heat, and stares at the pictures of naked women that adorn his walls. Frustrated, he gets into bed and drinks. Eventually there's a knock on his door. When he opens it, Scuggs finds Rosie, who enters, closing the door behind her.

ROSIE

Rosie notices the pictures that cover Scuggs's walls, and she offers to show him her private parts for a nickel. Reluctantly, Scuggs agrees, but while he checks the hallway to be sure that no one will catch them, Rosie poisons his dog and steals the cash box. Armed with a pistol, Scuggs pursues Rosie, corner-ing her in the alleyway next to their tenement. Hearing the com-motion, neighbors arrive and tell Scuggs to leave the girl alone. Then Scuggs returns to his basement apartment without hurting Rosie or getting his money back. Without explanation, Scuggs goes to the furnace and turns up the heat, perhaps sensing the cause of his misfortune. At this point, an officer knocks on Scuggs's door, demanding that he surrender. Before the police are able to break into the apartment and capture him, Scuggs uses the pistol on himself.

"COOKALEIN"

Benny: A fur cutter who fantasizes about meeting and marrying a rich girl while vaca-tioning in the mountains of upstate New York at Grossman's. His plan seems to work as Benny becomes informally engaged to Goldie, but when he learns that she doesn't have money Benny attempts to rape her, thus ending their relationship. Benny then marries Ruthie Fein, an heiress whom he is not attracted to.

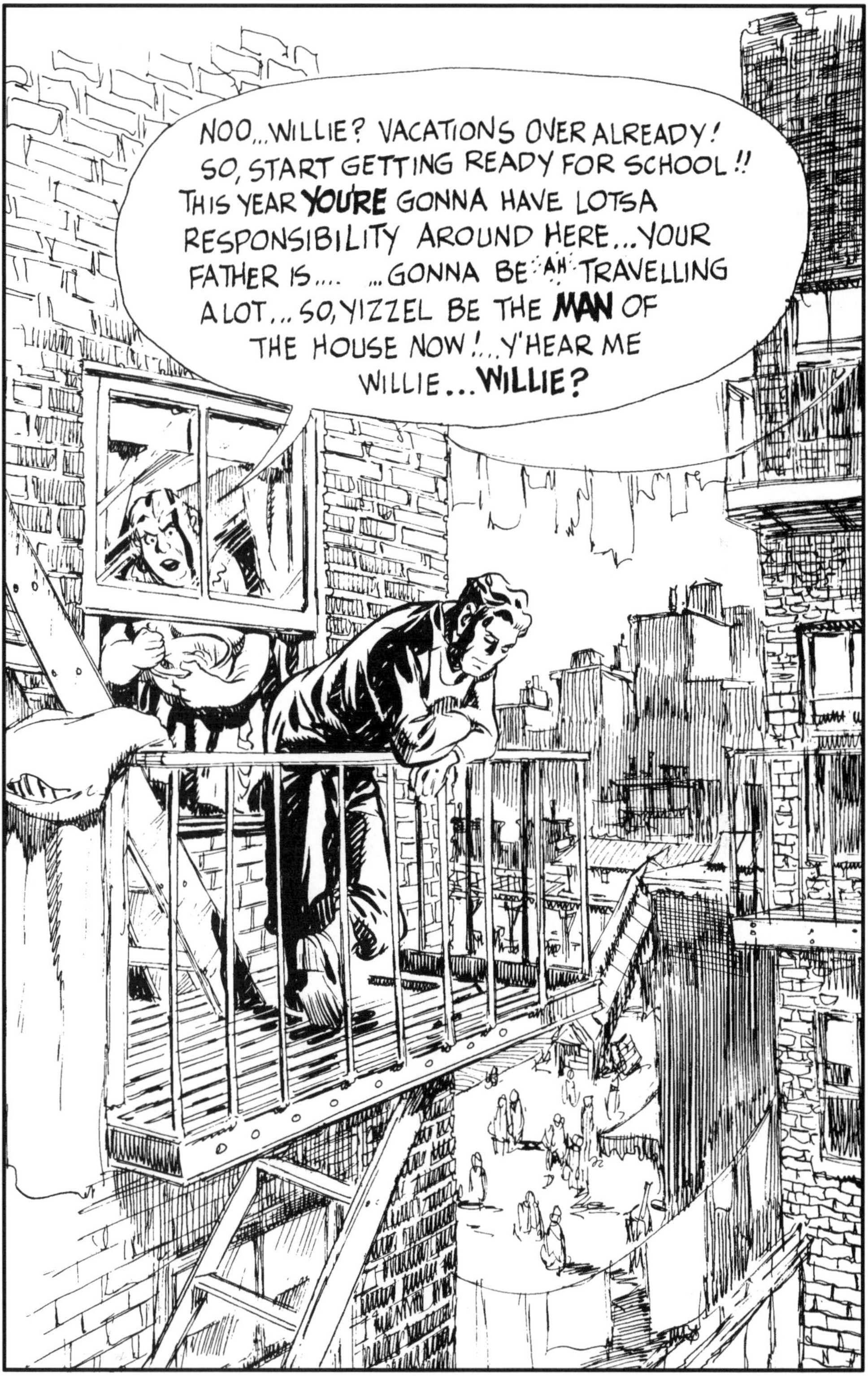
NOO...WILLIE? VACATIONS OVER ALREADY! SO, START GETTING READY FOR SCHOOL!! THIS YEAR YOU'RE GONNA HAVE LOTSA RESPONSIBILITY AROUND HERE...YOUR FATHER IS.... ...GONNA BE AH TRAVELLING ALOT...SO, YIZZEL BE THE MAN OF THE HOUSE NOW!...Y'HEAR ME WILLIE...WILLIE?

OH, SO YOU'RE ONE OF THE **HELP?** ...WELL...ER, I'M SORRY, I'LL BE-ER-BUSY!! YES, I GOT TO WASH MY HAIR!

GOLDIE

Goldie: A city girl who dreams of catching a rich eligible bachelor as she vacations in the mountains at Grossman's. Goldie very quickly becomes engaged to Benny, but when he learns that she isn't wealthy, their relationship ends when he attempts to rape her. After the incident, Goldie is comforted by Herbie, a doctor whom she initially mistook for a member of the staff. As the story "Cookalein" closes, Herbie and Goldie become engaged.

Willie: At fifteen, Willie hopes to impress an older woman as he and his family vacation in upstate New York. At a dance welcoming the husbands to the resort, young Willie spends much of the evening with Maralyn Minks, who believes her husband is away. After the dance is over, Willie goes to sleep in the barn, but is soon awakened by Maralyn, who comes on the pretense of bringing him a blanket. Her real intent is to seduce him. After Willie and Maralyn make love, Irving Minks, Maralyn's husband, arrives. Husband and wife proceed to make love loudly while ignoring Willie, who watches, terrified. Willie's story concludes as he returns to New York City with his family. He is emotionally torn over his family vacation, growing aware of his first genuine feelings of independence.

LIFE ON ANOTHER PLANET

Life on Another Planet stands out among Will Eisner's graphic novels because it is his only genre work, mixing adventure story techniques used so effectively in *The Spirit* with science fiction and espionage story elements. The book may also be read as social commentary.

JAMES BLUDD

"Alien first contact, rendered not as some goofy special-effects no-brainer, but as a panorama of tragic human foibles," Harlan Ellison has said about *Life on Another Planet*. "Is Eisner endlessly terrific, or what?"

Originally serialized in *The Will Eisner Quarterly*, the story was collected and initially published in color in 1983 by Kitchen Sink Press under the title *Signal from Space*. A black-and-white version of the graphic novel was later published under the title *Life on Another Planet* when the book was reissued by Kitchen Sink Press in 1995.

About *Life on Another Planet*, Will Eisner writes: "I became aware that the comic book audience had grown older, and it was clear to me that it was time for the medium to grow with them."

Bludd, James: An astrophysicist asked by the CIA to replace murdered scientist Cobbs. After reviewing Cobbs's notes, Bludd becomes convinced that, prior to his death, Cobbs had received a signal from space indicating life on another planet. When Bludd confronts colleagues Argano and Malley with this news, he learns that they were involved with the murder.

Before he is able to summon the authorities, Soviet agents, led by Bludd's secretary, Miss Bowen, confiscate Cobbs's notes and abduct Argano and Malley. The agents set fire to the house, leaving Bludd for dead. Amazingly, he survives.

After recovering, Bludd is employed by the Multinational Corporation, and assigned the task of restoring the captured scientists. In Germany, Bludd meets with Malley and Argano. The meeting is not fruitful. Information critical to Bludd has been left in the Soviet Union. Upon going there to retrieve the notes, Bludd is shocked to learn that his former secretary, now known as Nadia, has become Argano's lover. Bludd is able to get the necessary information, while killing Argano.

Returning to the U.S., Bludd is treated like royalty by the Multinational's Tripartite Commission. Bludd is skeptical of the commission's views, and disgusted by their attempt to politicize the implications of the space signal. His work done, Bludd is ready to leave the employ of the Multinational Corporation, but the commission isn't finished with James Bludd. Someone wants him dead.

When Bludd arrives at his apartment, a would-be assassin is killed by enemy agent Nadia, who attempts to persuade him to defect. She is very persuasive, and seduces Bludd in an effort to win him over. Soon, Nadia introduces Bludd to the World Action Group of Interplanetary Brotherhood, ostensibly a global organization, but in reality one arm of the Soviet Union's covert operation. After meeting with the World Action Group, Bludd accepts the assignment given him—to go to

Sidiami and stop the space launch that might well escalate the arms race between the U.S. and the U.S.S.R.

In Sidiami, Bludd receives unlikely help from Rocco Stilletto, a hit man. While attempting to infiltrate a missile compound, Bludd is captured and beaten. Bludd's rescuer is Stilletto, who hides him in a decaying building.

Bludd next appears in Istanbul, where he rescues Soviet agent Nadia from her tormentors. By now Bludd's idealistic streak has reached Nadia and she agrees to help him stop the space launch in Sidiami. With this in mind, he returns to Sidiami aided by Stilletto and a scientist named Jones. Bludd succeeds in delaying the liftoff because the passenger, a mutated plant, is stolen by Stilletto.

Back in the United States, the CIA informs Bludd that the Soviets have also been preparing a space launch, but the project was aborted by Nadia, who is now hidden in Paris. Bludd rushes overseas to rescue her. Nadia is badly beaten during their escape, and fatally poisoned while boarding an airplane.

Embittered, Bludd believes that his career as an agent is over, but he's wrong. While trying to stay hidden, Macready, CEO of the Multinational Corporation, finds him. From Macready, Bludd learns that the U.S. wants to launch its own spacecraft, and they want to use the mutated plant as a passenger, thus colonizing the planet where they believe the signal originated from. Macready has come to Bludd because he doesn't know where the mutated plant is, but knows that Bludd can find it. Bludd agrees to work for the Multinational Corporation, but these are his conditions: If the recovery project is successful, he will be awarded the post as director of Mount Head Observatory.

Next Bludd searches out Rocco Stilletto, still in possession of the plant. The price of success is high; both the hit man, Stilletto, and scientist Jones die while Bludd retrieves the plant. Before delivering it to Macready, he embeds an explosive in the plant, set to detonate after the spacecraft has been launched. After liftoff, the ship does explode, and Bludd has successfully averted an arms race between the superpowers.

The threat of arms race escalation apparently over, Bludd is contentedly settled in as director of the Mount Head Observatory. When one of his assistants informs him that they have received a signal from outer space, Bludd destroys the evidence.

Of all the protagonists in Eisner's graphic novels, James Bludd is closest to Denny Colt, the ironic hero of *The Spirit*, and is one of the comic creator's most complex heroes. However, Bludd is a Denny Colt in a more dangerous time, when the good guys question the motives of the forces they serve and use any means necessary to accomplish their ends.

Cora: A cocktail waitress with high ambitions, Cora becomes Marco's first follower when he proclaims himself leader of the Star People, a sect that will colonize planet Barnard, where it is believed that the signal from space originated.

When the Star People protest in front of the Multinational building, Cora slyly escapes the police by hitching a ride with George Macready, the CEO of the Multinational Corporation. Two days later, Cora is quietly protesting in front of the same building.

Caught in larger political events, Cora is sent to Sidiami, intent that she and ninety-nine other Star People will be among the first to colonize the new planet. Again, Cora reveals a cunning nature. Rather than go to Barnard, she hopes to become the concubine of General Ami, Sidiami's leader. However, this time it's Cora who is outfoxed. The General wants no involvement with her, and instead she is imprisoned. When Jones, a young man hoping to free Cora, arrives, she wants no part of his plan. Jones cannot offer her the good life, so Cora chooses to take her chances by remaining in the Sidiami prison. When Macready visits Sidiami, Cora seduces him and the two become lovers. When Macready leaves Sidiami, he brings Cora with him. Back in the U.S., he divorces his wife and marries sly Cora, fulfilling her desire to "be somebody."

Will Eisner is a master at creating female characters who use their male counterparts to their own advantage. Of all Eisner's desperate females, Cora may be the most remorseless and adept.

Macready, George: CEO of the Multinational Corporation, which influences the economies of fifteen countries, Macready is determined to push the United States and Soviet Union into an arms race that will benefit his company.

A random act of generosity works toward that end when he picks up Cora, a member of the Star People, during a riot. From Cora, Macready learns much about the Star People, and plots to use the organization toward his own ends.

Macready contacts James Bludd and tries to convince him of the necessity of beating the Soviets to planet Barnard in a ship with a genetically altered plant as a living passenger. Although Bludd isn't convinced that Macready is correct, George is now even more determined to reach the planet. He appears before a Senate committee, successfully defending the Multinational Corporation's right to assist the country of Sidiami as it contacts and colonizes Barnard.

Macready's personal life vastly differs from his professional one. He is unhappily married to an alcoholic whom he wed primarily to advance his career. He is disappointed in his gay son, whom he openly ignores even while the young man lies dying.

George Macready also makes easy alliances: he supports the reelection bid of former president Dexter Milgate, chiefly as a way to derail the administration. But, when the Senate supports Macready's plan to aid Sidiami, he abandons Milgate. When Macready visits Sidiami on business, the government there holds him prisoner until he agrees to fund their $100 million project to reach planet Barnard. While in Sidiami, Macready is seduced by Cora, another political prisoner, and formerly one of the Star People, a group of religious zealots in the U.S. determined to colonize Barnard as well. Cora wants to "be somebody" and sees her relationship with Macready as a way to access her dream.

Forces in motion are not easily stopped. Surprisingly, Milgate is elected President of the United States, Macready's infidelity with Cora develops into marriage, and the space race between the superpowers that Macready hoped to instigate accelerates.

Next, Macready engages James Bludd to find the mutated plant life, so he can use a living passenger on a spacecraft bound for planet Barnard. If the ship reaches the planet with a passenger, Macready believes that the United States will have rights of planet ownership. However, Macready's carefully laid plan fails; Bludd detonates the space launch on route to Barnard, while making the explosion appear to be caused by an electrical malfunction.

Marco: An alcoholic writer who crowns himself leader of the Star People, a sect intent on colonizing planet Barnard. At first Marco is successful, building a religious organization of several thousand members. However, Marco's motives are suspect, as he pines for a Cadillac while his organization funds research. When he leads a group of one hundred of the Star People to Sidiami in lost hope of joining a space launch that will colonize Barnard, he is abandoned by Cora, his first follower and apparent lover. Disgusted by his fall from grace and Cora's betrayal, Marco returns to the bottle for solace.

Milgate, Dexter: Ex-president Dexter Milgate (modeled in part on President Richard Milhous Nixon, who resigned in 1974 during the Watergate scandal) runs for the office of the presidency at the invitation of George Macready. Initially, Milgate's candidacy isn't viewed as a threat to the incum-

MARCO

bent, but Milgate's hard-line campaign does force the current administration to change its course. When the current president is wounded and chooses not to seek reelection, Milgate's victory is assured. As president, Milgate officially recognizes Sidiami as a colony of planet Barnard, the home of the signal from space.

DEXTER MILGATE

Nadia: An agent for the KGB, Nadia first appears undercover as Miss Bowen, secretary to James Bludd, when Bludd is sent to investigate the mysterious circumstances surrounding scientist Cobb's death in a New Mexico observatory. Bowen reveals herself as a Soviet spy when she leads a team that kidnaps two scientists and leaves Bludd apparently dead.

Next Nadia shows up as kidnapped American scientist Argano's lover, whom Argano attempts to strangle when she discovers Bludd hiding in Argano's closet.

Nadia has a knack for appearing at the right time, and some weeks later she rescues Bludd, while explaining that she wants to recruit him on behalf of the Unaffiliated People. Part of Nadia's tactics include seduction, and when Bludd meets the World Action Group of Interplanetary Brotherhood, he agrees to help.

Nadia next appears as a prisoner in Hotel Istanbul in Sidiami, where a launch is planned for planet Barnard. Nadia informs Bludd that the World Action Group is one of the

KGB's operations. However, this time, she convinces Bludd to help stop the space launch because it poses a threat to nuclear stability, and the two go their separate ways with separate missions.

In Paris, Bludd again finds Nadia, this time badly hurt while being interrogated. As Bludd helps Nadia escape, she is injected with a fatal poison by an umbrella in a crowded airport. Nadia's death leaves Bludd bereft and without aid in his quest to end the escalating arms race between the United States and the Soviet Union.

As far back as *The Spirit*, Eisner explored a love-hate relationship between the hero and a female who represented both good and evil. Nadia extends the role of females such as *The Spirit*'s P'Gell, but there is no humor in her story, given the seriousness of the possibility of nuclear war.

Stilletto, Rocco: A hit man and astrophysicist James Bludd meets on a flight to Sidiami. Rocco is searching for Vito Lupo, who is accused of murdering his wife. In Sidiami, Bludd is unable to hire a driver, and Rocco offers to help. Rocco finds and wounds Lupo, while freeing Bludd from a makeshift prison. As the two hide, Bludd convinces Rocco to join his cause to stop the Sidiami space flight. Later, when Stilletto informs his superiors that Lupo has become a form of mutated plant life, they are disappointed that Rocco has failed to bring Lupo back. Rocco is given a new assignment: assassinate the president of the United States. Stilletto wounds the president easily, then covers his tracks by killing his accomplice.

Redeemed in the eyes of his employer, Rocco hides out with Rosa, sister-in-law of Vito Lupo. Rocco is shot by Rosa when James Bludd appears at her door, looking for the plant.

The Dreamer is not an autobiography in the classic sense, although it takes place in a time through which the author lived. Will Eisner tells us that "It is a story that should satisfy those curious about life in and around a typical comic book studio of the middle 1930s. It is intended as a kind of graphic historical novel set in the primordial dawn of the comic book industry."

The book recounts the career experiences of a dreamer, Billy Eyron, a budding cartoonist, who finds the courage necessary to follow his heart.

About *The Dreamer*, Will Eisner writes: "A dreamer, in my definition, is one who imagines the fulfillment of an idea. Dreaming is a necessary prelude to financial accomplishment. Success depends very much on the skill of execution."

Bighero: A very successful comic book character, considered the first costumed super hero. Bighero catapults Donald Harrifield's comic book publishing company Bang Comics into the national spotlight. Bighero ("The Man of Iron") is based on Superman ("The Man of Steel"), and its creators—"two kids from Ohio"—were based on writer Jerry Siegel and artist Joe Shuster, co-creators of the seminal DC Comics super hero.

Eyron, Billy: An aspiring artist for Davis printing, Eyron is approached by the Giannini family and asked to draw some pornographic cartoons. As a result, Billy leaves the company, and while attempting to secure work as a cartoonist, he meets Jimmy Samson, an entrepreneur. Billy does some work for *Socko* magazine, but when it closes, Billy and Jimmy start a comic book packaging company. There, Billy is nicknamed the "Dreamer" because of his vision that comics might convey serious material. As Billy is the company's artist, he draws a lot of the material under pen names, such as J. Morgan Thomas, Spenser Steel, and Willis Rensie, hoping to give the impression that there's a large art staff on board.

As the workload increases, it is necessary to employ more workers. In order to fend off their competition, Eyron & Samson studios hire a staff rather than contracting freelance artists. The company becomes successful, with Billy filling the role of staff supervisor and Jimmy serving as manager of sales. Billy is so engrossed in his work that he ignores the advances of a female employee, but loses his virginity to a prostitute named Laverne, whom Billy believes (in a wide-eyed way) understands him.

A crisis arises when a publisher who has contracted work from Eyron & Samson is sued because of copyright infringement. A prominent publishing house claims that the smaller company blatantly imitated their very successful character. As the artist, Billy faces a moral dilemma: Should he lie and say that the character is his creation, or should he tell the truth, informing

the court that the smaller publisher instructed him to imitate the more successful character, hoping to capitalize on the original character's success? Billy chooses the truth and, as a result, Eyron & Samson lose a major account. However, the publicity generated by the court case brings Billy to the attention of a major comics syndicate. Syndicate heads Beansy Everett and Mike Henney make Billy an offer he can't refuse: to produce his own comic book section for weekly papers. Eyron accepts, and Eyron & Samson staffers Lew Sharp, Bo Bowers, and Chuck Mann, join him in his new venture.

The Dreamer is one of Will Eisner's autobiographical graphic novels, recalling his early years as a cartoonist. The packaging company of Eyron & Samson is based on Will Eisner's first company, Eisner and Iger. Staff illustrators such as Lew Sharp, Armand and Andrea Budd, Bo Bowers, Gar Tooth, and Jack King, are based on real life cartoonists such as Lou Fine, Bob Powell, George Tuska, and Jack "King" Kirby, all of whom were employed at one time or another at Eisner and Iger's studio.

Harrifield, Donald ("Donny"): A printer who becomes a comic book publisher by purchasing the properties of Captain Montrose B. Wilson, a failed publisher. Harrifield almost accidentally stumbles across a very successful character, the super hero Bighero. Harrifield is based upon Harry Donenfeld, then-publisher of DC Comics.

Heroman: A super hero character commissioned by a small publisher, Vince Reynard, in the hopes of capitalizing on some of the commercial success of Bighero. Heroman's adventures were created by the company of Eyron & Samson. When the publishers of Bighero sue Reynard for copyright infringement, protagonist Billy Eyron is forced to make a moral decision: Should he lie before the court, and say that he created Heroman, or should he tell the truth, openly admitting that Heroman was conceived by Reynard, a publishing rival, who blatantly stole many of Bighero's characteristics while creating Heroman?

Reynard, Vincent ("Vince"): An accountant for Donald Harrifield, who breaks away and opens his own comic book publishing company. Reynard enjoys early success in great part because he contracts Eyron & Samson to create a hero imitating Harrifield's star, "Bighero." When Reynard is sued for copyright infringement, he asks Billy to lie before the court, claiming that the rival hero, "Heroman," was his own idea. Billy refuses to lie, leaving Reynard with no plausible defense.

Eisner based the character of Vincent Reynard on Victor Fox, an accountant for DC Comics who had started his own comics company to create strips and comic books. Fox asked Eisner and Iger to create a caped super hero, and was sued by DC. In court, Fox tried to blame their studio for the resemblance, but Eisner told the truth on the stand: that Fox had requested a Superman-type character. Fox lost the case, and the Eisner and Iger Studio lost creative fees owed to them by Fox, as well as his future business.

Samson, Jimmy: Billy Eyron's business partner, co-owner of Eyron & Samson, a comic book packaging company. Initially, Samson hires Eyron to produce comics, but when his company goes under; Billy suggests that he and Jimmy go into business together producing comics. Samson's responsibilities include soliciting clients, whereas Eyron creates characters and concepts, and supervises staff. When Eyron leaves the business to start his own newspaper strip, Samson buys him out.

The Eyron & Samson studio is based on the real comic book packaging company of Eisner and Iger, and Jimmy Samson is based on Will Eisner's business partner, Samuel "Jerry" Iger. "The studio of Eisner and Iger continued for about eight years after I left," Eisner explains. "Selling my shares to Jerry was a very difficult decision. Going public and then going private in 1964 were both very difficult decisions."

WILL EISNER'S HAWKS OF THE SEAS

First published in 1986 by Kitchen Sink Press, then again in 2003 by Dark Horse Comics, this volume collects Will Eisner's work from 1936-1938. In the tradition of the popular swashbuckling films of the time, *Hawks of the Seas* is primarily an adventure story. *The Flame*, a forerunner of the *Hawks* series, had appeared in *Wow, What a Magazine!*, but when it ceased publication, Eisner reused much of the material to create *Hawks of the Seas* for Quality Comics' *Feature Funnies*.

About *Hawks of the Seas*, Will Eisner writes: "What is most significant to me about this work is that it represents the confluence of my writing and art at that point in my career. As a youngster, my main source of literary nutrition was Robert Louis Stevenson and Rafael Sabatini. These, mixed with James Fenimore Cooper, and later, the gritty pulp magazines, along with the short story genre extant at the time, formed the basis of my sense of what adventure was all about."

NEW YORK, THE BIG CITY

First published by Kitchen Sink Press, this 1986 volume collects a series of one- or two-page sketches (68 in all), sometimes wordless, depicting life in New York City. This perceptive graphic novel examines multifaceted metropolitan life, and all the flavor, color, and commotion that go with it. Stories fall under the headings "The Treasure of Avenue 'C,'" "Subways," "Stoops," "Garbage," "Street Music," "Sentinels," "Windows," "Walls," and "The Block."

About *New York, the Big City*, Will Eisner writes in his introduction: "I have, here, undertaken a series of vignettes built around nine elements which, taken together, are my portrayal of a big city...any city.

"Seen from afar, major cities are an accumulation of big buildings, big population and big acreage. For me it is not 'real.' The big city as it is seen by its inhabitants is the real thing. The true picture is in the crevices on its floors and around the smaller pieces of its architecture, where daily life swirls.

"Portraiture is a very personal thing, so in the end this effort reflects my own perspective. Because I grew up in New York City, its internal architecture and street objects are inescapably reflected. But I also know many other big cities, and what I show is meant to be common to them all."

In Will Eisner's collection *The Building* (1987), a series of intertwined stories explore the idea that a building itself may hold shared memories of its inhabitants, a theme discussed by writers as diverse as John Mitchell and Alan Garner.

In his foreword to *The Building*, Eisner wrote, "As I grew older and accumulated memories, I came to feel more keenly about the disappearances of people and landmarks. Especially troubling to me was the callous removal of buildings. I felt that, somehow, they had a kind of soul."

About the stories in this collection, Will Eisner said: "I did not empower the building with supernatural power. What appears supernatural is to me simply the 'psychic debris' that accumulates around objects that we live with. Objects that become part of our life, like desks or favorite chairs, are things we become attached to because they were part of our experience. Inanimate objects, I believe, absorb the radioactive fallout of emotions with which they were involved."

Benny: Gilda Green's poetry-writing lover, Benny is devoted to Gilda despite her marrying Irving Glumpen, a dentist. The two carry on a lifelong affair in front of the Hammond Building. Ostensibly, Gilda refuses to wed Benny because he is a financial risk. When Gilda and Benny are both senior citizens, Benny asks Gilda to leave her husband, proposing that they marry. Gilda turns Benny down, and shortly after that, when she doesn't arrive at their meeting place, Benny ventures into her apartment and discovers that the love of his life has died.

"Being a poet doesn't alter one's dimensions," Will Eisner explains. "One writes poetry because its form enables the author to deal with abstractions. What one has to say is more important than how it is said. Poetry, I think, is a more emotional style of writing."

Butts, Stephen T.: A corrupt building inspector who, at the instruction of P.J. Hammond, unethically charges the owners of the building, the Eton family, with code violations, thus making it possible for P.J. Hammond to purchase the property. After the purchase is final, Butts is fired as a result of charges related to the violations.

Green, Gilda: As a girl, Gilda Green was a "beauty" and the "golden girl of East City High," surprising everyone by falling in love with Benny, a poet. Their romance continues beyond high school—every day without fail, they meet in front of the Hammond Building.

BENNY AND GILDA GREEN

During one meeting, Gilda shocks Benny by announcing that she is going to marry Irving Glumpen, a dentist. Even as a newlywed, Gilda continues to meet Benny for their ongoing rendezvous in front of the Hammond Building, and these meetings blossom into a full-fledged affair. As Benny and Gilda age they continue to meet, until one day they are seen by Gilda's husband Irving.

Gilda is remorseful and goes to Irving's dental office, intent on making amends. Instead, she catches her husband in the midst of a romantic liaison of his own. Without being noticed, Gilda sneaks out of Irving's office. After this eventful day, the couple grows even further apart, eventually confessing their love affairs.

Benny and Gilda continue to meet in front of the building into old age, and finally, after years of having a clandestine relationship, Benny proposes, asking Gilda to finally leave her husband and marry him. Gilda gently refuses, telling Benny that she is too ill for such a major life change. Soon after the marriage proposal, she fails to appear at the appointed meeting place. Benny braves her apartment only to learn from Irving that Gilda has died.

Hammond, P.J.: "P.J. Hammond was born into a successful real estate family," and grew up amid wealth and power. Graduating from an Ivy League college, he goes to work

THE BUILDING

For over
80 years
the building
stood
astride the
intersection
of two major
avenues.
It was
a landmark
whose walls
weathered
the rain
of tears
and the
pelting
of laughter.

In time,
an invisible
accumulation
of dramas
ringed
its base.

IT'LL BE CALLED THE HAMMOND CENTER.

YOUR FATHER WOULD BE PROUD OF YOU, P.J.

P.J. HAMMOND

for his father. Initially, P.J. argues that the family investment firm should assume more social responsibility. After his father's death, P.J. inherits the company. As an entrepreneur, he appears to have lost his early sense of social responsibility, and dreams of owning an entire city block then remaking it into a thriving district called "The Hammond Center." When P.J. is unable to repurchase the first building his father had owned but later sold, he becomes obsessed and neglects his business.

After bribing Stephen Butts, the building inspector, into fining the Eton family, who owns the property, for false code violations, P.J. is able to purchase his father's former building. While owning the building, P.J. is charged with the same violations that he helped create, and loses an enormous amount of money while attempting to rebuild.

Consequently, P.J.'s advisor informs him that they have sold all his other properties to raise the funds needed to repair the ailing property. Now, a developer hopes to purchase this last building, tear it down, and put up a new building, naming it after him. Reluctantly, P.J. agrees, and thereafter withdraws even more deeply into himself, eventually committing suicide by jumping out a window.

The next spring the new Hammond Building is completed. One day a window washer's swing breaks. As he falls, the ghosts of Monroe Mensh, Gilda Green, Benny, P.J. Hammond, and Antonio Tonatti—all characters whose lives were heavily influenced by the original Hammond Building—are seen, as if coming back to life for a brief moment in time.

Pedestrians stand helplessly by as the ghost of P.J. Hammond tries to support the ledge that the man holds, and Antonio, the violinist whose music has always given strength to the weak, plays for the fallen window washer as he desperately clings to the ledge. The gorgeous music seemingly comforts the worker, who manages to hang on until the firemen arrive and bring him down him to safety.

"Incredible…how he survived!" someone from the crowd says. "A miracle!" says another. Most miraculous is that "the normal flow of life returned in front of the building," and that life does, indeed, move on.

Mensh, Monroe: A child of the city who "grew up anonymously, skilled in the art of city living," Monroe Mensh is a bachelor. His uneventful life takes an abrupt turn when he witnesses an innocent child killed in a drive-by shooting in front of the Hammond Building. After witnessing that violent act, Mensh (which means "a good man" in Yiddish) decides to become a fundraiser for the "Juvenile Charities Society." When he learns that this position doesn't involve working directly with children, he becomes a caseworker for the same organization.

When Chico, a child under Mensh's care, dies, it is recommended that Monroe either resign from the agency or return to his former position as fundraiser. Mensh chooses to resign, and goes into business with Charlie, creating the "Save the Kids Society." A few years into the business Monroe discovers that his partner Charlie has been embezzling funds and that the organization is bankrupt.

This news demoralizes Mensh, and he spends his time sitting listlessly in the park. One day, when a boy is struck by a car, Mensh chases the ambulance to the hospital, where he offers to donate blood in an effort to save the child. The boy does not survive the surgery. Mensh, who develops a blood clot during the operation, also dies.

Tonatti, Antonio: "From early childhood, Antonio Tonatti showed a talent for music that he displayed in the more affluent homes of friends and relatives." Unable to afford a piano, Tonatti's parents buy him a violin. Antonio plays into adulthood and dreams of a musical career, but he is told by a maestro that he isn't skilled enough to play professionally. Dejected, Antonio continues to play at weddings and family parties, eventually choosing to enter his family construction business, despite the fact that the physical wear on his hands makes playing the violin difficult.

After a work-related accident, Antonio is informed that he will be impaired for the rest of his life, unable to work again. In retirement, he returns to violin playing, entertaining noontime crowds in front of the Hammond Building. Antonio's playing has a joyful, magical quality that enhances love affairs, mends rifts, and infuses the weak with resolve. While the building is being demolished and rebuilt, Antonio, now an old man, grows weaker, eventually dying before the new Hammond Building is completed.

Now Antonio returned to his true love ...the violin. And every day at noontime he appeared at the entrance of the building where, for a few hours he played for the passers-by.

Robert Crumb called *A Life Force* "genuinely touching and honest...an uplifting book! It inspired me to keep going in this field!"

Originally serialized from 1983-1985, *A Life Force* was collected by Kitchen Sink Press and published in 1988. It is perhaps Will Eisner's most realized graphic novel, telling the story of Jacob Shtarkah, an out-of-work carpenter who approaches life with a philosophical bent ("*shtarker*" is Yiddish for "a stout fellow" or "a strong person") and the lemony taste of a rekindled, long-lost love.

About *A Life Force*, Will Eisner writes: "I do not consciously look for themes contrary to current trends. I concentrate on themes that I believe ought to be addressed, or ones that I feel compelled to write in sequential art form.

"My influences (those that I'm aware of) come from the short story writing of the 30's. As for structure in my graphic novels, I lean on my memory of Dostoyevski's works, which have a very discernible architecture.

"*A Contract with God* and *A Life Force* remain my favorites because in them I demonstrated what I believe a graphic novel could be."

Aaron: A homeless man, presumably in his twenties, with an unidentified mental disability. Aaron resides in an abandoned building, after a normal childhood that slowly revealed his

problems, and spends his days "talking back" to real and imagined tormentors. One day Aaron dares to confront God, and afterward finds himself ready to reenter the real world to "find reality." However, the real world holds terror. In an alleyway, Aaron almost collides with a child on a go-cart. As he comes across a mobster, Aaron accidentally causes the gunman's self-inflicted assassination. Looking for safety, Aaron returns to the abandoned building that was his home.

Fiore, Angelo: A neighbor and lumber yard business partner of protagonist Jacob Shtarkah. Angelo is indebted to gangster Moustache Pete, a leader of the organization known as the Black Hand. When Gino, one of Pete's henchmen, surprises Fiore at the lumber yard while searching for evidence that might incriminate Moustache Pete in a murder case, Angelo almost perishes in the fire started by Pete's henchman Gino.

Gold, Frieda: A former lover of Jacob Shtarkah, Frieda surfaces thirty years after their affair asking for his help in escaping Nazi Germany. After several false starts, Jacob is able to bring Frieda to the United States, where he wants to rekindle their romance. Frieda admits that she does "feel something" for Jacob, but discourages him from thinking of their reunion as anything long lasting, even as she accepts an apartment and a job from him. Jacob plans to leave his wife Rifka and move in with Frieda, but suddenly Frieda's daughter reappears in

FRIEDA GOLD

Palestine, and Frieda chooses to join her. Jacob offers to accompany her, but she refuses him, saying that the best path is for the two of them to keep in touch and watch how their relationship evolves.

Max: A tailor who works for Morris, Max is a good-hearted employee. When gangsters (appearing to be union members seeking new recruits) appear at Morris's shop, Max, loyal to the owner who treats him well, tries using brute force to remove them. Amid the struggle, one of the gangsters, Gino, hits Max, causing permanent brain damage. Because Morris is very fond of Max, he takes him into his own house and treats him like family.

One day Willie, Morris's son, takes Max with him as he does errands. While out, Max spots Gino and follows him into the lumber yard, where Gino has started a fire. Max carries one of the owners, Angelo Fiore, to safety. Then Max returns to the burning yard where he struggles again with Gino. This time both of them perish.

Moustache Pete: A gangster who helped Angelo Fiore emigrate to the U.S. illegally. As a result, Angelo owes Pete a significant amount of money. When Pete and his henchmen try to collect, Fiore tells them that he has gone into the lumber yard business with Jacob Shtarkah, and therefore is able to pay the funds back.

MOUSTACHE PETE

Pete takes advantage of Angelo's new business venture by selling Fiore lumber at low prices, thus making the lumber yard a success. Moustache Pete also helps Jacob Shtarkah bring his former lover, Frieda Gold, to the U.S. illegally. Pete's luck begins to turn when he has a man killed and tries to hide the body in the lumber yard. This indirectly causes the deaths of Pete's hit man Gino, and Max, a brain-damaged tailor, bringing the lumber yard to the ground in flames.

Shaftsbury, Elton: A disenfranchised socialite, Elton Shaftsbury sells his family's axe-handle factory, only to find himself among the casualties of the 1929 stock market crash. By the winter of 1933, broke and unemployed, Shaftsbury is reduced to selling apples on the corner of Wall and William Street. Shaftsbury lives in the same building (55 Dropsie Avenue) as Jacob Shtarkah. He is introduced to the Shtarkah family one Saturday when they unknowingly call him back from a suicide attempt by asking him to turn on their electricity. Elton catches the eye of Rebecca Shtarkah, and the two begin spending days together. Meanwhile, Elton becomes a bond runner for a local bank, but seems resigned to drop in social status.

When Jacob Shtarkah informs Shaftsbury that the lumber yard where he buys his supplies has foreclosed, Elton recommends to his superiors that they purchase the lumber yard and set up Shtarkah and his partner Angelo Fiore as new owners, in the hope that the yard will profit, making selling the company shares an option for the bank. His superiors take his advice, and Shaftsbury is promoted.

While this is happening, Elton and Rebecca are having a torrid love affair despite their religious and cultural differences. As a result, Shaftsbury keeps a very close eye on the happenings at the lumber yard. From a neighbor, he learns that a murder victim was hidden in the yard. Upon investigation, Shaftsbury realizes that the yard's supplier, Moustache Pete, has been selling Shtarkah and his partner Angelo Fiore stolen merchandise. When the lum-

ELTON SHAFTSBURY

ber yard burns because Moustache Pete wants to destroy evidence, Shaftsbury helps Shtarkah and Fiore successfully claim that the fire was accidental, so they can collect from their insurers.

Shortly after the fire, Rebecca tells Shaftsbury that she is pregnant and the two elope immediately, determined to build a life together. In a change of heart, Rebecca's father Jacob blesses their marriage.

"Elton Shaftsbury," Will Eisner explains, "was meant to personify the fragility of class-based social position. I've known people like him. Money is ephemeral and wealth is transitory, as the recent history of the dot-com millionaires demonstrated."

Shtarkah, Daniel: The son of Jacob and Rifka, Daniel becomes a doctor. He would otherwise be a source of great pride to his parents, but he marries out of the Jewish faith. Daniel tries to be independent, but he is easily manipulated by his mother, who hopes to come between Daniel and his wife.

Shtarkah, Jacob: When we first meet Jacob Shtarkah he is destitute, completing a five-year job, building a study hall at the local synagogue. With no new work prospects available, Jacob, a part-time poet as well as a carpenter, ruminates about his life as he walks home while suffering an attack related to his weak heart. After reviving, in a sudden burst of compassion, Jacob saves the life of a cockroach ("Izzy"). Over dinner, he tells his wife Rifka that that compassionate act was the day's accomplishment. Not long out of work, Jacob is asked by Rabbi Bensohn to build a small room for his wife Beckeleh, who is ill. Because of Jacob's weak heart, he believes he needs a partner, so he asks his neighbor, Angelo Fiore, to help him build the room.

Jacob and Angelo's hopes of a partnership are shattered when they learn that the lumber yard where they purchase materials is being foreclosed by the bank. On the steps outside his apartment house, Shtarkah explains to a neighbor, Elton Shaftsbury, that his supplier is going out of business. Shaftsbury works for a rival bank, and presents Jacob's problem to the company president as an expansion opportunity. The president agrees with Shaftsbury, and Jacob and Angelo are set up as "owners" of the foreclosed lumber yard, with the bank as share-holders. Shtarkah and Fiore are back in business.

The lumber yard becomes a successful venture, primarily because Jacob and Angelo buy stock very cheaply from Moustache Pete, a gangster who some years ago helped Fiore emigrate to the United States.

Even though they are moderately successful businessmen, Jacob and Angelo contin-ue to build the room for Rabbi Bensohn. One day the rabbi receives a letter from Frieda Gold, a woman Jacob knew romantically thirty years before in Germany. It's 1935 and Gold and her family are being persecuted by the Nazis.

Jacob does everything in his power to bring Gold to America, but his first attempts are unsuccessful. He then enlists the aid of Moustache Pete, all the while knowing that this illicit partnership may come back to haunt him.

Jacob hasn't told his wife Rifka about his attempts to bring Frieda to the U.S. because he wonders if he is still in love with her.

After Gold arrives, Jacob sets her up with an apartment near his own, and employs her at the lumber yard. Although unsure what he feels for Frieda, Jacob is sure that whatever it is, it's stronger than what he feels for Rifka. Meanwhile, the bank goes public with the lum-ber yard stock, which sells at a significant profit, making Angelo and Jacob wealthy men.

By now, Jacob is determined to leave Rifka and marry Frieda Gold. Frieda admits hav-ing feelings for Shtarkah, but discourages him from leaving his wife. Gold must be ready in case her daughter, who is in hiding, needs her.

While all this is happening, Shaftsbury discovers that the lumber yard's supplier, Moustache Pete, is running an illegal operation, after a dead body is discovered there by a child. When one of Pete's henchmen, Gino, surprises Fiore at the yard while searching for the dead man's clothes, Gino starts a fire in order to destroy the evidence of the murder. Max, a man who has been following Gino, carries Angelo out of the burning yard to safe-ty, and then returns to the fire, where he and Gino both perish. Because the insurance com-pany believes that the fire was accidental, Jacob and Angelo pocket the funds. In the inter-im, Gold's daughter makes her whereabouts known. Gold immediately plans to leave the U.S. and join her daughter in Palestine. Although Shtarkah offers to accompany her, Frieda is not ready to make a commit-ment to him. She does offer some hope; they should keep in touch and see how their relationship evolves. Hope, Shtarkah muses as he returns to his wife Rifka, "is more than a cockroach has."

"Jacob Shtarkah," Will Eisner explains, "was a stereotype, an everyman. A human cockroach."

Shtarkah, Rebecca: The daughter of Jacob and Rifka, Rebecca is a school teacher smitten by Elton Shaftsbury, one of the upper class disen-franchised by the crash of 1929, now living in her tenement building, 55 Dropsie Avenue. As their romance evolves, Rebecca resists the idea of marriage because Shaftsbury is not Jewish. However, when Elton helps her father out of some business difficulties while ascending the bank's corporate ladder, Rebecca softens. When she tells Shaftsbury that she's pregnant, the couple elopes without delay, despite the mixed reaction from Rebecca's parents.

REBECCA SHTARKAH

Shtarkah, Rifka: The wife of Jacob Shtarkah, Rifka accepts the disappointment in her life: her husband Jacob is a dreamer who can't provide the stability that she craves, her son Daniel is a doctor but marries outside of their religion, as does her school teacher

RIFKA SHTARKAH

daughter, Rebecca. Although Jacob and Rifka have been married for thirty years, they don't get along well; her habit is to nag him, and his general response is to ignore her. Rifka is a master manipulator, who feigns a small heart attack in order to convince their son not to miss the Sabbath meal together. When Jacob threatens to leave her, Rifka takes to bed, but rises quickly when Jacob changes his mind.

Willie: A young artist who attends a union meeting, Willie is inspired to work toward the downfall of the bourgeois. After the meeting, Willie and his friend Ken return to Willie's apartment to make signs for a rally. Unfortunately for Willie, on the very same day of the meeting, some members visit his father's shop and try to force the employees to join a union. While both the owner (Willie's father) and the employees agree that unionization isn't necessary, one representative, Gino, hits an employee, Max, on the head, causing permanent injury. When Willie's father is greeted at home with news of workers' oppression, he throws Willie's friend Ken out of the house, ending Willie's very short stint as a union man.

This collection of 32 "graphic essays," first published in 1989 by Kitchen Sink Press, offers glimpses of city life, almost as if readers are allowed to peer into the artist's sketchbook, gleaning his personal experiences. A sequel to *New York, the Big City*, the essays center on an examination of three facets of city life: Time, Space, and Smell. Eisner brings to this task a lifetime of memories and shares them with consummate skill.

About *City People Notebook*, Will Eisner writes in his foreword: "Much of this book's content emanates from an accumulation of sketches, notes, and 'thumbnail' outlines intended for stories or graphic novels. Some were part of the research I did for 'Big City,' a series that ultimately was collected and published under the title *New York, the Big City*.

"During my relocation to Florida, these files were unearthed and the idea of harvesting this unused crop presented itself. As it always seems to happen, simple ideas quickly become complex projects, and soon I was at work 'tightening' sketches, filling gaps, and finally inking the whole shebang to fit a book format.

"I suppose in all honesty I would have to present this effort as a book based on 'out-takes.'"

Set against the backdrop of the Great Depression, *To the Heart of the Storm* tells the story of Willie, a strong-willed child with artistic leanings who grows up to be a successful cartoonist. It is also the story of Willie's mismatched parents—Sam, his idealistic father, and Fannie, his practical mother—who had only their wits and experience to protect Willie from the looming specter of anti-Semitism.

First published in 1991 by Kitchen Sink Press, *To the Heart of the Storm* is widely regarded as Will Eisner's finest autobiographical work, in which his mastery of storytelling,

art, and dialogue combine with universal themes to make this his most moving and powerful graphic novel.

"I had begun this book with the intention of writing about what I believed to be the 'biology of prejudice,'" Will Eisner explains. "Rather than use dry scholarly documentations, I thought it would be more interesting to report my own personal experience. About one-third into the book, I realized that I was producing an autobiography. It gave me serious pause, for writing a self-revealing account of one's life takes considerable courage. It took me a year to produce.

"At the end it turned out to be a period of deep therapy. I had to deal with untrustworthy memory and the residue of guilt about the fairness and accuracy of the portrayal of loved ones."

Buck: A German boy who first fights with Willie, then becomes his best friend. Their intense friendship continues over the course of the year prior to high school, as Willie and Buck work very hard to build a boat despite several setbacks. During their year-long friendship, the duo encounters many adventures, one involving Buck's Aunt Lena, who catches Willie watching as she bathes. As Willie and Buck prepare to attend high school, they sell the boat they've built and buy a car. During high school, the two grow apart.

Many years later, Buck and Willie meet again, now young men. By this time the United States has entered the Second World War, and as the two reminisce over coffee, Buck demonstrates that he's blatantly anti-Semitic. When Buck turns to formally invite Willie to dinner, he finds that Willie has slipped away without saying goodbye.

Fannie: Willie's mother, Fannie, was born on a boat sailing from Romania to the United States. Fannie grew up in a house peopled with siblings and half siblings—Irving, Mike, Rose, Goldie, and Bobby. On Fannie's tenth birthday, her mother died. Later that year, her father, Isaac Wolf, died. Several of her siblings fled or moved away, but Fannie stayed, taking care of the house. As a young woman, Fannie went to work as a seamstress in Siegel's factory, while shouldering much responsibility for her younger siblings, perennially in trouble. In an effort to bring her siblings Goldie and Bobby in line, Fannie attempts to enlist the

help of her brother Irving, but Irving has converted to Christianity and wants no part of the family, therefore Fannie must manage alone.

Fannie's difficulties at home are compounded as a dentist named Max courts her. When Max proposes, Fannie turns him down, in part because her sister Rose argues that Fannie isn't smart enough for him. Instead, Lilly the Matchmaker finds Fannie a distant cousin to marry, Sam, Willie's father. Anxious to get away from Rose's clutches, Fannie agrees to the matchmaker's match.

The cousins, it turns out, are poorly suited for each other. Sam is restless and talented, but has difficulty making a living as a scene painter. As a result, Sam engages in a series of business ventures, but he is unsuccessful. Sam isn't really interested in business, and the Great Depression adds to his financial difficulties.

Fannie and Sam have three children: Willie, the book's protagonist, his brother Julian, and a baby. The baby doesn't figure prominently in this book, but Julian does have a cataclysmic role: After being victimized as a result of anti-Semitism, Julian (whom the kids call "Jew-leen") changes his name to "Pete," at Willie's request.

ROSE

Heidi: A German girl, attracted to young Willie, Heidi is unaware that he's Jewish. The news humiliates her, proving she isn't strong enough to overcome her inbred anti-Semitism.

Helen: Helen is a girlfriend of Willie's whose father is a boat builder. She is a great help to Willie and Buck as they build their own boat. Although Willie finds her attractive, he chooses not to pursue their relationship because of Helen's socialist, alcoholic father.

Rose: Willie's aunt, Rose is a half-sister to his mother, Fannie. After Fannie's mother dies, Rose takes the ten-year-old girl into her home. By day Rose works in a sewing factory, taking home piecework at night. "But Rose was looking for a man!" Fannie recalls, and one day she announces her marriage to Louie, a newspaper salesman.

Rose and Louie appear to be happily married, but after a few years Rose's overbearing nature proves too much for Louis, and he becomes an alcoholic.

Sam: Willie's father, originally an apprentice to a successful church artist in Austria prior to the First World War. The Austrian master artist had a habit of humiliating his assistants, so Sam, a natural leader, tampered with one of the master's paintings. In a drunken rage, the master destroyed his own defaced painting. Following that incident, the master showed new respect for his apprentices.

With the outbreak of the First World War, Sam leaves a bohemian Viennese lifestyle for the United States. Shortly after arriving, he meets Fannie, and proposes. Fannie agrees to their marriage despite worries that the two are not well matched.

Marriage necessitates that Sam find suitable employment, and Sam works as a scene painter for a theatrical company, but as the Depression worsens, work becomes scarce. After leaving the theatre company, Sam embarks on a series of unsuccessful business ventures, many of which require the family to move. Despite failing, Sam repeatedly proves himself to be a leader and consensus-builder among those whom he employs and among other employees.

As Willie (the protagonist of *To the Heart of the Storm*) matures, Sam is a steadying influence on his son, teaching him clever ways to combat anti-Semitism while supporting his son's dream of becoming a cartoonist.

"The person whom I regard as being most influential to me was my father," Will Eisner explains. "He appears as Sam in *To the Heart of the Storm*."

Uncle Shimon: Shimon, Willie's father's brother, is a very successful businessman, to whom Willie's

SAM

father Sam is indebted. Following Sam's decision to leave the furniture painting business because of health problems, Shimon backs Sam in a variety of business ventures, none of them financially successful. After Shimon's partners grow tired of Sam's failed ventures, Shimon himself supplies funds needed to embark on yet another business opportunity.

Willie: In *To the Heart of the Storm* we follow Willie's childhood through his early adult years. As a boy, Willie faces several serious encounters with anti-Semitism. These interactions form the core of this graphic novel.

The story is told from memory: Willie, on a train to boot camp during World War II, looks back and recalls both subtle and direct confrontations with racism, and the ways he learned to overcome them. These interactions range from fights with neighboring kids to feeling the shame of having to sneak away from a teenage girl's party after he overhears her reaction to learning that he is Jewish.

The book also follows Willie's boyhood friendship with Buck, a German boy, as the two of them work very hard to build a boat. Their friendship cools after they complete the boat, but they meet again as young men. The happiness of their meeting is marred when Buck displays an open hatred for Jews.

Willie's story is one of a child who has moved constantly, unable to form lasting friendships because of his father's many failed business ventures. His father, however, imparts some very positive values on young Willie: He teaches his son to handle the many forms of anti-Semitism he encounters, and encourages Willie's artistic interests. Like Will Eisner himself, as an adult Willie becomes a cartoonist.

To the Heart of the Storm is also a story about accepting responsibility. Although Willie's artistic interest grows into a successful career, and it appears that he will not be drafted into the armed forces to fight in the Second World War, the book ends with Willie informing disappointed business partners that he has chosen to enlist.

Wolf, Isaac: Willie's grandfather, who emigrated from Rumania around 1880. After settling in the United States, Isaac became a traveling salesman and over the years has several sexual liaisons. After the death of his wife, Isaac returns to Rumania to marry his deceased wife's younger sister, who becomes Willie's maternal grandmother. Fannie, Willie's mother, is born on the boat trip to the United States, although Isaac is 70 years old at the time. After returning to the states, Wolf resumes his career as a traveling salesman, rarely seeing his family. On Fannie's eleventh birthday, Isaac Wolf dies. Because her mother has passed away earlier that same year, Fannie moves in with Rose, her older half-sister.

Subtitled "Seven Graphic Stories by a Comics Master," this anthology, first published by Kitchen Sink Press in 1991, collects stories originally serialized in 1985 and 1986 in *Will Eisner's Quarterly* nos. 6-8. Unlike other story collections, *The Will Eisner Reader* is not thematically based. Stories range from the ironic—"A Sunset in Sunshine City"—to the period piece "The Long Hit." Also included in this volume is an adaptation of Franz Kafka's classic work *The Trial*—"The Appeal"—as well as "Detective Story," "Winning," and "Humans."

"Hang-Up" appears as the last segment of a story called "The Telephone" and demon-

strates Eisner's mastery of the form, telling a poignant, familiar story by focusing on facial expression and body language, letting the reader fill in the details. While the technical expertise lies in Eisner's illustration skills, the story's theme of ironic frustration is one that all readers are able to call their own.

The stories in *Invisible People* were originally serialized as a three-volume miniseries in 1992. They were collected by Kitchen Sink Press and published as a graphic novel in 1993. The first story, "Sanctum," tells the consequences of a mistakenly printed obituary notice. The second, "The Power," focuses on a healer. The last story, "Mortal Combat," features repressed Hilda and Herman, middle-aged lovers.

"This book was written in anger," Will Eisner explains. "In 1991, I came upon an item in my local newspaper about the suicide of a poor woman, Carolyn Lamboly. Disabled, impoverished, and alone, she had for over a year applied again and again for help from the community. But her case became lost in the county computer system and she had become an invisible person.

"A few days before Christmas 1990, sick, alone and in despair, Carolyn Lamboly hung herself. Her body lay unclaimed in a funeral home for two months. She was finally buried on February 27, 1991 in an unmarked grave in a public cemetery in Memorial Park, Dade County, Florida.

"The stories in *Invisible People* grew out of my dismay."

SADIE GLOTZ

"SANCTUM"

Glotz, Sadie: The editor of the newspaper's obituary page, Sadie Glotz mistakenly prints Pinkus Pleatnik's death notice, inadvertently setting into motion the forces that cause his death. Upon her retirement, Glotz is awarded a medal and a $5,000 bond for being an "errorless" editor.

Pleatnik, Pinkus: Pleatnik, retiring by nature and a bachelor by choice, is a clothing presser by profession. One day the newspaper mistakenly runs his obituary notice. Pinkus is unable to convince his apartment building superintendent that the obituary is a mistake. When he attempts to convince his employer, Abe Shmotter (in Yiddish "*shmatte*" means "rag"), that he is still alive, Tony, Pleatnik's replacement in the dry cleaning store, calls in union henchmen "Joe the Delegate." In an effort to silence him, Pinkus is taken for a drive to New

PINKUS PLEATNIK

Jersey. There he dies attempting to escape from a moving car, thus making the newspaper's mistake a prophecy.

"THE POWER"

Gypsy Lil: A fortune teller, Lil uses Morris's healing powers to make her business successful. When Morris questions the morality of her enterprise, the gypsy throws him out.

Years later, Lil seeks Morris's help when she surprises him with the knowledge that she bore his son. The child, now seven, is disabled. Unable to heal him, Morris wants to raise his son. Lil is unmoved by Morris's wish, but is willing to let the child choose. The child chooses his mother, leaving Morris forever.

Morris: From an early age, Morris possesses an ability to heal people and animals. This "power" seems to be recalled whenever necessary. As an adult, Morris is compelled to help others, and seeks work as an orderly, a farm hand, and a circus magician. Claiming to feel phony and dishonest, Morris is dismissed from the circus, only to fall in with Gypsy Lil, a fortune teller. Seven

GYPSY LIL

MORRIS AND HIS SON

years later, after he questions her enterprise by calling it a "cheap scan," Lil throws Morris out. "It's all over...you're no good for me anymore!" she exclaims. "We're finished!"

Dejected, Morris takes company with homeless men Grifter and Charley Gimp. After Morris heals Charley's leg, he becomes employed in a soup kitchen by Pastor Brown, but he is again dismissed, this time because of his healing abilities, which the pastor considers "cheap sorcery."

Morris sets up shop as "Holy Morris the Healer," and the new business is successful. Some time later, he receives a surprise visit from Gypsy Lil, his former lover. She explains that she and Morris had a child after his departure, and that their seven-year-old boy is disabled. Surprisingly, Morris is unable to heal his own child. Moved by his son, Morris asks if the boy might live with him. Lil gives Morris twenty minutes to convince their son to choose which parent to live with. The boy seems receptive to living with Morris, but finally decides to stay with his mother. The story ends with the boy and Gypsy Lil leaving a despondent Morris, who ends up among the "invisible people," living on the street.

Will Eisner explains: "I meant to portray Morris as a man who *wanted* to become invisible."

Morris's son: A boy about seven, Morris's son is unable to speak or walk without crutches. His father, Morris, a healer, fails when using his amazing restorative powers on his own son. Morris, however, requests that the boy remain with him, as he and the boy's mother, Gypsy Lil, live apart. Lil decides to let the boy choose which parent he wants to live with, and although Morris pleads, the boy chooses to remain with his mother. As the story closes, both the boy and his mother leave with no intention of ever seeing Morris again.

Pastor Brown: Brown is a pastor who employs Morris at a neighborhood soup kitchen, then dismisses him because he fears that Morris's healing powers are "cheap sorcery." Later, after Morris sets up shop as a healer, Brown visits Morris and witnesses him taking money from a woman with a sick child. Saddened, the pastor leaves.

"MORTAL COMBAT"

Gornish, Hilda, and Herman: Hilda Gornish (in Yiddish "*gornisht*" means "nothing") is a forty-year-old "spinster" whose father's death frees her to pursue her own life. She soon meets Herman, a fifty-year-old bachelor who is employed in the children's section of the same public library where Hilda staffs the circulation desk. Hilda and Herman become romantically involved, but Hilda is resistant to the idea of marriage, fearing that Herman's mother, Yetta, will disapprove. Hilda's fears are well founded; Herman's mother doesn't want the two to marry. Regardless, Herman finds the resolve to inform Yetta that he and Hilda intend to marry.

In a freak accident, Herman's mother is poisoned by oven gas. Hilda and Herman continue their marriage plans while Yetta recovers. Their story ends tragically as Herman's mother crawls from her bed, knocking over a candle and igniting the gas stove. The explosion kills both Yetta and Hilda, leaving Herman disabled.

Dropsie Avenue: The Neighborhood, first published by Kitchen Sink Press in 1995, explores a recurring theme in Will Eisner's books: City blocks have life spans just as buildings and people do.

Dropsie Avenue is a fictional street representing Eisner's "hometown" of the Bronx, and has appeared as a location several times in his work, most notably in *A Contract with God* and *A Life Force.*

In his introduction to *Dropsie Avenue: The Neighborhood*, Will Eisner writes: "If you come from a big city, the street on which you were born, grew up, and matured was your 'hometown,' and it was always referred to as the 'neighborhood'. Residency defined you as surely as did national origin, and gave you a lifelong membership in a fraternity held together by memories."

In *Dropsie Avenue*, Will Eisner follows the pageant of almost 500 years of United States history, played out in the lives of the dreamers, the strivers, the reformers, and the criminals. It is the saga of the death and rebirth of a New York neighborhood where Dutch, Irish, Italian, and Jewish immigrants built a city and a nation.

Brown, Ruby: Ruby is the daughter of Jim Brown, the super at Svenson's apartment building on Dropsie Avenue. Much to the distress of the neighbors, Ruby is befriended by Rosie, a white girl. After Svenson sells his building and Ruby's father is out of work, the neighborhood pulls together, finding employment for Brown because they want Ruby and her father to stay in New York City. As an adult, Ruby becomes City Planning Director, and works with aged millionaire Rowena Shepard and attorney Abie Gold to redevelop their old neighborhood, Dropsie Avenue.

RUBY BROWN

Cash, Izzy: Initially a ragman, Cash emerges as one of the neighborhood's success stories, buying and reselling tenements. Although he denies it, Cash has a generous heart, and with a little arm twisting, he donates a storefront to be used by the neighborhood as a youth center. As an old man, Cash leaves his estate to his secretary, Miss Bernstein.

After Abie Gold is no longer City Councilor, Cash retains him as his attorney. After Cash's death, Gold merges his estate with Rowena Shepard's, using the combined funds to remake Dropsie Avenue.

Consuelo: A resident of Dropsie Avenue, Consuelo and her husband Adolfo have a bad marriage. Consuelo is disgusted by what she perceives as her husband's lack of drive, as well as his inability to secure employment. With the aid of a mystic, Adolfo tricks his wife into believing that he has been transformed into a dog. In reality, Adolfo has run out on Consuelo. After her dog bites her, Consuelo treats her "husband" with more respect than she had given him when he'd been human, and the two appear to have come to an understanding. Later, when her dog dies, Father Gianelli refuses to perform last rites because the participant is an animal. Crying hysterically, Consuelo is taken to the local hospital.

Dropsie Avenue Property Owners Association: The Association is a neighborhood group run by Mr. Kelly, with the purpose of making the German residents so uncomfortable that they leave the neighborhood. Ironically, Kelly's own son Kyle impregnates a young German woman, Heidi, whom he's romantically involved with. When Heidi's father (known only as "Klaus") discusses the situation with Kelly, Kelly denies that his son Kyle is in any way responsible. Klaus then takes his family, including his pregnant daughter Heidi, to live in upstate New York, away from Dropsie Avenue.

Gold, Abie: As a boy, Abie was exempted from neighborhood prejudice because he was a star baseball hitter. As a teen, Gold becomes romantically involved with Marie Leone, to the consternation of those who felt that Jews and Italians shouldn't intermarry. Initiating a new tradition on Dropsie Avenue, Gold and Leone are married by both Father Gianelli and Rabbi Goodstein. As an undergraduate, Abie represents the Dropsie Avenue Parent Association, forcing land baron Izzy Cash to donate a storefront to be used as a youth center. Gold's second case as a young military attorney during World War II is to defend Aldo Nero, another child of Dropsie Avenue. Although Nero has been charged with selling government goods on the black market, Gold successfully defends him.

After the war is over and back on Dropsie Avenue, Abie represents Izzy Cash in a suit covertly sponsored by politician Polo Palermo. Although adversaries, Polo sees a future politician in Gold and helps Abie win a seat on the city council.

Abie proves to be an able councilor. His greatest strength lies in his ability to read the changing face of the neighborhood he represents, and he is one of the street's best advocates for many years. When Palermo is killed, Gold loses his backing and is no longer a strong political force. Returning to private practice, he is again retained by Izzy Cash, this time as the executor of Cash's large estate. However, Abie's most important client is Rowena Shepard, now a very old woman and owner of the Rowena Corporation, valued at several million dollars. Shepard's new project is to redevelop Dropsie Avenue by turning the street into single family homes. Although unable to exactly realize Shepard's dream, Gold is able to use both Shepard's and Izzy Cash's estates to revitalize Dropsie Avenue. In the course of one lifetime, Abie proves to be a stabilizing force and a hero in the neighborhood, first as a baseball star, then as an undergraduate representing parents, then as a councilor, and finally as an attorney executing the estates of the wealthy.

RAFA GORGOL

Gorgol, Rafa: Gorgol is a wife beater whose violence affects other street residents. After neighbors alert the police, they learn that the authorities can't stop Gorgol without a formal complaint being filed. One day, in full view of other residents, Gorgol kicks his wife

POLO PALERMO

for dropping a bag of groceries. Soon after, neighbors hear gunshots coming from inside Gorgol's apartment. After the police arrive, Gorgol is carried out on a stretcher, apparently dead, and Gorgol's wife leaves in handcuffs. The tale of Rafa Gorgol and his wife is a sad commentary on both the inability of people to rescue themselves early on and the inefficiency of the judicial process.

Palermo, Polo: Polo rises to almost immediate celebrity in the neighborhood because he bests "Irish" Mike in a boxing match, symbolizing Italian superiority on the street. Smartly, Palermo uses his fame to win a seat on the neighborhood council. At first a voice for the Italians, Polo is able to stay in office because he responds to the changing wave of power-wielding ethnic groups. After a long political career, Palermo is assassinated by Sarge, a disabled hit man hired by convict "Crazy" Bones in retaliation for Palermo's justified role in Bones's imprisonment.

Red/Sarge: Red first appears as an idealistic young man on his way to serve in the Vietnam conflict. Red's only regret is that the girl he feels for opposes the military intentions of the country he serves, and refuses to "wait" for him. When Red does return, he is known as "Sarge," now a legless embittered veteran who is able to move by using a dolly. Fearless, Red becomes an enforcer for Mr. Bones, an imprisoned murderer and drug dealer. After purchasing a tenement on Dropsie Avenue, Bones doesn't redevelop it, but instead turned the dilapidated building into a drug palace. While Red tries to collect on a debt, he dies in a fire in the very building owned by his employer, Mr. Bones.

Shepard, Rowena: Rowena is a teenager, disabled and bound to a wheelchair. She loves flowers and lives with her grandmother on Dropsie Avenue. One day a mute thief escapes pursuit by crashing into Rowena's garden. Surprisingly, she isn't angered by this intrusion and inconvenience, declaring happily that her "Prince Charming" has arrived. As he tries to leave her, Rowena immediately informs the thief that she will scream, alerting the police. That settled, "Prince Charming" lives up to Rowena's expectations and defends her house against other thieves.

Time passes and Rowena and her prince marry and move to Westchester. As a very old woman, Rowena reappears on Dropsie Avenue. She now heads the Rowena Corporation, a multimillion-dollar flower enterprise. She has returned to her old home because she wants to develop the crumbling neighborhood, revitalizing Dropsie Avenue by converting it to single family homes. Rowena engages attorney Abie Gold, who was also raised on Dropsie Avenue. The two of them meet with Ruby Brown, the city planning director, another neighborhood alumnus. Brown arranges for Rowena to purchase the tenements on Dropsie Avenue and fulfill her dream of redevelopment. However, Rowena is an old woman, and she does not live to see her plans realized. That task is left up to Abie Gold, the executor of her estate.

Rowena Shepard's story encapsulates two of Will Eisner's recurring themes: that periods of decay and renewal are cyclical, and that, given the right circumstances, the disabled can heal one another and flourish.

"I regard everyone as disabled in one way or another," Will Eisner explains. "I employ disabled characters to emphasize or portray graphically the human struggle to survive against the implacable force of life."

Smith, Danny: A returning World War II hero, Danny becomes planning director for the city. Initially, Danny is a strong director, concerned chiefly with public safety. However, as he and his wife fall into the debt of mobster "Big" Ed Casey, Danny enjoys a lifestyle beyond his meager salary, and Danny extends political favors to Casey to cover his debts. Following a murder that could implicate Smith, Casey arranges for Danny to receive a promotion, allowing him to leave Dropsie Avenue.

Family Matter, first published in 1998 by Kitchen Sink Press, is one of Will Eisner's most biting books. It tells the story of familial love and betrayal, focusing on a family reunion to celebrate the 90th birthday of Ben, the protagonist. In the span of twenty-four hours, the darkest family secrets are revealed. Long-suppressed memories surface—betrayal, abuse, greed, and worse. The strained family comes together, only to be torn apart.

About *Family Matter*, Will Eisner writes: "Families are little tribes. They provide identity and survival. *Family Matter* was not homily, it was reportage. It related an incident in the life of a family. It was social observation, you might say."

Al: One of Ben's sons, Al lives in Texas trying to strike oil. When Al appears at his father's 90th birthday party, he is greeted with hesitation. Also attending the party is Al's estranged son Sammy, whom Al hasn't seen in ten years, since Sammy's mother died.

The siblings try to decide what's best for their ailing father, both in terms of his health care and their own financial security. As a young man, Al's father, Ben, caught him stealing from the family business but chose not to report the theft to the police. Despite this, Al's primary concern is not to risk his own investments.

Ben: Following a stroke, Ben is confined to a wheelchair. Unable to speak, he lives with his daughter Greta in a New York City apart-

ment. When he was younger, Ben was a successful businessman selling scrap metal, beating out his competition by playing smart and working hard. He expected the same from his children, but was disappointed by them. When he caught his eldest son Al stealing from the business, he chose not to prosecute. In addition, his son Leo entered the legal profession against his wishes. We also learn that Ben sexually abused two of his three daughters.

Later in life, Ben developed more compassion for others, and was a great help to his grandson Sammy when Sammy's mother died. Ben also ended his terminally ill wife's life at her request.

Despite the stroke that rendered Ben mute, he is able to hear and comprehend. As his grown children, all harboring their private grudges against him, discuss which nursing facility to place him in as well as their disappointment in their dwindling inheritance, Ben is disappointed as well as shamed. When his grandson Sammy, also overhearing the decisive conversation, appears, he offers Ben an overdose of his medication. Ben knowingly accepts it, choosing to end his own life.

Greta: Ben's daughter, who, along with her husband Harry and their child (Kiddo) has taken her ailing father into her home. For the occasion of her father's 90th birthday, Greta has planned a party and invited all of her siblings, most of whom have grown distant. During the course of the day, Greta recalls her childhood, and how her father abused her. Surprisingly, she appears to harbor no malice toward him, perhaps because their relationship made her feel special to him.

When her siblings arrive, Greta is horrified as she hears them talk openly about their inheritance. However, when her husband announces that his company is bankrupt, her thoughts also turn to her father's estate. After she and her siblings decide that they will place their father in an inexpensive nursing facility, it falls upon Greta to tell Ben. She intends to break the news to him as positively as she can, but when she enters his room, she discovers that he had taken an overdose of pills, committing suicide.

GRETA

Leo: A ne'er-do-well attorney, Leo is Ben's second son. As a young man, Leo had the strength to defy his father's wishes and study law rather than enter the family business. Apparently, winning that battle depleted him, leaving Leo with little resolve. Now middle-aged, Leo is spent. As an attorney, some of his responsibilities are to execute his father's estate. As the family gathers to celebrate Ben's 90th birthday, the discussion turns toward needed medical placement for the old man. Leo is increasingly anxious; he has received bad news—medical costs would most likely dry up Ben's accumulated fortune. This leads to the touchy subject of the death of their mother some years earlier. Although the insurance company determined that her death was a suicide, Leo has rightly guessed that, at their mother's request, their father discontinued her life support.

Later that very same day, Ben purposefully overdoses on medication, ending his own life.

Sammy: Sammy is Al's son, Ben's grandson. Sammy has been estranged from the family since his mother died, ten years earlier. Extremely depressed, Sammy lives on welfare and spends his time in therapy. Years before, when his mother died, his grandfather was one of his true lifelines. Sammy is reluctant to attend his grandfather's 90th birthday celebration because he is afraid of his father Al, also attending. However, at the urgings of his therapist, Sammy joins the family reunion, hoping to reconnect. However, just as he anticipated, he and his father Al don't get along. Sammy muses on what ties families together, even as he discovers close-

ness with his grandfather, now mute as the result of a stroke. While his father, aunts, and his uncle discuss what's best for the old man, Sammy visits with his grandfather and intuits that he would prefer to die rather than enter a nursing facility. In an effort to help his grandfather, and possibly paying a debt from years gone by, Sammy gives him an overdose of his medication, allowing him to end his life.

Selena: A former actress, Selena now works for a department store. As she joins her family to celebrate her father's 90th birthday, she appears content with her accomplishments.

However, her actions prove otherwise: Either out of spite for her snobby sister Molly or out of genuine desire, Selena seduces Molly's husband Charlie while remembering that her father sexually abused her. When Selena was a young woman, her father purposefully interrupted her sexual encounters. As her siblings debate the benefits of placing their father in a nursing facility, Selena's assessment of the situation is frank and unsentimental.

THE PRINCESS AND THE FROG

The first in a series of fairy tales and literary adaptations springing from Eisner's work in television, this playful retelling of the story originally appearing in the 1812 seminal publication *Grimm's Fairy Tales* is aimed at readers young and old alike (published by Nantier, Beall, Minoustchine Publishing, 1999).

THE LAST KNIGHT: AN INTRODUCTION TO "DON QUIXOTE" BY MIGUEL DE CERVANTES

A lighthearted adaptation for young readers of the epic 1605 Spanish novel *Don Quixote*. In this version (published by Nantier, Beall, Minoustchine Publishing in 2000), Eisner turns his pen and brush to humorously capturing one of history's most well-known literary characters, focusing on Don Quixote's gallantry and sense of humor. A colorful and entertaining look at the Man of La Mancha and his faithful assistant, Sancho Panza.

LAST DAY IN VIETNAM: A MEMORY

Six short stories of life during war time. From World War II to Korea to Vietnam, Eisner was there as a soldier and later as a correspondent for *P.S. Magazine*. These true stories, drawn from memories and experiences, present the reader with a unique perspective on the lives of both soldiers and civilians in a war zone.

In this unusual collection from Dark Horse Comics (2000), readers are treated to a series of monologues presented by nameless protagonists offering slices of military life. In the title story, an officer takes a middle-aged reporter on a tour of the military base, one of the officer's last responsibilities, as he is to be discharged the next day. Although it begins harmlessly, the walk-through turns deadly serious, as both the reporter and the officer survive an explosion and sniper fire.

About *The Last Day in Vietnam*, Will Eisner writes in his introduction: "I arrived in Vietnam during the autumn of 1967. I was based in Saigon, and my tour was only to last about a month. It wasn't until the Tet Offensive in January of the following year that Saigon was partially overrun by the Viet Cong, and America became truly aware that it was losing the war."

"Long ago and once upon a time back when uncles were heroic, cousins were clever, and miracles happened on every block." That is how Will Eisner describes *Minor Miracles*—at least in its subtitle. He has also described it as "perhaps the most enjoyable book I've done so far. It was the closest experience to telling a joke."

The first original graphic novel by Will Eisner to be published by DC Comics (2000), *Minor Miracles* is a collection of four stories tinged with nostalgia and a bit of magic. One thing it displays is Eisner's range within the comics format. The stories vary from humorous to mysterious to poignant. The first story, "The Miracle of Dignity," is a drama of extended family. The second story, "Street Magic," tells of a confrontation averted. The third story, "A New Kid on the Block," is a fable of sorts, and the last story, "A Special Wedding Ring," is a tale of healing.

In the foreword to *Minor Miracles*, Will Eisner writes: "It is hard to make a case for miracles. Either you believe in them or you don't. I believe in them.

"The stories in this work resemble the stories my parents referred to as '*meinsas*.' And while they are apocryphal, they were nevertheless distilled from my remembrance of those that were the common property of our family.

"I tell these stories out of an abiding sense of wonder which time and age have not altered. I wonder at the good or bad fortune of friends. I wonder about the appearance and departure of people I knew and the miraculous endurance of impossible alliances. The wonder of it all still remains vibrant in me, which is a wonder in itself."

COUSIN IRVING AND UNCLE AMOS

"THE MIRACLE OF DIGNITY"

Cousin Irving: Well-to-do Irving bumps into his downtrodden cousin Amos and, in an act of generosity, lends him $10,000. With the loan, Amos opens up a furniture business. Amos's business is not successful, and he repeatedly asks for an extension repaying his debt to Irving. Finally, Irving agrees to buy Amos's unsold stock in lieu of repayment.

Like Amos, Irving is unable to sell the merchandise. However, the two cousins see each other at family gatherings, and Amos attends the bar mitzvah of Irving's son Julius. When Julius is disappointed in Amos's small congratulatory gift, Amos decides to pay for the boy's education.

Julius: The son of Irving, Julius is given a five-dollar gold piece as a bar mitzvah present by well-off Uncle Amos. Julius, however, is disappointed, expecting something larger. To compensate, Amos agrees to pay for Julius's education. Ten years later, Julius is a successful attorney and Amos's business is failing. In an attempt to save Amos's dignity, Julius buys up the business.

JULIUS

Uncle Amos: Down and out, Amos's wealthy cousin Irving offends him by offering him five dollars. To repent for the insult, Irving loans Amos $10,000. Irving also sets Amos up as salesman at a prime storefront. When Irving tries to collect the debt, Amos, short on funds, has a solution: Irving should purchase Amos's $20,000 dollars worth of merchandise in lieu of the $10,000 debt. Irving agrees, but is unable to sell the goods. When Irving approaches Amos again, one year later and even more desperately in need of funds, Amos has a second solution. He will take over Irving's failing business.

This transaction raises Amos's status within the family. At his nephew Julius's bar mitzvah, Amos gives the boy a five-dollar gold piece. However, the small amount offends young Julius, and in an effort to make amends, Amos pays for his college education.

Ten years pass. Amos, now insolvent, sells his business to Julius, who buys it to preserve Amos's dignity. Amos spends the rest of his days in the park, feeding pigeons and giving advice to anyone who will listen.

"STREET MAGIC"

Cousin Mersh: Mersh is a clever boy who casually escorts his cousin through what he calls "enemy" territory, a block inhabited by anti-Semitic bullies. In an effort to appear both intimidating and fair, the enemy boys ask Mersh to pull a piece of paper out of a hat. If Mersh chooses the blank paper, as opposed to the one that reads "guilty," he and his  cousin may go free. The bullies, however, have loaded the game: both pieces of paper in the hat read "guilty."

Mersh picks and deftly eats the paper as all the boys watch on in wonder. Then Mersh asks the bullies to read the one paper remaining in the hat. Of course the paper says, "guilty." "Well, then, I swallowed the blank one!" Mersh declares, as he and his cousin continue their walk unharmed, never looking back.

"A NEW KID ON THE BLOCK"

Boy: A young man appears out of nowhere, late one afternoon, speaking an indecipherable language. While taking refuge in an alleyway, the boy is given a stolen cashbox temporarily by two thieves. Not realizing what he has in his possession, the boy stumbles into Melba's Books, and presents Melba, the owner, with the cashbox.

Melba comes to understand that "Boy" is homeless, and finds him a decent place to live with the Rizzos. Although he displays animal-like tendencies, Boy has a healing effect on those around him: husbands and wives stop bickering, and small miracles and acts of goodness appear in his wake.

Unfortunately, Boy's stay with the Rizzo family ends abruptly when Marie Rizzo decides that the boy is her deceased son Silvio, returned from the dead.

After fleeing the Rizzo household, Boy takes refuge with Melba, who teaches him to speak. Armed with language, the boy tells Melba that he was kidnapped. Melba researches kidnappings from fourteen years earlier and concludes that Boy is the lost son of Boyard Rensalier, a wealthy man.

A truant officer eventually traces the boy's whereabouts to Melba's apartment. Terrified by the officer's presence, Boy flees, never to be seen in the neighborhood again. With the boy gone, his healing effect on the neighborhood wanes, and neighbors and spouses return to their bickering ways.

BOY AND MELBA

The "wild child" or outsider is a recurring figure in Will Eisner's work. However, the boy in this story differs from his predecessors (such as Aaron in *A Life Force*) in the sense that his is a healing presence and someone who has grown apart from society.

On May 26, 1828, an unusual young man of roughly sixteen years of age showed up on the streets of Nuremburg, Germany, bewildered and incoherent. His name was Caspar Hauser, and he was murdered five years later. Not much is known about this young boy, but his mysterious life has served as the basis for much fiction, including the boy in Eisner's tale.

Melba: Melba first recognizes that the mysterious young man who suddenly appears in the neighborhood is special when he returns her stolen cashbox. Melba is entranced with the boy, and arranges for him to stay with the Rizzo family. When the boy gets scared and runs away from the Rizzo household, he finds refuge with Melba in her apartment, where she teaches him to speak, coaxing his life story out of him.

Melba learns that he was kidnapped as a young child. Researching kidnappings from that time, she theorizes that the boy is heir to a fortune. However, because the child was

MARIE AND SALVATORE RIZZO

missing for so many years, the funds from the estate were dispensed to charities. When the boy runs away from a truant officer, Melba spends days searching for him, but ultimately gives up in despair. She remains unmarried but stays in the neighborhood running her store, Melba's Books.

Rizzo, Marie and Salvatore: Marie and her husband Salvatore take in the mysterious boy at the request of Melba, who runs a local bookstore. After staying with the Rizzos for a time, Marie becomes convinced that the boy is their son Silvio, who died of polio ten years before. Her love and enthusiasm frighten the boy, and he flees.

Despite the boy's departure, Marie continues fantasizing that her child has returned from the dead, and is determined to find him. She enlists the aid of Father Vincent. After being questioned by truant officer Bogen, she becomes so overwrought that she suffers a fatal heart attack, all the while contending that her son Silvio has returned.

"A SPECIAL WEDDING RING"

Emmis, Shloyma: Shloyma Emmis (in Yiddish, "*emmis*" means "the truth") is known as a "good Jew." Every Friday night and Saturday morning he goes to shul, walking three avenue blocks through the "Valley of Shadows," as he calls the "*goyisher*" neighborhood on the south side of Dropsie Avenue. The rest of his week is devoted to a small business selling cheap diamonds, which he gets on consignment. Emmis lives alone and has an interest in books and mysticism. Emmis sells "Missis" Fegel a wedding ring, promising that the ring itself will bring her son Marvin and his fiancée Reba Grepps happiness. It appears that Emmis is correct; marriage seems to make the couple, a cripple and a deaf-mute, blossom. As a result, Emmis's business booms. Coinciding with the purchase of this

special ring, the neighborhood experiences a period of good fortune.

Business continues to thrive for the old jeweler, so much so that he is followed home one night and murdered for his wealth. Shloyma's death seems to end the time of miracles for the people of Dropsie Avenue.

MARVIN FEGEL AND REBA GREPPS

Fegel, Marvin: Marvin Fegel (in Yiddish, "*feygele*" means "an effeminate or gay male," literally "a little bird") is a disabled, successful writer who weds deaf-mute Reba Grepps. Marvin helps Reba learn to communicate, encouraging her to become an avid reader. A year later she mysteriously regains her hearing and is able to speak. However, Reba's newly found abilities make her want more freedom than life with Marvin can offer, and the two separate following an ugly incident at a party.

Reba moves in with her mother and is then stricken blind as a result of a stroke. Marvin goes to Reba, and the two reconcile. He remains a very devoted husband, supporting his wife, doing all the cooking and cleaning as well as reading aloud romance novels to her, which he abhors.

Grepps, Reba: Reba is a deaf-mute whose marriage to disabled writer Marvin Fegel is arranged by her mother. After her marriage, Marvin helps educate Reba. A year later she mysteriously regains her hearing and is able to speak.

Reba Grepps (in Yiddish, "*greps*" means "to burp") now finds life with her disabled husband confining, and pursues an active social life, virtually ignoring him. Finally, after Marvin feels abandoned by Reba at a party, the two frankly discuss whether or not their marriage has a future. Reba admits that she wants a divorce, and she moves back in with her mother. However, about two months later, she experiences headaches and is blinded by a stroke. Following her stroke, Marvin reappears and the two make amends, culminating with Marvin giving Reba back her ring.

This retelling for young readers is taken from the 1851 classic American novel by Herman Melville. Published by Nantier, Beall, Minoustchine Publishing in 2001, it recounts the story of Ishmael, who takes a position on a whaling ship in the early 1800s, after years away from the sea. Ishmael has unknowingly signed on with Captain Ahab, who has sworn vengeance on Moby Dick, the white whale, who had "remped away" the captain's leg during an earlier encounter. The crew realizes that Ahab is on a death-quest but is unable to stop him. In the battle with Moby Dick, Ishmael alone survives to tell this cautionary tale.

Published by DC Comics in 2001, *The Name of the Game* is a graphic novel in the epic tradition, a multigenerational saga that chronicles the rise and decline of the powerful Arnheim family over the course of nearly a century. The foreword is written by Eisner as if it were from Abraham Kayan, the father of Aron Kayn, the poet protagonist.

Arnheim, Conrad: The preferred son of Isadore and Alva Arnheim, Conrad is the heir to the extremely successful Arnheim Corset company. Conrad grows up spoiled in a household where his parents refuse to see his manipulative side. When he turns twenty, his father arranges for him to enter the family business and marry Lilli Ober of the prestigious Ober family. The two are poorly matched, and Conrad constantly escapes his marriage by fleeing to Europe. On a trip to France, he learns that his father has died. Eventually, Conrad is welcomed back to the United States by his mother and alcoholic brother, Alex.

Alva, Conrad's mother, has big plans for him: With Izzy gone, he will run the company. However, Conrad has his own plans: He intends to live like a gentlemen and let the business run itself. After strengthening the company by securing a large loan, Conrad sails for the Bahamas in his yacht while his wife suffers a miscarriage. As the Arnheim Corset Company fails, Conrad starts an investment company, Arnheim Stocks & Bonds. Through social connections, Conrad is able to pull together an impressive client portfolio. One of his

first employees is his cousin, Roland Sydney. At this time, Conrad's wife Lilli again becomes pregnant, dying during childbirth. Not wanting to be hampered by raising a child, Conrad farms his daughter Helen out to her grandparents, the Obers.

The crash of 1929 is not good for Arnheim Stocks & Bonds. The family is reduced to selling valuables in order to maintain the appearance of wealth. At this time, Conrad's second wife, Eva Krause, enters his life. A beauty from Nebraska, Conrad is completely taken with her, and the two marry. However, Eva is also a poor wife for Conrad. He quickly learns that she married him chiefly to elevate her social position.

After his mother Alva's death, Conrad wants to have children, in the hope of preserving the Arnheim legacy. When Eva refuses to bear a child, Conrad reclaims his daughter Helen. A bitter quarrel over custody ensues with the Obers, which indirectly causes the death of Helen's grandfather. Now in custody of Helen, an unhappy child, Conrad is disappointed. While Helen is away at school, Conrad rapes Eva, and the two have a child of their own, Rosie. When Helen, now a young woman, announces her engagement, Conrad pays her fiancée $25,000 dollars to leave the Arnheim family alone. Heartbroken, Helen dies in a skiing accident.

CONRAD ARNHEIM

Conrad's other daughter, Rosie, grows up a defiant child, who doesn't value the Arnheims' need for social position. When Rosie marries poet Aron Kayn, Conrad chooses not to interfere, but offers Aron a position at his investment firm when Aron is no longer able to sell poems. Quite pleased with his son-in-law's work performance, Conrad promotes him repeatedly. After his 80th birthday, Conrad retires, making Aron company president. Aron immediately merges with the Sydney Company, run by Conrad's cousin and former employee, Roland Sydney. Shocked when learning of the merger, Conrad becomes so enraged that he suffers a fatal heart attack.

Arnheim, Eva: The daughter of David and Edna Krause, Eva Krause grew up in Cranston, Nebraska. From an early age, she was considered to be a stunning beauty. Although many young men called on her, Eva wasn't interested in their attention, and accepted a modeling position in New York City. Through her mother Edna, Eva was introduced to socialite Conrad Arnheim. Smitten with her, Conrad proposes, and Eva accepts.

On their honeymoon, Conrad learns much about his new bride who is repelled by his advances. To the outside world, Conrad and Eva appear happily married, but behind closed doors they are distant and disinterested in each other. The emotional vacuum takes its toll on Eva, who drinks in part to come to terms with her husband's numerous sexual affairs. When Conrad requests a divorce, Eva refuses, unwilling to leave a life of privilege. When

EVA ARNHEIM

Conrad suggests that they have children, Eva again refuses. To counter Eva, Conrad brings Helen, his daughter from a previous marriage, into their house.

Eva is cold and a poor substitute mother. One day while Helen is away, Conrad rapes his drunken wife. The couple soon have a daughter: Rose. As with Helen, Eva shows little interest in being a mother. After Helen tragically dies in a skiing accident, Eva does turn her attention to Rose, and supervises her education. As her daughter matures, Eva enjoys watching young Rosie stand up to her father. However, when her daughter declines to marry into the well-off Klegheimer family, Eva is disappointed.

When Rosie does marry, it is to a poet from a working class family. Eva is shocked and disappointed in her daughter's choice for a husband. However, she learns to appreciate her son-in-law after he becomes employed at Conrad's investment firm. Some years later, at her husband Conrad's death, Eva is unmoved, concerned primarily that she will remain a member of the exclusive clubs that she and Conrad joined previously.

Kayn, Aron: The son of Polish and Dutch immigrants, Aron wants to be a poet. He meets his future wife, Rosie Arnheim, at a poetry reading. After the two marry, Aron supports his family by selling poems to *Modern Poetry Monthly*. But when the magazine no longer needs new material from Aron, he begins working for his father-in-law, Conrad Arnheim, at Arnheim & Co. Stocks & Bonds. This career change infuriates Rosie, who married Aron in part because she believed him to be the polar opposite of her father.

The same intelligence that helped Aron Kayn create poems helps him thrive in the investment business, where he shrewdly takes care of key clients. Aron rises quickly, in part because of his skills, and in part because his father-in-law owns the company. However, success comes with compromises. In order to facilitate growth, Aron is away most evenings from his wife Rosie. Some of these evenings are spent in sexual liaisons with Arnheim & Co. clients. When Conrad Arnheim retires, he makes Aron the company president. One of Aron's first executive decisions is to merge with the Sydney Company,

ARON AND ROSIE

another investment firm. When Conrad learns of the merger, he becomes so upset that he suffers a fatal heart attack.

Aron's continued faithlessness is no more evident than the night his wife Rosie gives birth. While Rosie is in labor, Aron spends the evening with his secretary. Disappointed in their marriage and in him, Rosie confronts her husband, and Aron tries to hit her. Instead, Rosie beats him. Then she informs Aron that, for the sake of their child, they will stay married.

The aspiring poet has been a recurring figure in Will Eisner's graphic novels. However, previous poets, such as Jacob Shtarkah in *A Life Force* have retained their poetic instincts even as they plied other trades. Aron Kayn's life is perhaps best understood if one examines it as the result of what happens when one consciously shuts off one's poetic instincts.

Kayn, Rose ("Rosie"): The only daughter of Conrad and Eva Arnheim, Rosie rebels against her aristocratic upbringing by declining an offer of marriage from a member of the well-off Klegheimer family, by quitting her private high school, and by attending a city college, where she studies poetry. Her plans to attend graduate school are sidetracked when she meets and marries struggling poet Aron Kayn. Rosie is disappointed when her husband joins her father's investment firm after learning that he can no longer sell poetry. Her disappointment hardens into feelings of betrayal as Aron rises in the company, eventually becoming president, all the while forsaking his poetic ambitions.

After their first child is born, Rosie confronts Aron, telling him that she knows about his perpetual infidelities and his lack of moral compass. However, she decides that she will

CONRAD AND ROSE

not leave Aron. Divorce is not the way the Arnheims do things, and she and her husband will maintain the appearance of a loving marriage while living separate lives. Rosie has come full circle; her attempt to escape the Arnheim legacy has failed. She has now become the very thing that she rebelled against as a child.

Ober, Abner: The son of a German immigrant, Abner managed a dry goods store before going into banking. Wealthy and successful, the Obers long to be respected and to rise socially, and so they cooperate with journalists doing features about them. When the Arnheims invite Lilli Ober, Abner's daughter, to spend the summer with them, Abner wonders what they have in mind. Meeting with Izzy Arnheim, Abner learns that the Arnheims are looking for a wife for their son Conrad, who will inherit the family business. Abner agrees

ABNER OBER

that the pairing of his daughter Lilli with Conrad Arnheim will benefit both families.

The Obers are unhappy with their daughter's marriage. Lilli seems sad and depleted, and Conrad travels constantly. They become so disappointed that eventually the bank that the Obers head up stops lending the Arnheims funds.

When Lilli dies in childbirth, the Obers raise their granddaughter Helen until Conrad, Helen's father, steals her, taking Helen home. Although Helen lives with her father and stepmother, the Obers are intent on bringing her up and initiate a legal battle for custody. When Conrad learns of this, he angrily confronts the Obers. The heated conversation causes Abner to suffer a fatal heart attack.

This retelling of the Mali tale about Sundiata and Sumanguru recounts old lessons: If you ignore the weak they may grow strong enough to hurt you, and evil acts eventually receive just punishments.

This African tale for young readers (published by Nantier, Beall, Minoustchine Publishing in 2003) is based on "The Lion of Mali," the part-historical, part-mythical stories of a West African king.

Published by Doubleday in 2003, this reinvention of the classic Charles Dickens novel *Oliver Twist* (1837) expands magically on the groundwork Eisner laid in previous adaptations of *Moby Dick* and *Don Quixote*.

The story is told from the point of view of Moses Fagin, whose family emigrated from Bohemia to London. Orphaned at thirteen, Fagin becomes a house servant (a "houseboy") for Eleazor Solomon, a wealthy Jewish merchant. As a teen, Fagin is assigned the task of preparing an old building to become a school for Jewish children, where he will receive an education. However, a brief love affair with the owner's daughter lands Fagin on the sidewalks of London.

Fagin's education now comes from the streets, where he learns the ways of petty crime and is sentenced to ten years of servitude. Moses ends up working faithfully for Jack Dawson, who promises to set him up in business. However, Dawson dies before he can act on his promise.

His sentence completed, Fagin returns to London, where he enters into a partnership with Bill Sikes. Their business: thievery. Because he treats destitute children well, Fagin develops a troop of children adept at picking wallets out of the pockets of the wealthy.

At this point, Fagin's life intersects with Oliver Twist's, and the story we are familiar with is retold, but from Fagin's perspective. Fagin is eking out a living through theft and the funds brought in from the children. His one rule is that violence will not be tolerated. However, when Nancy, Bill Sikes's lover and a member of Fagin's band, risks herself to save young Oliver Twist, Sikes becomes so enraged that he murders her.

This brings the police to Fagin's door, and he is first interrogated, and then sentenced to be hanged. Unknown to Fagin, another life had opened for him: His old benefactor Eleazor Solomon has died, and made Fagin the heir to his fortune. Had he known this, his whole life as a criminal could have been avoided.

But that doesn't change the consequences delivered as a result of the life he did live. While awaiting his hanging, Moses Fagin has two visitors in prison: the first one is Oliver Twist, needing help to reclaim his birthright. Even at the point of death, Fagin is merciful,

and gives Oliver the information he needs to identify himself as the illegitimate child of Sir Leeford, insuring a good life for Oliver Twist. Fagin's other visitor is the author Charles Dickens, who listens carefully to the story of Moses Fagin's life, assuring him that "in my later books I'll treat your race more evenly."

In telling Fagin's story, Eisner looks at prejudice, poverty, and anti-Semitism prevalent in classic literature. About *Fagin the Jew*, he writes in the afterword: "Fagin, created by Charles Dickens in *Oliver Twist*, ultimately became one such 'profile' of a Jew that embedded itself in popular culture and prejudice. In truth, the author never intended to defame the Jewish people, but by referring to Fagin as 'the Jew' throughout the book he abetted the prejudice against them. Over the years, *Oliver Twist* became a staple of juvenile literature, and the stereotype was perpetuated."

THE WILL EISNER SKETCHBOOK

Published by Dark Horse Books in 2003, this oversized hardcover bears the same title as a previously published sketchbook from Kitchen Sink Press issued in 1995. This latter volume is divided into sections comprising rough concept sketches, character studies, and preliminary drawings from *The Spirit, A Contract with God, A Life Force, The Dreamer, To the Heart of the Storm, Dropsie Avenue, Family Matter, The Princess and the Frog, The Last Day in Vietnam,* and *Minor Miracles.* Also included is the unpublished *Spirit* story "The Last Hero." Each section contains an introduction by Eisner himself, where he discusses the intent of his graphic novels and specifics about the artwork. *The Will Eisner Sketchbook* shows the evolution of Eisner's art from his first working ideas to the final narrative, providing readers with invaluable insight into the creative process.

In his first nonfiction graphic novel, *The Plot*, Eisner tackles the subject of anti-Semitism. Here he expands on the theme that haunts the pages of his autobiographical works like *To the Heart of the Storm*, and which he addresses directly in the metafictional *Fagin the Jew*.

The Protocols of the Elders of Zion is one of the most influential and pernicious anti-Semitic works ever published. Eisner dramatizes its creation by the experienced expatriate forger Mathieu Golovinski, a propagandist who worked for Pierre Ratchkovski, head of the Paris branch of the Okrana (the Russian secret police). *The Protocols* was written in 1903 to influence Czar Nicholas II and persuade him to turn against modernization and the granting of rights to Russian Jews.

In *The Plot*, Eisner shows how the book was created, using a previously published volume from 1864 by the French liberal writer Maurice Joly, *Dialogue in Hell Between Machiavelli and Montesquieu*. This imaginary debate between an Enlightenment philosopher and the man whose name has become synonymous with ruthless governance was intended as political satire—an attack on Emperor Napoleon III. Years later, as recast by Golovinski, the book is rewritten as the purported secret minutes of an imaginary Zionist meeting where unnamed, international Jewish leaders—bankers, journalists, and financiers—plan world domination. *The Protocols* was subsequently revealed as a forgery, first in 1921 by reporter Phillip Graves in the *Times* of London, and again in a 1935 ruling by the Court of Berne, Switzerland.

Eisner dramatizes the fabrication in a story that begins with Graves discovering a copy of the *Dialogue* in Cairo. Eisner then turns to the horrors of Nazi Germany, including the role of *The Protocols* in the Holocaust—Adolf Hitler cited it in his 1925 memoir *Mein Kampf [My Struggle]*, using it to justify his attempt to exterminate Jews during World War II.

Eisner's work traces the forgery's horrifying history, including its U.S. serialization from 1920-22 in the *Dearborn Independent*, a Michigan newspaper published by Henry Ford (yes, *that* Henry Ford) to attack Jews and Communists.

Even after *The Protocols* was exposed as a forgery, Ford continued to cite the document as proof of a "Jewish conspiracy" until he was forced to recant in the wake of a defamation lawsuit in 1927.

Deeply personal, *The Plot* serves as a warning about the renewed use of this reprehensible propaganda by right-wing and anti-Semitic groups, as well as its continued circulation by Muslim extremists in the Middle East.

In a February 23, 2004 interview with Steven Lee Beeber for *The New York Times*, Will Eisner remarks that he set out to "create a work that would be understood by the widest possible audience." Although this book has not been published at the time of this *Companion*'s completion, *The Plot* (W. W. Norton, 2005) promises to be as sweeping and powerful as any of Eisner's previous graphic novels.

At age 87, Will Eisner continues to reinvent himself and the genre he helped to create.

SERGE NILUS (UPPER LEFT, CENTER) AND COURT ATTENDANTS

AFTERWORD

I first met Will Eisner at an early Phil Seuling comic book convention in New York City in 1971, during the height of the Vietnam War. The nation was polarized by the "conflict," much as it is today. Newsstand comics (there was no network of specialty shops) were in gradual decline. Underground comix, a movement I was part of, were raising eyebrows and proliferating in alternative outlets nationwide. The Seuling con was the first such industry event for both of us. I certainly respected Eisner's work but had no expectation of meeting him. He was already a legend in the field, even though he was still years away from inventing the modern graphic novel. In addition, he was an "old guy" (about the age I am now) and the generation gap was no small thing in 1971. Thus it was rather amazing to me at the time—though not in retrospect—that Will sought me out for a private meeting. I found myself fielding serious questions about the way my fledgling company, Krupp Comic Works/Kitchen Sink, was distributing comix on a radical non-return basis to non-traditional outlets. My attempts to interject questions about *The Spirit* were handled graciously, but Will Eisner was not at the convention to bask in nostalgic reverence. He was there to learn something new about the most mundane, and yet essential, of publishing topics: distribution. We took an instant liking to each other.

That an already well established, balding, no-nonsense businessman/artist, then working for the U.S. Army, would hit it off with a much younger, anti-war, long-haired hippie entrepreneur/artist was somewhat improbable. But that seminal meeting began a longtime personal and business relationship. I've served various turns as Will's publisher (nearly thirty years), editor, literary agent, and art agent. Will served for a while on the Board of Directors of Kitchen Sink Press, Inc. We "jammed" on comic pages. Eisner Awards hang on my wall. My oldest daughter, Sheena, was named after an Eisner creation before Will and I ever met. He has been a mentor and, particularly during tough times, he has been a surrogate father.

So, on many levels, I'm delighted to see this *Will Eisner Companion* become reality. The well-organized information about significant characters from *The Spirit* and Will's many graphic novels, the time lines, and other information guarantees this will be a well-thumbed reference in my library. Chris Couch and Stephen Weiner have provided a valuable resource to collectors, readers, and researchers. As essential as this book is, I hope fans do not unrealistically expect every street lamp, every Eisenshpritz, and every Will Eisner creation to be indexed. This is *not* the *Eisner Encyclopedia*. Eisner's artistic career includes numerous pre-*Spirit* 1930s comics stories and covers created during the Eisner-Iger and Quality shop era, and posters and hundreds of publications (*Firepower, Army Motors,* and *P*S*) created for the U.S. Army. Countless more educational comics were created during his American Visuals period for such disparate clients as the Job Corps, the American Dental Association, and General Motors, to educational materials aimed at grade-schoolers. It's a long, prolific, and fascinating career, one that is far from over, so the twelve-pound multi-volume encyclopedia will have to wait. In the interim I'm going to be thumbing through *The Will Eisner Companion.*

Denis Kitchen

DENIS KITCHEN

Amherst, MA
June 2004

WILL EISNER:
A SELECTED BIBLIOGRAPHY

All About P'Gell: The Spirit Casebook, vol. 2. Northampton, MA: Kitchen Sink Press, 1998.

America's Space Vehicles: A Pictorial Review. New York: Sterling Publishing, 1962.

Bringing Up Your Parents. New York: Scholastic, 1980.

The Building. Princeton, WI: Kitchen Sink Press, 1987; New York: DC Comics, 2000.

The Christmas Spirit. Northampton, MA: Kitchen Sink Press, 1994.

City—A Narrative Portfolio. Hollybrook Graphics, 1980

City People Notebook. Princeton, WI: Kitchen Sink Press, 1989; New York: DC Comics, 2000.

Comics & Sequential Art. Tamarac, FL: Poorhouse Press, 1985.

A Contract with God and Other Tenement Stories. New York: Baronet Press, 1978; Princeton, WI: Kitchen Sink Press, 1985, with an introduction by Dennis O'Neil; New York: DC Comics, 2000.

Dating & Hanging Out. With Wade Hampton and Keith Diazun. New York: Scholastic, 1966.

The Dreamer. Princeton, WI: Kitchen Sink Press, 1986; New York: DC Comics, 2000.

Dropsie Avenue: The Neighborhood. Northampton, MA: Kitchen Sink Press, 1995; New York: DC Comics, 2000.

Fagin the Jew. New York: Doubleday, 2003.

Family Matter. Northampton, MA: Kitchen Sink Press, 1998.

Gleeful Guide to Communicating with Plants to Help Them Grow. New York: Poorhouse Press, 1974.

Gleeful Guide to Living With Astrology: An Everyday Manual for Coping with People, Events, and Afflictions through Astrology. Researched and edited by Ivan Klapper. New York: Poorhouse Press, 1974.

Gleeful Guide to Occult Cookery: The Saucerer's Apprentice. With Ivan Klapper. New York: Poorhouse Press, 1974.

Graphic Storytelling. Tamarac, FL: Poorhouse Press, 1996.

How to Avoid Death & Taxes...and Live Forever. New York: Poorhouse Press, 1975.

Incredible Facts, Amazing Statistics, Monumental Trivia. Edited by Ivan Klapper. Research by Jason Hanson. New York: Poorhouse Press, 1974.

Invisible People. Princeton, WI: Kitchen Sink Press, 1993; New York: DC Comics, 2000.

Last Day in Vietnam: A Memory. Milwaukie, OR: Dark Horse Comics, 2000.

The Last Knight: An Introduction to Don Quixote by Miguel de Cervantes. New York: Nantier, Beall, Minoustchine Publishing, 2000.

A Life Force. Princeton, WI: Kitchen Sink Press, 1988; New York: DC Comics, 2001.

Life on Another Planet. Introduction by James Morrow. Originally published as *Signal from Space*. Northampton, MA: Kitchen Sink Press, 1995; New York: DC Comics, 2000.

Minor Miracles. New York: DC Comics, 2000.

Moby Dick by Herman Melville. Retold by Will Eisner. New York: Nantier, Beall, Minoustchine Publishing, 2001.

The Name of the Game. New York: DC Comics, 2001.

New York, the Big City. Princeton, WI: Kitchen Sink Press, 1986; New York, DC Comics, 2000.

101 Outer Space Jokes. New York: Baronet Publishing, 1979.

The Outer Space Spirit, 1952. With Jules Feiffer and Wallace Wood. Princeton, WI: Kitchen Sink Press, 1983.

A Pictorial Arsenal of America's Combat Weapons. Introduction by Major General J. B. Medaris. New York: Sterling, 1960.

The Plot. New York: W. W. Norton, 2005.

The Princess and the Frog by the Grimm Brothers. Retold by Will Eisner. New York: Nantier, Beall, Minoustchine Publishing, 1999.

Robert's Rules of Order. New York: Bantam Books, 1986.

Signal from Space. Princeton, WI: Kitchen Sink Press, 1983.

The Spirit Archives, Vol. 1- . New York: DC Comics, 2000- .

Spirit Casebook. Princeton, WI: Kitchen Sink Press, 1990.

Spirit Color Album, Vol. 1-3. Princeton, WI: Kitchen Sink Press, 1981-1983.

Spirit Coloring Book. New York: Poorhouse Press, 1974.

Spirit Jam. With Brent Anderson, et al. Northampton, MA: Kitchen Sink Press, 1998.

The Spirit Portfolio. Collectors' Press, 1977.

Star Jaws. With Barry Caldwell and Keith Diazun. New York: Baronet, 1978.

Sundiata: A Legend of Africa. Retold by Will Eisner. New York: Nantier, Beall, Minoustchine Publishing, 2003.

To the Heart of the Storm. Princeton, WI: Kitchen Sink Press, 1991; New York: DC Comics, 2000.

The White Whale: An Introduction to Moby Dick. Tamarac, FL: Story Shop, 1991.

Will Eisner Color Treasury. Text by Catherine Yronwode. Princeton, WI: Kitchen Sink Press, 1981.

Will Eisner Reader: Seven Graphic Stories by a Comics Master. Princeton, WI: Kitchen Sink Press, 1991.

Will Eisner Sketchbook. Introduction by Alan Edelstein. Northampton, MA: Kitchen Sink Press, 1995.

The Will Eisner Sketchbook. Milwaukie, OR: Dark Horse Comics, 2003.

Will Eisner's Hawks of the Seas. Introduction by Al Williamson. Edited and with an afterword by Dave Schreiner. Princeton, WI: Kitchen Sink Press, 1986; Milwaukie, OR: Dark Horse Comics, 2003.

Will Eisner's John Law: Dead Man Walking. With Gary Chaloner. San Diego, CA: IDW Publishing, 2004.

Will Eisner's John Law, Detective. Forestville, CA: Eclipse Comics, 1983.

Will Eisner's Shop Talk. Milwaukie, OR: Dark Horse Comics, 2001.

Will Eisner's Spirit Casebook of True Haunted Houses and Ghosts. New York: Tempo, 1976.

Will Eisner's 3-D Classics featuring the Spirit. Princeton, WI: Kitchen Sink Press, 1985.

FOR MORE ABOUT WILL EISNER...

Throughout the course of Will Eisner's long career, much attention has been paid to him by comics industry publications as well as by mainstream media. Listed here is a sampling of Eisner-related books, articles, movies, and academic conferences. They range from entries in encyclopedias to interviews and career profiles, all indicating the influence Eisner has had on the field of comics and on the evolution of popular culture.

Books

Andelman, Bob. *Will Eisner: A Spirited Life*. Milwaukie, OR: Dark Horse Comics/M Press, 2005.

Bails, Jerry. *Who's Who of American Comic Books*. Detroit, MI: J. Bails, 1973-1976.

Chabon, Michael. *The Amazing Adventures of Kavalier & Clay*. New York: Random House, 2000.

Clute, John, and John Grant. *The Encyclopedia of Fantasy*. New York: St. Martin's Press, 1997.

Feiffer, Jules. *The Great Comic Book Heroes*. New York: The Dial Press, 1965 and 1977; Seattle, WA: Fantagraphics Books, 2003.

Goulart, Ron. *The Great Comic Book Artists*. New York: St. Martin's Press, 1986.

Graham, Judith, ed. *Current Biography Yearbook*. New York: H.W. Wilson Company, 1994.

Greenberger, Robert. *The Library of Graphic Novelists: Will Eisner*. New York: The Rosen Publishing Group, Inc., 2005.

Harvey, Robert C. *The Art of the Comic Book: An Aesthetic History*. Jackson: University Press of Mississippi, 1996.

Steranko, James. *The Steranko History of Comics, vol. 2*. Reading, PA: Supergraphics, 1972.

Wiater, S., and S.R. Bissette, ed. *Comic Book Rebels*. New York: Donald I. Fine, 1993.

Weiner, Stephen. *Faster Than a Speeding Bullet: The Rise of the Graphic Novel*. New York: Nantier, Beall, Minoustchine Publishing, 2003.

Yronwode, Catherine, and Denis Kitchen. *The Art of Will Eisner*. Introduction by Jules Feiffer. Princeton, WI: Kitchen Sink Press, 1982.

Articles

Barson, Mike, Ted White, and Mitch Berger. "A Talk with Will Eisner: '...And I Threw In a Hat...'" *Heavy Metal*, vol. 7, no. 8. November 1983.

Beeber, Steven Lee. "Wrath of a Pulp Patriarch: Will Eisner Draws Rebuttal to the Notorious 'Protocols.'" *The New York Times*. February 23, 2004.

Beronä, David A. "Breaking Taboos: Sexuality in the Work of Will Eisner and the Early Wordless Novels." *International Journal of Comic Art*, vol. 1, no. 1. Spring/Summer, 1999.

Cooke, Jon B. "A Spirited Relationship: Will Eisner Discusses His Experiences with Jim Warren." *Comic Book Artist*, no. 4, Spring 1999.

Eisner, Will. "Getting the Last Laugh: My Life in Comics." *The New York Times Book Review*. January 4, 1990.

Eisner, Will. "The Finest: Will Eisner's Eulogy for Dave Schreiner." *Comic Buyer's Guide*, no. 1558. September 26, 2003.

Fingeroth, Danny. "The Spirit of Comics: The Will Eisner Interview." *Write Now!* August 2003.

Fitzgerald, Paul E. "Every Picture Tells a Story: His Pen and Wit Sharper than Ever, Graphic Novelist Will Eisner Takes on Religious Intolerance." *The Washington Post.* June 3, 2004.

Hembeck, Fred. "Face Front, True Believers! The Comics Industry Sounds Off on Stan Lee." *The Comics Journal*, no. 181. October 1995.

Jennings, Dana. "The Angouleme Convention." *The Comics Journal*, no. 89. March 1984.

Kitchen, Denis. "How I Met Will Eisner, Businessman." *Comic Buyer's Guide.* November 29, 1996.

Vaughn, Susan. "A Pioneering Spirit in Pen and Ink." *Los Angeles Times.* January 7, 2001.

Movies/Television/Video

Comic Book Confidential. A film by Ron Mann. 1988.

The Spirit. ABC made-for-TV movie starring Sam Jones, written by Steven E. de Souza, directed by Michael Schultz. 1987.

Stan Lee Presents: The Comic Book Greats: Will Eisner, vol. 11. Livonia, WI: Stabur Home Video, 1992.

Academic Conferences

"The Graphic Novel: A 20th Anniversary Conference on an Emerging Literary and Artistic Medium." The University of Massachusetts/Amherst. Conference program booklet contains a brief essay by Will Eisner, "Twentieth Anniversary Reflections on *A Contract with God*." November 13, 14, and 15, 1998.

INDEX

Bold numbers denote primary entries.